My GPO Family: Trilogy E

Seven Ages on the Phone

People of all ages use the telephone
It makes them feel so much less alone.

At first the baby crying into the alarm
Its parents listening to ensure no harm.

Next the infant, *iPad* on *Skype*
Young ones quickly learn to type.

Teens on mobiles glued to their ears
Later deafness, radiation fears?

Business colleagues ever in touch
Never used the phone so much.

Middle-aged women gossiping free
On a supermarket shopping spree.

Into retirement contacts still there
Glasses, bad teeth and thinning hair!

Then when the final call rings
A silent sadness overall brings.

Cover photo: Doctors' switching and referral of calls switchboard at Southend AMC (1971)

The Seven Ages of Man totem pole at BT's Baynard House, London 2015 (see Outlet 20: Heritage Trail)

"*This Sculpture commissioned by Post Office Telecommunications and created by Richard Kindersley after inspiration from Shakespeare's seven ages of man was unveiled by Lord Miles of Blackfriars on 23 April 1980.*"

My GPO Family: Trilogy Edition

John Chenery

The author in Basildon ATE (1995)

A Light Straw Presentation 2018

Quote from *Job in a Million* (1936): *"On your faithful performance of a public service will depend the future greatness of the Post Office. It's a vast organization, and you as a small part of that will be called upon to put public service before anything else."*

Important Note(s)

The thoughts and explanations expressed in this book are solely those of the author and contributors. They are not intended to imply any endorsement from trading units of Royal Mail Group Ltd., Post Office Ltd., British Telecommunications Plc., or any of their associated companies.

Copyright © 2017 John Chenery
ISBN 978-0-244-63598-5

All rights reserved. This book or any portion thereof may not be reproduced or used in any manner whatsoever without the express written permission of the author, except for the use of brief quotations in a book review, or scholarly journal.

First published Feb 2017. Second Edition May 2017.
Trilogy Edition (abridged and edited) Oct 2017. Revised Oct 2018.

A Light Straw presentation formatted at Fynevue.

www.lightstraw.co.uk/mygpofamily

My GPO Family is the first in a planned trilogy of books unravelling the history of the General Post Office, and its successors.

As a child, the Post Office influenced my life from an early age. I loved working for British Telecom, so it made complete sense to write the story of *My GPO Family*. This tome has been crafted with a large dose of due diligence, and collaborative checking.

Dedication

This book is dedicated to:

- All GPO, Post Office and BT staff, past and present.
- My parents, who never tired of my constant playing of *Post Offices* and *Telephone Exchanges*!

Memorandum

TO:
My GPO Family Member:

....

FROM:

Contents

Acknowledgements viii
Foreword xi
Preface xiii
Introduction 1
Timeline 3
Outlet 1: Beginnings 11
Outlet 2: Going Postal 27
Outlet 3: College Years 49
Outlet 4: Traffic 63
Outlet 5: Sales CO 81
Outlet 6: Mechanisation of Order Handling 99
Outlet 7: TAG Telephone Accounts Group 115
Outlet 8: CSS Customer Service System 127
Outlet 9: Southend Telephone Area 135
Outlet 10: Office Machinery 149
Outlet 11: Billing One 161
Outlet 12: Billing Two 177
Outlet 13: Scheduling 195
Outlet 14: End Game 205
Outlet 15: Post Office Tower 211
Outlet 16: Bleeping Computers 241

Outlet 17: ERNIE 249
Outlet 18: Location, Location, Location 257
Outlet 19: Retrospective 265
Outlet 20: Heritage Trail 275
Outlet 21: Faraday Building 303
Outlet 22: BT Archives..311
Outlet 23: Bletchley Park..317
Outlet 24: Traffic Record Final Tally 337
Outlet 25: Supplied for the Public Service 347
Glossary..351

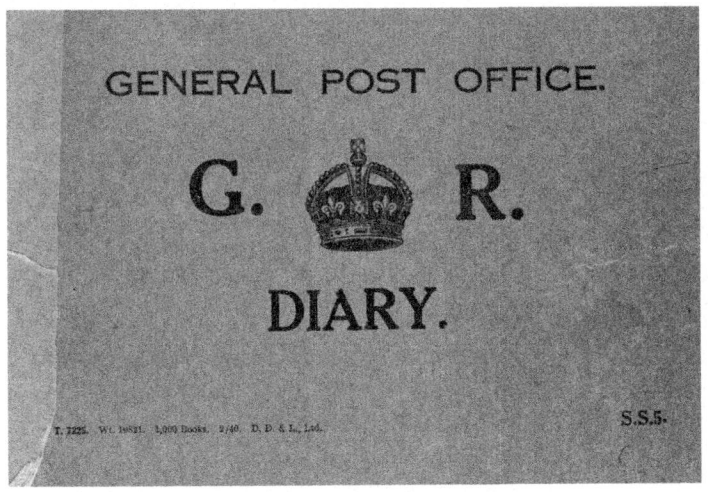

GPO G.R. Diary (Book SS5)

Acknowledgements

Thanks to: Adam Oliver, Tommy Lowe, Brian Henwood, Yve Collins, Dawn Wigley, Andrew Herbert, Malcolm Knight, Jason Ford, David Chaplin, and John Tythe.

Special thanks to: Chris Hogan of the Post Office Vehicle Club for help with the GPO/Post Office/BT Timelines. Andrew Emmerson for assistance with proofing. Also to David Hay/BT Heritage and Archives for making access to historical documents possible.

For an ongoing historical review of *The Company* see also my *Light Straw* website: www.lightstraw.co.uk

Illustrations:

Page vii	GPO G.R. Diary (Book SS5)
Page xvi	ISOCC ticket cartoon by Arthur Wallace (1970s)
Page 2	A 3124 compliments slip (1970s)
Page 26	Join the headset (1980)
Page 62	Job offer letter (1979)
Page 80	Scan from leaflet PH 2028 (12/76)
Page 125	NBS leaflet PH 2023 (1977)
Page 148	Buzby promoting PO Telecoms (c1977)
Page 176	British Telecom INPHONE tag (circa 1983)
Page 203	BT Museum leaflet PHME 7665
Page 204	Welcome to the telephone service (1970)
Page 273	Van poster (c1970)
Page 315	BT Archives leaflets
Page 334	Van poster (c1977)
Page 343	Make your career in the Post Office (1969)

Page 344 GPO Lamp No.13 (Ken Pike)
Page 347 S.O. Book 616
Page 348 Tally Card (A 521)

Photographs:
Photos © John Chenery:

Frontispiece *Seven Ages of Man* totem pole (2015)
Page xii The Enfield CB1 Switchboard (2012)
Page 6 Post Office Telephones van ELO 688 (2010)
Page 7 British Telecom van GHM 578W (2014)
Page 8 BT Ford Transit in Piper livery (2000)
Page 9 Openreach 'Superfast fibre' van (2015)
Page 114 MOH Computer Room (circa 1986)
Page 194 Telephone House, Southend (1991)
Page 210 BT Tower (2006)
Page 248 Disused TV control centre BT Tower (2015)
Page 256 ERNIE Mk1 at Science Museum (2010)
Page 264 Telephone House, Manchester (1983)
Page 274 Disused TV control centre BT Tower (2015)
Page 296 Keybridge House (2013)
Page 302 Southend ATE (2016)
Page 310 Faraday (North Block) plaque (2016)
Page 316 BT Archives (2016)

Photo © Harold Chenery:
Front cover *'Doctors' switching Board'* Southend AMC (1971)
Page 61 The author in Southend AMC (1973)

Photo © Crown copyright:
Page 336 Engineers at Bletchley RTC (1966) [Kindly supplied by Mark Hembling]

Photo © Andy Greenwood:
Page 10 - Openreach van FP17 UFR (2017)

Photo © Godfrey Hunt:
Page iii - The author in Basildon ATE (1995)

Photo © R. Henstridge:
Page 126 - QIT winners (1991)

Photo © Adam Oliver:
Page 240 - The author standing on an upper aerial gallery of BT Tower (2015). Used with permission.

Inspiring book list:

Between the Lines
by Robert C. Morris

Please Wipe Your boots
by Stanley George

Transmitting Signals:
The early and working life of R. Neil M. Alston

Hold the Line Please: The Story of the Hello Girls
by Sally Southall

Telephone Service Vehicles since 1906
by Bill Aldridge

Post Office/British Telecom Factories 1870-1994
by Ken Govier, David Proctor, John Spanton, Charles Reynolds

Foreword

In recent times a number of retrospective books have been written about life in the telephone service. By and large these very worthy publications have all been written in connection with the technology used and/or from a senior management perspective. This book is different, however, because it is concerned with the non-technical support operations carried out in what used to be called the Telephone Manager's Office.

Subjects covered therefore include Accounting, Billing, Customer Service, Sales and the mysterious-sounding topic of Traffic, along with the relevant interfaces with the technical processes that they supported. Although these matters might sound 'bread and butter' in their nature, you can rest assured that John paints a vivid and highly engaging picture of these operations, with a leavening of humorous incidents and reflections on office politics, all written in highly readable language and as little jargon as possible.

But that's not all this attractively illustrated book covers. Other chapters describe the Post Office Tower, Bletchley Park, the Premium Bonds computer ERNIE, and the Colossus and Tunny equipment designed by the Post Office to underpin vital codebreaking activities in World War Two.

Authentic, articulate and engaging are all words that describe this book accurately. So prepare to be fascinated; I shall not delay your entertainment any longer.

Andrew Emmerson, President of the Telecommunications Heritage Group and one-time Technical Press Officer for British Telecom.

January 2017

The Enfield CB1 Switchboard (2012)

Preface

The Post Office - What a Good Idea, was part of a catchy advertising campaign created by the Publicis agency in 2001. From an early age, I'd always thought that too, and *The Post Office* was often my chosen subject whenever I was asked to write a project. Over the years, the UK Telecom Heritage scene had steadily become more prevalent with the growth of the Internet, self-publishing and social media. As early as 1997, I had created my website, *Light Straw* so named from the paint colour (from 1959) of the equipment racks of the GPO (General Post Office) telephone exchanges. BT Archivists, knowing of my passion, had occasionally suggested that a book of my memoirs would be welcomed. A trusted manager, Angela Jane, said,

"I think it would be great! Even if the wider market didn't 'get it', there would be lots of BT people that would enjoy the trip down memory lane I'm sure."

And so, here it is - a retrospective of my life with the Post Office...

A cumulative work of notes, memories and feelings over many decades. An eclectic compilation of stories, reports, poems and thoughts written to encapsulate everything that was and is the General Post Office. A snapshot in time of some of the processes; as accurate as memory and notes permit. My personal 'take' on how I perceived the events, usually as a somewhat introverted self-effacing individual, with a sense of wonderment at how people and the world functioned. Always with a never-ending drive to observe, record, take note, express my opinion and contribute as only I could.

As I was growing up, Tony Benn - the Postmaster-General of the time - was shaping the GPO into an organisation of new technologies and ideas with which to provide a universal public service of both telecommunications and banking. Some of his ideas were radical, though politics aside, his name will forever be associated with the Post Office.

In October 1964, Anthony Wedgwood Benn (his given name) became the Postmaster-General. In his autobiography, *Out of the Wilderness: Diaries 1963-1967* he wrote:

"The General Post Office, as it was then called, was one of the oldest and biggest enterprises in Britain and, with responsibilities ranging from posts and telephones to broadcasting and satellites, was effectively a ministry of communications. But the restraints imposed on the GPO and the apathy into which it had fallen, mainly as a result of the anomalous position as a Civil Service department instead of an independent public corporation, were immediately apparent."

Fast forward to September 1979 when I joined Post Office Telecommunications, which was the name of the telephone division of the public corporation of the Post Office. Reorganisation was proceeding to enable the much-needed cash for exchange modernisation and growth to be found, without the constraints of having to cross-subsidise the postal service. The future was optimistic; it was hoped that the new *System X* digital exchange technology would change the world. Thus, I entered an increasing turmoil of headlong competition in what had been a lumbering state monopoly. Much was achieved in those early years of British Telecom and those staying on after the reorganisation scheme known as *Project Sovereign* (circa 1991) worked hard to adapt to the requirements of an ever-progressive company.

It was later proved that the reorganisation of British Telecom, in preparation for privatisation, had been sufficient to release enough working capital, without the 'sell-off' of shares being necessary. However, as Professor James Foreman-Peck of Cardiff Business School observed (BBC news article 2004),

"BT was profitable, but the investment necessary to maintain this position counted as public borrowing so long as the business was owned by the state."

Inevitably, the enforced competition with increasing regulation against BT was almost certainly responsible for what some respected commentators observed as a wasted opportunity for building a first class 'Broadband Britain'. On a personal note, the loss of many thousands of jobs was the additional price which was ultimately paid. I saw much change during my time with BT as the technology that improved the services was always the enabler for greater change.

As for many others before me, when I felt that I could no longer adapt to the latest environment, it was time to leave. I took with me memories of serving the customers with integrity and understanding; it had been a privilege to serve and had been exciting to be involved with such a large organisation.

It's an almost impossible quest to capture every memorable event or to recount my story without mentioning at least a few of my friends and colleagues. However, I count everyone, with whom I worked, as part of *My GPO Family,* in spirit and soul, and this book is dedicated to all staff, past and present.

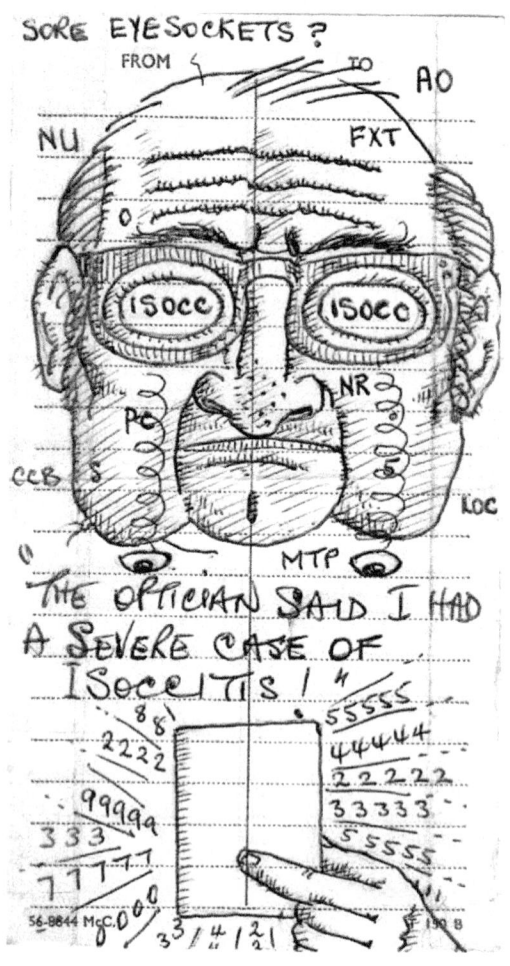

ISOCC ticket cartoon by Arthur Wallace (1970s)

Introduction

The most engaging histories written about the GPO (General Post Office) tend to be a mix of factual and personal recollections. For those of you who have worked for *The Company*, little explanation is necessary, suffice to say that *Living the BT Values* is a phrase which equally lends itself to retrospection throughout the GPO years, as much as it does in modern times.

Working for the GPO was indeed a way of life and had to be experienced at first hand to be fully believed, comprehended and possibly, understood! The ethos was absorbed after working for *The Company* for a lifetime (more than 30 years) and was often either loved or hated in equal measures, by all those concerned.

Facts and perceptions gradually fade into a rose-tinted mist of time, as past hardships, long working hours and 'difficult' customers merge into a collective memory of friendship, achievement and above all loyalty to one another.

Descriptions and recollections may be intricate or outline, but all should be read in the context of an era of stability throughout, with an underlying trend of unprecedented, ever-advancing change!

I look upon my GPO colleagues and friends, endearingly as my 'extended family' and they will always be *My GPO Family*. Through this book, I hope to convey just some of the personal excitement of being 'part of the Post Office'.

My GPO Family: Trilogy Edition

This book is a personal recollection of my 'GPO life'. *My GPO Family* refers to everyone (from *The Company*) with whom I lived, worked, played, and talked, during my journey through life.

The Company is all entities of the GPO (General Post Office), Post Office, British Telecom and BT, as detailed in the 'Timeline'…

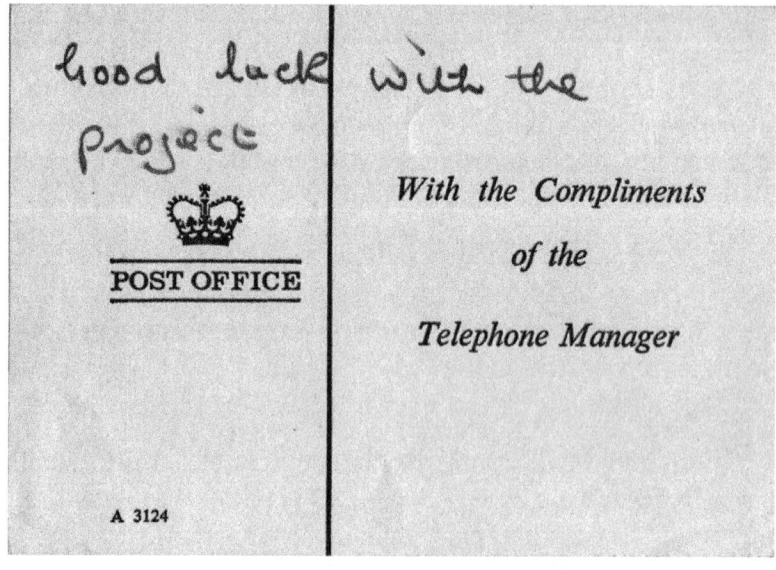

A 3124 compliments slip (1970s)

Timeline

Timeline
The all-encompassing, General Post Office (GPO) was once the sole supplier of both postal and telephone services in the UK. This was certainly the situation as the stories in this book began. Postal departments included Post Offices and Royal Mail, though primarily it is the telephone side of the business which is featured throughout.

An overview of *The Company* timeline is essential to comprehend how the organisation and regulation of the era contributed to the commercial and financial drivers, which in turn dictated the evolution and direction of the business.

Branding of everything from notepaper to telegraph poles showed the diversity of the GPO's influence. Its vehicle fleet markings and logos, over the years, reflected many of the organisational changes and were useful to inform the public of its latest identify and chosen name(s). Its extensive telephone network of ducting, with footway covers marked 'Post Office Telephones' ensured that particular entity lived on, long after 'British Telecom' had been established!

1660 General Post Office (GPO)
The origins of the GPO can be traced back to the 17th century when the Post Office Act of 1660 was passed to legally recognise the formation of the organisation. In 1661, under the Postmaster-General, Henry Bishop, the first British postmark was introduced. The first public postage stamps (Penny Black) went on sale on 1 May 1840.

My GPO Family: Trilogy Edition

1846 The Electric Telegraph Company

The Electric Telegraph Company, from which BT is ultimately descended, was established on 18 June 1846. The Telegraph Acts of 1868-70 gave Her Majesty's Postmaster-General the right to acquire and operate the existing inland telegraph systems in the UK.

1912 Post Office Telephones

From 1 January 1912 the General Post Office became the monopoly supplier of telephone services with the exception of the remaining municipal services in Hull, Portsmouth and Guernsey.

1920

The term 'Engineering Department' was displayed on vehicles used for telephone duties, as well as variations of 'Post Office Engineering Depart.' though from about 1931, 'Post Office Telephones' became the recognised name, qualified by 'Sectional Engineer'.

1935-1940

Between 1935 and 1940 the Telephone Area structure was established. This combined the admin from Telephone Districts and local engineering activities from Sectional Engineers into a number of self-contained units with responsibility for smaller geographical areas. Thus, Telephone Area Offices (TAOs) headed by a Telephone Manager (TM) were created. Van fleets began to display 'Post Office Telephones' together with the designation 'Telephone Manager' and the Area.

1941-1965

Another variant displayed on fleet vehicles was 'GPO Engineer-in-Chief' (generally after World War Two). The staffing of Telephone Exchanges was the responsibility of the Head Postmasters, but

Timeline

telephonists based in towns with Telephone Manager's Offices were their responsibility. Post Offices and Telephone Exchanges usually shared the same premises as the GPO was responsible for both.

1966-1968 Post Office Telephones
During this period of reorganisation, the Engineering Department was divided into separate telephone and postal organisations with the abolition of the post of Engineer-in-Chief. The telephone section was merged with the Inland Telecommunications Department to create Telecommunication Headquarters (THQ).

The remaining telephone operating staff were transferred from the control of Head Postmasters to Telephone Managers as a prelude to the streamlining of the postal service and the elimination of many of the smaller Head Postmasters' areas.

Each of the provincial regions, except Northern Ireland, were divided into separate telecommunications and postal regions. The GPO thus became effectively two separate organisations at all three levels (headquarters, regions and areas) with only a very limited number of common services such as legal and investigation.

1969
On 1 October 1969 the Post Office became a Public Corporation no longer under direct control of HM Government. In May 1968, the GPO Board had decided to change the colour of telephone vans from *Mid-Bronze Green*, on safety grounds, and this timely change produced the ubiquitous *Golden Yellow* fleet of vehicles.

1975 Post Office Telecommunications
The telephone part of the service was rebranded to be become Post Office Telecommunications. The now yellow vans of the new era

My GPO Family: Trilogy Edition

were to be seen with the red 'Post Office Double Line' lettering which had been created in 1972 by the design agency of *Banks and Miles*. With the hatching of the telephone cartoon character Buzby, in 1976, the once rather once sober image of the Post Office was becoming more dynamic.

Morris 8, overhead lineman's van ELO 688 at Amberley Museum Post Office Telephones, Sectional Engineer, HQ, Brighton

Timeline

1980 British Telecom – part of the Post Office

In May 1980 British Telecom was revealed as the new name for the telephone side of the business, although it was still 'part of the Post Office'. Another unique branding was once again created by *Banks and Miles*, with their striking 'dot-dash' lettering.

"This is only the beginning of what we hope will penetrate into every part of the Telecom business and become the banner of British Telecom, as familiar in time as the old GPO."

British Telecom Bedford HA van in Golden Yellow livery GHM 578W

1981 British Telecom

After Vesting Day on 1 October 1981, British Telecom was the trading name of the British Telecommunications corporation, entirely separate from the Post Office.

My GPO Family: Trilogy Edition

1984 British Telecommunications plc
On 6 August 1984, British Telecommunications became a public limited company. British Telecom was the first in a series of state-owned utility privatisations as HM Government initially offered 50.2% of its shares to the public and employees. The shares floated on the Stock Market at 130p on 3 December of that year.

1991 BT
On 2 April 1991, BT became the new (simplified) trading name for British Telecommunications Plc. The unique *Piper* logo led the way, until a more global image was adopted in April 2003.

BT Ford Transit one-tonne utility with custom-made Anglian bodywork, fitted out by Papworth. The livery shows the updated (1999) BT Piper logo in distinctive red and blue, on a white background.

Timeline

2006 Openreach – A BT Group Business
On 11 January 2006, Openreach was spun-off as a stand-alone division to service the network (local-loop) for all Telecom Providers.

Connecting the Nation to Phone, Broadband and TV services... Openreach Vauxhall Vivaro van FD64 WMW in a typical 'Superfast fibre' livery.

2016 BT merged with EE
T-Mobile Holdings and Orange acquired 12% and 4% respectively of BT's issued share capital as the merger with the mobile phone giant, EE took place in January 2016. A *sell-down* by Orange in June 2017 reduced its shareholding and aided BT's ongoing share buyback scheme.

BT relinquished its original mobile arm when it sold O_2 in 2002.

My GPO Family: Trilogy Edition

2017 Openreach Ltd
On 24 March 2017 Openreach Ltd was incorporated as a separate company, although still part of BT Group. In July, the new branding was announced. The demarcation from BT was to satisfy OFCOM that Openreach would treat all Service Providers equally.

The new branding excluded any reference to BT.

New Openreach livery on Vauxhall Vivaro FP17 UFR.

Quote from 2013: *"Our role at Openreach is to keep you connected to your provider. So when you order a new service, or have a problem with your connection, contact your provider, but expect Openreach!"*

On 24 March 2017 Openreach Ltd was formed. On 1 Oct 2018 31,000 BT employees were TUPEd into the new company.

Outlet 1: Beginnings

Setting the Tone

To me, the Post Office was, and is, my family, my work, and my life. Casual readers may not understand this all-encompassing concept, but as with most things, you have to have been there and experienced it to really know. Towards the end of my time with BT, I used to joke that we had been institutionalised and perhaps this was correct, as the routines and outlook were just so familiar that they had long become a way of living.

The stories are mainly in chronological order, though retrospections may be repeated in parts to add emphasis and aid explanations. This book contains special memories for me. For you, it may trigger 'Essence of *Oildag*' or the sharpness of paper-cuts, flecked with tints of quips, poems and lots of abbreviations. At the very least you will form images of a changing public service. Dip into it as the mood takes you back to another time, and perhaps recall your own memories too.

As an only child, I learned at an early age to occupy my time and reflect upon what the world is, or might be, and to realise not to fight too hard against one's destiny. One could try to change the world, but through the years I realised that if the timing isn't right, it will fail, regardless of how badly you want something, or how much effort you apply.

Some of these lessons I conveniently forgot during my long career as I balanced my need for stability, against my limited worldly skills and my reason for being. My strong sense of right and wrong guided me throughout, though 'office politics' and the 'operational

My GPO Family: Trilogy Edition

needs of the department' often ignored these principles!

The underlying philosophy…

For me, work was always a compulsion, a mix of

I. What I had to do (for the money).
II. What I could do (my ability).
III. What I wanted to do (my desire).

Of course, many things in the world are a compromise and may turn out better or worse than one's expectations of how to survive, develop and prosper. Conformity, followed by security, and lastly, enjoyment, all played a part too!

Many readers may not appreciate the seemingly mundane routine and conformity of which a business as old and established as the GPO affords. Others of you may identify completely with an innate sense of belonging in a powerful corporate organisation. I grew up in a GPO family such that my fascination began at a very early age. To me, the GPO was my heart and soul, and although it wasn't always easy or straightforward, I still remain privileged to have been a part of it.

I'd forgotten quite what a proliferation of writings, projects and investigations I'd produced over the years, regarding the Post Office in all its many guises and it's something of which I never tire, as there is always a different aspect to engage my attention and desire to learn.

Beginnings

The Beginning...

My GPO (General Post Office) story begins just after WWII against a setting of the Cold War, the Cuban Missile Crisis, and a state of continued threat against the UK. It was a time of strict moral codes, Government departments, and the OSA (Official Secrets Act). 'The times they were a changing', but the solid, state-owned GPO was as staid and regimented as ever could be. Procedures, processes, abbreviations, and routine were the norm and had been for many decades past.

Perhaps it was a gentler way of life back then? Many shops had 'half-day closing' on a Wednesday. Supermarkets were tiny in comparison with today's stores. Most shops closed after 5 pm on Saturday, right through until Monday morning. Computers were only used in large companies to calculate the payroll; the days of home computing were several decades away. BBC and ITV were the two television channels available, in black and white, and most sets were rented. Radios used valves, not transistors and records were played at 78 rpm on a turntable, though 45s and LPs were becoming popular! Most telephones had dials, not buttons, and 'trunk calls' (calls over 15 miles) were expensive and had to be connected via an operator. Not everyone had a landline; if you wanted to contact someone urgently, you went to the public telephone box on the corner. Or you wrote a letter, or sent a telegram. The GPO could be relied upon. It was the one (and only) place to go for all your communications needs. Getting services from the GPO was the norm. In towns, Post Offices could be found within a half-mile walk. Main Post Offices, Crown and sub-Post Offices; many had both a pillar box and telephone kiosk outside. It's not surprising that the Post Office organisation employed over 358,000 * people in its heyday.

My GPO Family: Trilogy Edition

*[Source: *An Introduction to the Post Office* – training booklet December 1959.]

As a Government department, the GPO was often seeking ways to increase revenue and in November 1956 the Treasury launched the Premium Savings Bonds scheme, more popularly known as ERNIE. Thus, in late 1959, my father purchased my first 'ERNIE Bonds'. As I grew up, I bought more bonds from the Post Office and I marvelled at the thought of illuminated prize numbers from the Electronic Random Number Indicator Equipment (ERNIE). Early Bond numbers such as 2FL could be thought of as 'two flashing lights' of the machinery. The playing of 'Post Offices' had begun...

My father grew up and worked in London, but moved to Southend when his parents retired to the seaside. In 1961 he joined GPO Telephones, at 221 London Road, as a Night Telephonist on a starting wage of nine pounds and eighteen shillings per week, less deductions. During the daytime he worked as a manager for Mence Smith's hardware shop and had fill-in jobs as a Kleeneze representative (salesman) and he also conducted surveys for Gallup Poll. Later he was doorkeeper at Olympia Bingo, when it was first established.

My father once remarked that he had connected calls in Faraday Building, London, during wartime with the RAF and it's possible that he had previous GPO service before he joined Southend TE. [I spent some time searching the microfiche records of the Postal Archive, for telephonist enrolments, but didn't find any trace of his service. The Archivist remarked that many appointments during the war weren't recorded, possibly due to the many thousands of placements and the temporary nature of the work.]

Beginnings

The inner workings of the GPO were confidential and the interception of messages or telephone calls was forbidden by the Official Secrets Act. In this respect, my father's work had an element of secrecy surrounding it and he rarely went 'to the Telephone Exchange', instead he used to 'go up *The Building*'. This mystery was further extended to any would-be listeners when he used to wave, and shout out goodbye to mother and I, before he departed for a Sunday morning shift; *"Og-in tower hot k-row wan"*, was the strange utterance. The translated spelling of butcher's back-slang 'Gniog tuo ot krow won' is remembered by me as 'Going to work now'!

'What daddy did' was more obvious when he was filling in his buff-coloured overtime dockets or writing out a note of his shifts for the forthcoming week. Terms such as 'an all-night' meant I did not see him from one teatime until early the next morning. A 'nine to six' on a Sunday was quite the norm too.

Invariably, there was often a blank Telephone Ticket (TT223) in his jacket pocket, and before long I learnt how an operator's ticket was filled out with call pricing details. To store these practice tickets, he made me a little wooden drawer in which they could be indexed (with stiff cards) and filed. I could now play at 'telephone operators'!

It was many years before we 'went on the phone' at home, in spite of the fact that there was telegraph pole just outside our property! At one time it was actually our pole, because it was replaced and we somehow ended up with a section of it, to saw up as 'plod logs' to burn on our coal fire. When we used to get taxis home from days out, my father always used to say, to the driver, *"The house is the third telegraph pole on the left."*

My GPO Family: Trilogy Edition

* Plod logs. Dad bought a bow saw to cut up a section of old telegraph pole for our coal fire. The logs were stumpy and heavy to carry up the path, hence we plodded along with them – plod logs!

To gain experience and earn extra money, my father worked away in Ipswich Telephone Exchange (Portman Road) for one week. With the ever-growing demand to connect Trunk Calls, my father had the opportunity to volunteer and work at Cambridge Telephone Exchange (Tibbs Row – demolished 1972) for three weeks in June 1964. He stayed in lodgings and wrote home to mother and (a four-year-old me).

In one of the letters my mother wrote…

"Guess what, the strut has been taken away from our telegraph pole, it looks all bare. You know what the bedtime story tonight will be, this letter travelling all night on a train while we are asleep, that will please John."

PPS
"John says I've got to tell you they took the wood off the top of the telegraph pole."

My father wrote…

"The work at the Exchange is a little different from Southend; it's a much older place and old fashioned, the size is equal to Southend, it's situated in the Main Shopping Centre, and below there is a large Post Office."

"Have done 9 to 1pm overtime this morning and was on 6 to 11pm yesterday."

Telephonist training for Home Counties was at Bletchley Park and my father attended there in 1965, although this seems rather late considering he joined the GPO in 1961. It was not until many

Beginnings

decades later that knowledge of the park's key role in the war was revealed. My GPO connections with Bletchley Park go back to about 1940 when my mother was lodging in Letchworth and worked at BTM (British Tabulating Machines) machining precision parts on a lathe for the CANTAB project. CANTAB was the code name for the Enigma Bombe machine which was a vital part of the wartime code-breaking operation at Bletchley. As well as the precision, mechanical parts, the Bombe also utilised GPO 'telephone-type' electromechanical relays.

In between 'pricing telephone tickets' I used to play *Toy Town* Post Offices with a date stamp and ink pad, just like at the real counter where they stamped my Post Office Savings Account book. My practice telephone tickets were soon covered with date stamps!

At school, I always chose to draw or write something about the Post Office, though the telephone side was still a bit of a mystery as we didn't have a phone at home, other than the toy telephone intercom set which I was lucky enough to get one Christmas. In the GPO, 25 December was another work day and the switchboards still had to be manned to deal with emergency and assistance calls. It wasn't a particularly onerous duty and a taxi was always laid on, because public transport didn't run on Christmas Day! It was only for a few hours, but it was strange for daddy to rush about and put his suit on as though it was a normal day.

In 1968 there was an open day at Southend Telephone Exchange. I knew where it was, as many times I'd ridden there on my bicycle to meet daddy when he came off shift on a Sunday morning. I think he was one of the designated guides to show people around. So, my parents and I all got on the bus and it stopped opposite Baum's Furriers and we walked into the exchange. It was quite exciting, but I was very young and nervous. I hadn't envisaged the Switchroom

My GPO Family: Trilogy Edition

being on another floor, and as dad was registered disabled (*Green card scheme) we used the small brown-painted lift (in what was later known as the 'old building'). I hadn't been in many lifts and this one made my tummy go funny as it accelerated (presumably as gravity has a greater effect on a smaller body). I don't tend to notice that nowadays!

* The 'Green card scheme' was part of 'The Disabled Persons (Employment) Act 1944' which originally had a quota scheme whereby companies who employed many staff had to have a percentage of disabled.

I thought we would go straight to where daddy worked, but he left me alone to join the tour. Other than my toy intercom phones, I wasn't used to a 'real' phone, but the man doing the demo expected me to dial a number. People who I didn't know were being polite and asking if I'd like a cup of tea (I never drink tea), but all I wanted to do was to see where daddy did his work. I wasn't used to social situations, I needed to go home and it had to be now! Of course, once I got outside of the building, I calmed down, but dad was annoyed with me for showing him up, so there was no choice, and home we all went. That was the shortest ever telephone exchange tour! We did come away with a couple of leaflets entitled *Welcome to Your Telephone Exchange.*

One of my favourite library books from the era was *The Post Office* by Nancy Martin. From the Exchange Open Day leaflet and library book, I wrote a story for school. I think this was my first 'GPO story' that I wrote. I also cut up another telephone leaflet so that I could include three photos in my exercise book.

Beginnings

The Telephone Service (written in 1968)

Have you ever thought when you pick up your telephone, about all the work involved in connecting you with another person...

First of all on picking up the handset, a signal goes to the exchange then when you dial machines start working and complete the line. The cables coming from the exchange going to different places sometimes join in a cabinet which is painted green. Faults are passed onto the engineer who at his own control panel identifies the fault. Also, you can ring the operator to dial the number you want, for you. A telephone cable haves all the wires in it coloured different, so as not to get mixed up. In London, there is a building called the Post Office Tower, which is 620 feet high. It is built to handle telephone calls and television programmes. The top turns round and people in the restaurant can see all over London. In telephone exchanges meters count the cost of the calls we make. They are photographed every so often to avoid human error.

In the street there are telephone boxes with telephones in them. So far there have been six different call boxes, the fifth and sixth are in use at the moment. Most of them were designed by Gilbert Scott. Telephone exchanges are different from other buildings because, unlike others they need a year to dry out, because of all the electrical things which will go in them. Graham Bell was born in 1847 and he made the first telephone. Times have changed a lot since then. Sometimes repairs have to be carried out then, men lift up the inspection covers and make the repairs. They come in a greenish van which is now being changed to yellow for safety.

There is more than one sort of telephone, for a start you can [get] one called Trimphone that is the latest one. The Trimphone is a new telephone because, it is a different shape to the ordinary one; it

My GPO Family: Trilogy Edition

also has a volume control which the ordinary telephone has not got. There is more than one ordinary telephone, the most common one is in picture number one. In picture number two you can see the wallphone, ideal for shopkeepers. In number three you can see the intercom telephone in which you can have two or three telephones all linked up together.

After the explosion at the Post Office Tower in 1971, visits to all Telephone Exchanges were more strictly controlled and it was not until 1973 that I got to see where my father worked. At home, there were always a few blank telephone tickets around to remind me of Post Office Telephones. On the reverse of my tickets you may have found characters from *Winnie the Pooh in Fuzzy Felt*, and I discovered that the telephonists drew on the back of their tickets too! Arthur Wallace (TPST) was a budding cartoonist who used to doodle on whatever tickets or dockets were to hand. The drawings were often slightly derogatory and humorous. One depicted an ignorant subscriber who had called 100 for assistance and the caption read, '*Can you get it for me, I'm pickin' me nose?*' Making calls with a dial was a real chore back then! Another (from 1974) showed a man with 'popping out eyes' as a result of ISOCC (tickets) eyestrain, '*The optician said I had a severe case of ISOCCitis!*' Eye strain was a serious problem and THQ (Telecommunications HQ) had been running trials of alternative colour tickets. The outcome was that the figures in the marking field were made bolder and sharper. Arthur's cartoons were 'spot-on', though sadly only the ISOCC example survives.

By now I was at secondary school. During the 1970s, one of my school friend's father, Gordon Wales owned a factory (Wellview Tubes) which rebuilt cathode ray tubes (mainly for television sets)

Beginnings

by a method of baking them in an oven. Parts of the factory processes were controlled by cam-switches and timers. There was a bank of three ovens with chain-operated doors which slowly lowered like a portcullis as the processing began. Many of the electrical switch components had been sourced at *Southend Electronics* an 'Aladdin's Warehouse', that was a short bike ride away from the factory.

The warehouse was full to bursting of all kinds of new and surplus equipment including telephones, relays, uniselectors and cable, which originated from STC (Standard Telephones and Cables) Private Comms. Division in Footscray, Kent. I spent many a happy hour sorting through the masses of cardboard boxes both on the floor and on the extensive shelves of the warehouse. As stock was gradually sold, then more 'finds' of older batches of equipment and components were discovered. Boxes full of new 3000-type Post Office relays in polystyrene packing were among the parts unearthed. I usually chose a selection of as many as the carrier on my bicycle would allow, subject to buying them for just a few pounds. The owner was always generous to us 'kids'.

Two other popular places for surplus and electronic components were 'Bi-Pre-Pak' and Bill Fleming's 'Radio Constructor's Centre'. Maplin Electronics began in this decade too, and was a good source for transistors and early integrated circuits. Bi-Pre-Pak had stacks of recovered (ex GPO) black Bakelite 300 series telephones, as well as dials and relays, but my pocket money only went so far. And I had to convince my parents that our home could accommodate a few telephones in each room! The telephones were used, but in good order and only needed a clean. Sometimes they still had the original 'dial number labels'. One dial displayed 'Bedford 65150' and there was a list of handwritten numbers in the small pull-out drawer of the base of the phone. H. Thewlis Black

My GPO Family: Trilogy Edition

54081, Dr. Sewrey Bfd 64158 and others. Also, noted...'chimney sweep June 14, 10.30'. It was all rather intriguing and I tried to imagine the household from whence it had come.

During that era, Philips brought out an *Electronic Engineer* kit in which BC148 and BF159 transistors could be clipped onto a spring-loaded hardboard backing, together with resistors and capacitors, to make working circuits. And one of my favourite circuits could generate 'the pips' – the pay tone which could be heard from Public Payphones. We weren't 'on the phone' at home, so I have mixed memories of traipsing down the road, with mum, to the red kiosk several turnings away and (in the early days) perhaps being sat on the parcel shelf while mum pressed button A or B. And, in later times, looking up at the POA (Pay On Answer) mechanism, in a smoky smelling modern kiosk, listening for the 'pips' and for mum to press home the money which was balanced on the coin slots. Of course, on the occasions that we rang the operator (or supervisor) to report that dad was 'resuming to a day off', after being on sick leave, those calls were free.

I think it was my 14th birthday (1973) and my father had asked if I wanted anything in particular and I mentioned that a visit to see where he worked would be good. My father had to get permission from the day supervisor and I remember walking up a flight of rather sweeping stairs, as the Switchroom was in the old building (the new exchange was still in the process of completion). My father was waiting outside the double doors on the landing and we went through a second set of doors into a comparatively dim setting (by today's standards) of the operators' inner sanctum. The Switchroom was quiet, save for the operators working on the Board, answering and connecting calls, as the * Free Line Signals blinked along the strips of jacks, and the status of junctions changed in real time.

Beginnings

* Free Line Signals (FLS) were simply that: signals to indicate that a junction was not in use and could therefore be plugged into to make an outgoing call.

The outgoing multiples were labelled with the first two digits of the exchange number, e.g. Southend 54xxxx, such that the operator making a call to a Rochford number only had to dial the last four digits, as there were junctions directly to that exchange (and others). The operators wore headsets, but a telephone handset could be plugged into one of the two jacks on the front of the Board, for listening in, usually by a supervisor. The mahogany woodwork looked somewhat worn and it's possible that it was all the original equipment as installed when the linked numbering schemes were devised, circa 1929. The recently fitted push-button keysenders in lieu of the telephone dials were a stark contrast to the otherwise timeless façade. We plugged a handset into the jack on the front of the switchboard and made a call to my dad's twin sister in London and said hello. I don't think we wrote out a ticket for that one!

As night staff, my dad and his colleagues were responsible for the security of the building, so it was not unusual that he was familiar with some of the equipment floors as well as his own work area. As we did a quick tour of the building, he pointed to the 'tick-tick' * box which was clicking away on a desk. He explained that if the speaker stopped clicking, then we would have just four minutes (possibly) before the end of the world! I hoped that the box wouldn't stop clicking as we carried on, to visit other parts of the exchange.

[* This was a WB400 receiver used as part of the UK's Civil Defence Early Warning System. In the event of a possible nuclear attack, instructions on what to do would be broadcast over the speaker. Large telephone exchanges had these advance warning devices as maintaining telephone services in the event of a war was vital.]

At home, with one of the PO Type 2 uniselectors, from *Southend Electronics* I was able to connect a lamp strip of 10 or 20 lamps No.2 and have my own 'Free Line Signals (FLS)'. However, the uniselector had to be stepped with pulses from interacting relays, as self-homing was too fast for the lamps to give an authentic display. Figuring out how to connect all the bits was never too difficult as 'everything GPO' was manufactured to work together! If I found a power supply marked 'PO Batch Sampled' it was sure to match at least some of the kit! It was always fun buying a piece of equipment and figuring out how it worked or what it was supposed to do. Some of the relay sets were 'second hand' and again, it was interesting to note how the wiring had been laced and to study the multi-coloured wires and to decode where the power was connected. The uniselector was mounted on brackets screwed to a wooden table which at one time had hosted my model railway layout! The FLS strips were sandwiched between pieces of blockboard and painted opal green (as we had a spare tin of paint). I had the beginnings of my own telephone exchange!

It wasn't long before I had rigged up a telephone line (along the fence) between the garden shed and the lounge, controlled via relays and pay tone from my bedroom. The bells were on separate circuits as I hadn't (at that time) figured how to use a 'ring-trip' relay. But it was all immense fun and you could dial a number to switch the shed light off or on. As we didn't have mains power to the shed, the lights were actually a string of parallel wired GPO No.2 six-volt lamps powered over-the-line.

Following on from the Telephone Exchange visit... In October 1973, I wrote to the Post Office as part of another school project. I

Beginnings

was pleasantly surprised when my doorbell rang and someone from the local TMO (Telephone Manager's Office) actually called at my house to hand me some booklets and a very large wall chart: a map of the world showing all the major telephone cables between the various countries. I think it was the only time that a rep from a large company called at our house. Of course, those were the days when doctors and even opticians still did house calls.

I remember marking (on the wallchart) the route of CANTAT 2, which had been recently been completed. CANTAT 2 ran from Widemouth Bay, Cornwall, UK to Beaver Harbour, near Halifax, Nova Scotia, Canada. It was laid by two cableships, *Mercury* and the Canadian ice-breaker/cable layer, *John Cabot*. At the time, it was the biggest single cable to be laid across the Atlantic Ocean.

From adverts in the *Post Office Telecommunications Journal* (which my dad occasionally brought home), I wrote to major telecom manufacturers for info. These included Standard Telephones and Cables (several divisions), Plessey, and Associated Automation. Plessey replied that it was not company policy to give out details of operating systems. STC sent a good selection of telephone and cable brochures, as well as a hardcover book, *Progress in Telecommunication Cables*. From an STC leaflet listing all of their divisions in the UK, I was able to write off to more locations. It was rather exciting receiving a whole host of A4-sized postage-franked envelopes containing professionally printed company literature. GEC (General Electric Company) sent brochures of their range of telephones, although the specifications for their plansets appeared to be for use on private systems rather than the Public network that I was expecting.

Associated Automation sent leaflets of their payphone mechanisms and even invited me to visit them, though it was never really

My GPO Family: Trilogy Edition

convenient for me to do so, as we rarely went to London, especially not in term time.

I also borrowed Atkinson's *Telephony* volumes I and II from my local library. Atkinson was the 'official' book for anyone who wanted to make a serious study of the subject. My third-year school project filled nearly two exercise books and helped me understand how to research the topic. I did another two reports, though these were on A4 size loose-leaf paper: *The Post Office Tower* and a critical write-up of *Various Aspects of Post Office Telecommunications*. At this point the pressure of the exam system was taking its toll and these projects were stretching my time and resources!

In my final year at secondary school, I took the Post Office aptitude test for an engineering apprentice, but my imagining of geometric shapes wasn't good and my science could have been better. To improve my chances of a decent job I applied to take an OND (Ordinary National Diploma) in Technology (Engineering). This was a two-year course roughly equivalent to A-Levels, though was not sponsored by an employer and there was still no guarantee of job at the end of it. As I didn't quite meet the entry standard, I did a one-year pre-Dip course to get me up to speed.

London Telephones — Join the headset

Post Office (LTR) leaflet (circa 1980)

Outlet 2: Going Postal

As Royal Mail celebrated 500 years of service in 2016, I recalled my fascination with the postal business and how it related to *My GPO Family* and everyday life. A condensed timeline is included below to aid an understanding of the structure of the businesses and the different trading names used through the years.

Timeline

1516 Royal Mail
Royal Mail's origin can be traced back to 1516 with the appointment of a Master of the Posts, Brian Tuke. This was formalised with Oliver Cromwell's parliament establishing the 1657 'Act for the Setling of the Postage of England, Scotland and Ireland'.

"From henceforth there be one General Office, to be called and known by the name of the Post Office of England....And one officer....under the name of Post Master General."

1660 General Post Office (GPO)
However, Charles II disputed Cromwell's laws and so the Post Office act of 1660 was passed to legally recognise the formation of the organisation: 'An Act for Erecting and Establishing a Post Office.'

Thus, the General Letter Office, subsequently known as the General Post Office, was formed in London. Henry Bishop was appointed Postmaster-General in 1660.

My GPO Family: Trilogy Edition

1950s GPO
During the 1950s the GPO organisation (as part of the Civil Service) was responsible for both Posts and Telecommunications which included:

- Royal Mail Letters and Parcels
- Post Office Counter Services
- Post Office Savings Bank
- Post Office Telephones (and Telegraphs)

1969 The Post Office Corporation
On 1 October 1969 the Post Office became a Public Corporation and no longer had a Postmaster-General. The Post Office Savings Bank remained with the Exchequer and became National Savings. The telephone division was split to a separate corporation, British Telecommunications in October 1981, which was finally privatised in 1984.

- Royal Mail
- Post Office Counter Services
- National Giro (which became Girobank plc in 1988 and was sold to Alliance and Leicester in 1990.)

1986
The Post Office was reorganised into three divisions in October 1986.

- Royal Mail Letters
- Royal Mail Parcels (later renamed Parcelforce)
- Post Office Counters (later became Post Office Ltd)

Going Postal

2001 Consignia
With the passing of the Postal Service Act, the Post Office holding company was renamed Consignia plc. This new name was not popular with the public, thus it was changed to the Royal Mail Group plc in 2002.

2002 Royal Mail Group plc
Royal Mail Group became the parent company name with trading units of:

- Royal Mail
- Post Office Limited
- Parcelforce Worldwide

2012 Post Office Ltd
On 1 April 2012, Post Office Limited was demerged from Royal Mail Group to report directly to the Government. This was the only part of the original 'Post Office' that had not been privatised. A 10-year inter-business agreement between Royal Mail and the Post Office allowed for the handling of stamps, parcels and letters throughout the network of Post Offices. The Government retained ownership of Post Office Ltd via the Postal Services Holding Company plc.

2013 Royal Mail plc
In October 2013 70% of Royal Mail was sold. By October 2015, the Government had sold its remaining holdings. Trading groups were:

UKPIL (Parcels, Internationals and Letters)
GLS (General Logistics Systems)

My GPO Family: Trilogy Edition

Within UKPIL, Parcelforce Worldwide was the express parcels unit. GLS was a Europe-wide parcel delivery service which was acquired by the Post Office in 1999.

My GPO Family

The General Post Office (GPO), as it was once known, provided a comprehensive public service, and I never tired of wanting to be involved with it, although it was more by chance than design that I eventually did.

My intrigue with the GPO in the 1960s was encouraged by my parents who supported the products and services of the Post Office, which was the place we visited during our shopping trips. In those early days, cash was used for all transactions; only well-off people had cheque books, and credit was hire purchase, 'on the never' (weekly cash payments against items put by in a shop). Coincidentally, we had a *Never Never Land* in Southend (as part of the seafront illuminations), although that was always a fun place to visit! Credit cards had only just been launched in the UK and were not something that would have been accepted by my thrifty parents.

From early on, I had a Post Office Savings Bank account opened in my name and, by about age seven, I sent off a specimen of my signature so that I could operate the account myself. Any deposit or withdrawal was hand written in the book and then date stamped by the counter clerk. The round metal date stamp always made a 'thump-thump' sound as the clerk pressed first on the ink pad and then stamped in the book. I spent many a happy hour date stamping everything in sight, with my *Toy Town* Post Office set, though the sound was never quite the same!

Going Postal

Premium Savings Bonds were purchased for me and the thrill of listening to the radio to hear which bond ERNIE, the Electronic Random Number Indicator Equipment, had drawn for the weekly £25,000 prize was always fun, although it was never us!

Stamp collecting was enhanced with the irregular appearance of *First Day Covers* with the issue of new stamps. And many sub Post Offices also sold sweets and stationery, so a visit was always quite a treat! In a letter to my father, when he was working away, in 1964, my mother wrote...

"You know what the bedtime story tonight will be, this letter travelling all night on a train while we are asleep, that will please John."

And of course, it did!

When I bought my Tri-ang Hornby OO model railway, it had to have the Travelling Post Office (TPO) carriage, which picked up mailbags from a trackside hook, and then deposited them into a bin further round the track. TPOs never ran from Southend, and it was not until 2009 that I was able to watch the real apparatus in action!

In 1966 the mail train from Glasgow to London, Euston featured prominently in the news; it was the Great Train Robbery! Cash to the value of approximately £2.6 million was stolen, but why was Royal Mail transporting banknotes? In 1930, the HVP (High Value Packet) scheme had been introduced as a service to the banks for special handling of notes, cheques and securities. To aid identification, HVPs were carried in separate mailbags and thus became a lucrative target for the robbers. The 1960s were a time of

My GPO Family: Trilogy Edition

great change and audacity in both culture and business as new opportunities were forged by everyone. I was still rather young to understand these elemental forces, and why such a fuss was created by appearances of The Rolling Stones, or Alf Garnett in *Till Death Us Do Part* on television.

National Giro (bank) was introduced in 1968, and my father soon opened an account, so terms such as 'Giro cheque' and 'Giro transfer' quickly became familiar words in our household. This was postal banking and all correspondence was pre-paid (free), as National Giro was also part of the Post Office. Cheques payable to 'self' could be cashed at the Post Office Counter. National Giro was *the peoples' bank* with *a chequebook for everyone*, and was the idea of the Postmaster-General, Tony Benn. In 1964, he had written:

"My attraction to the Post Office was that I saw it as an essential public service that ought to develop in all sorts of creative ways."

By 1970, a favourite library book of my childhood was *The Post Office* by Nancy Martin. This detailed all aspects of the modern-day Post Office organisation, which included the Post Office Railway and the Post Office Tower. Both of these held my attention and I wondered if I might ever visit them? London was a very busy city and we didn't go there very often. Regardless, the book fuelled my passion for all things 'GPO' and I never ceased to be excited by them.

Years later, the term 'giro cheque' was more frequently associated with welfare payments than the cheques written by personal customers of National Giro, but nevertheless this shows how

Going Postal

widespread their use had become! To other banks, National Giro was never a serious contender and today, as part of Banco Santander, it performs well, but is simply another public service which has been lost to the UK.

Pre-printed envelopes for National Giro changed addresses in 1974 as Bootle was rezoned from Lancashire to Merseyside. Premium Bond correspondence was once postmarked 'Fylde Coast' referring to Lytham St. Annes, but in 1978 the operation moved to Blackpool. These changes were significant as our family always guessed the content of incoming post by the postmarks, or the return address. With the rattle of our letter box, it was always exciting (and still is) to rush to the door and see what the postman had delivered.

By 1974 postcodes had been allocated to the whole of the UK to aid mechanised sorting of mail, so I grew up with the habit of finding the correct code for an address, whenever possible. During the 1980s all of this address information was collated by Royal Mail to form the PAF (Postal Address File), containing the full and correct address for every known household and business. Much later, I was to experience use of the PAF with 'CSS address matching' in British Telecom.

At secondary school, I did a project about the early days of Royal Mail stage coaches and the beginnings of mechanised sorting of mail. Suffice to say that every aspect of the Post Office was of interest to me.

Trips to the local Post Office have remained constant throughout my life. The dimly lit premises of 555 London Road where the

My GPO Family: Trilogy Edition

counter towered above me as I was so young (and little). The chatter of Mr and Mrs Nash at Inverness Av. as they worked diligently to explain the many forms, as well as serve in their sweet shop. The polite staff in Waitrose who calmly calculated the best parcel rates from the ever-changing tariffs. Post Offices still accept 'Giro' envelopes (free of charge) for onward processing at Bootle! Girobank was one of the early partners in the 'Link' cash machine network. At the launch in 1985 there weren't any machines in Southend, so I eagerly drove to the nearest one in Basildon Town Centre to be able to try out my brand-new card. I inserted my card in the slot, entered my PIN number, and carefully followed the instructions on the screen to withdraw cash. The cash magically appeared and a transaction slip popped out of another slot. I retrieved my cash, but was so busy studying the machine in wonderment that I didn't notice the time-out on my card and within a few more seconds the machine had quietly swallowed it! It wasn't supposed to do that, or was it? I had to write a letter to Girobank and they sent me a new card a week or so later. That was one way of learning about new technology!

Over the years, *First Day Covers* (new stamps) continued to be a novelty to collect with generally one trip to the Post Office to buy the special envelope in advance and then another journey to get the stamps and post the cover in a dedicated box at the main Post Office on the actual day. Covers were hand franked 'First Day of Issue' and 'Southend-on-Sea', so were quite unique! Nowadays the issues are bought on-line with the generic postmark, 'Tallents House'; far easier to do, but less fun and perhaps not so valued? Each issue has multiple product lines of Presentation Packs, stamp cards, mint stamps, stamps books, and more recently, *Post and Go* stamps. All very slickly designed and co-ordinated to encourage

Going Postal

maximum spending on the hobby.
Mail for Southend used to be sorted locally, first at Tylers Avenue, then at Bircham Road and later (from 1986) at Short Street, adjacent to Southend Victoria railway station. A rail terminal allowed mail trains direct loading from the sorting office. In the 1960s additional sorting offices were to be found along Southchurch Road and also the London Road. With 'volumes of scale and economy' in mind, a large out of town facility was developed in Chelmsford and as a member of the Post Office Vehicle Club (POVC), I joined a tour...

South East Anglia Mail Centre (SEAMaC) Chelmsford (2005)

The building was of warehouse proportions, rather like a large B & Q store, but with restricted areas; mail handling is confidential. After we had collected our visitors' passes we were ready for a tour of the handling and sorting area. Four shifts cover a 24 hour, 7 days a week operation, with a staff base of approximately 800. This is centred around the two-tier mail system, 1st and 2nd class letters (and small packets) which are all sorted to strict deadlines. The postal regulator imposes penalties if the targets are not met. To have a single letter left at the end of a shift, although almost inevitable, can count as a failure. Chris Kennedy, our manager-guide explained with obvious passion about the many inadequately enveloped items that are posted by the general public. Children's birthday cards with badges, which tend to jam the sorting machines. Pound coins and notes sent in packets without return addresses. These go to charity if the sender cannot be traced. All different sizes of postcards, envelopes and packets can legally be posted and accepted for delivery; this doesn't help, because the sorting machines have to cater for such a wide range of possible shapes, thicknesses and designs. Some envelopes made from recycled paper tend to fall apart as they go through the machines!

My GPO Family: Trilogy Edition

Certain DVD envelopes, which have perforated edges tend to follow a similar fate. Letters which are too poorly addressed to deliver are returned if a sender's address is found on the outside of the envelope. Letters without return addresses are forwarded to the 'dead letter office' in Northern Ireland, because they are authorised to open the envelopes and search the contents for clues.

Letters for sorting are tipped onto one of four conveyors, which lifts them about six feet into a large drum, which rotates at 4 miles per hour. Slots in the drum allow letters of the desired size and thickness to fall through into the next stage of sorting. Oversize items are rejected for manual handling. Metal detectors reject items (seemingly apart from badges) which might otherwise jam the machines. An intrinsic part of the process allows for letters to be orientated with the longest end and face forwards before they pass to the next stage.

After the letters have been correctly orientated they are scanned and the process allows 14 seconds for a match with the PAF (Postal Address File) before they are rejected for manual checking. Every attempt is made for automatic sorting; once scanned the images can pass to one of four UK centres, where operators troubleshoot a vague address from their remote computer screens. Such letters can be fed into the sorter a second time when the correct coding details can be added, by phosphor or similar marking. A correct house number and postcode is the minimum requirement for a match. Correctly addressed letters are machine sorted and batched into their 'walks' i.e. they are 'Walksorted' for despatch to a local office.

The letter sorting machines are about the size of an office photocopier with many belts and rollers. For the complete process, about twenty sections of machine are joined together. Each

Going Postal

machine has a prominent blue 'stop' button to isolate it in the event of a jam! A display on the batching machine confirms which 'plan' is being worked at any moment, e.g. 'MS27' (MailSort 27).

MailSort items (usually high-volume mailings from large companies) are presented in window envelopes. The machine reads just the special barcode inside the envelope to determine the correct mailing destination. Batched mail is bagged and placed on *York* containers, which are lined up in an orderly fashion in one of 34 despatch bays. The larger 'blues' RSCs (Rigid Stackable Containers) are also stacked ready for collection to destinations in the UK and abroad.

After the tour of the building we took photographs of the many Royal Mail vehicles parked at the Centre. Typical vans of the time were the Vauxhall *Combo* and LDV *Pilot*.

All sorting of Southend's post was moved to SEAMaC (by now renamed Chelmsford mail centre) in early 2012. By 2015 five DOs (Delivery Offices) had closed: Rochford, Leigh-on-Sea, Shoeburyness, Canewdon and Great Wakering. The Short Street centre is now the only DO for Southend and the surrounding areas.

Mail by Rail

Travelling Post Offices (TPOs) were purpose-built carriages for the Post Office to transport large volumes of mail across the rail network, usually overnight. Mailbags were picked up and dropped off at intermediate stations along the routes. Individual letters and small packets were manually sorted into pigeonholes by staff as the train progressed along its journey. By the time the train reached its final destination, all mail had been sorted, bagged and tagged, ready for local delivery.

TPOs abolished the trackside picking up and setting down of mail in 1971. Poor infrastructure maintenance by the privatised Railtrack in 2000 led to service delays of the TPOs and subsequently this was a factor in their demise. The last TPO ran on public rails in 2004. Many carriages were donated to preserved railways and it was at the Nene Valley Railway that I finally got to see a full sized TPO exchanging mailbags.

Nene Valley Railway (July 2009)

I caught a fast train from Kings Cross to Peterborough and walked the 20 minutes or so in the hot July sunshine to arrive at the Nene Valley Railway in time for the midday steam train. The *City of Peterborough* no. 73050 a 4-6-0 engine with coal tender was eventually sighted and I was soon on board one of the carriages heading towards Wansford. At Wansford, British Railways Deltic diesel D9009 *Alycidon* was coupled to *Brian White* NSA 80337 a Royal Mail TPO sorting carriage complete with 'apparatus' (a traductor arm and net). I carefully stepped aboard and it seemed a little odd to be in a carriage without any seats! I sat up on one of the benches as the train started its journey to Sutton Cross where the mail pick-up and drop off was to be demonstrated. The sorting tender door was open, so we could watch the countryside going by, while a postman stood against the single metal bar guarding the opening.

At Sutton Cross there was no platform at which to alight, so a set of metal stairs was positioned to allow us to descend to track level. We stood a safe distance away from the 'apparatus' and waited while the postmen, dressed in period buff workcoats, climbed the trackside ladder, then strung and tied three heavy mailbags to the lineside hooks. The train made a pass with the net on the carriage

Going Postal

extended to catch the mailbags. It all happened so very quickly and smoothly! The postmen walked a few yards down the trackside to retrieve the mailbags which had been dropped into the lineside net.

Although I'd never seen a mail exchange before, it was as if we'd gone back in history to another time, to perhaps when the world was more organised and had better routines? Clearly, everyone had enjoyed the demo, especially the men who were effectively playing with a real train set! I returned to the carriage and the train trundled back to Wansford.

Note: Although TPOs no longer run in public service, a few Royal Mail trains (the 325 class) still transport mail between London, Warrington, Glasgow and Gateshead.

Blythe House (2010)

Much GPO history is centred on London, such that the Post Office Savings Bank (POSB) HQ once occupied the North Block of Faraday Building in the days before the telephone service began there.

Blythe House is a magnificent and imposing building which was designed by Sir Henry Tanner and was built in the late 1890s to become the new headquarters of the Post Office Savings Bank. It gained Grade II listing in 2004. The move of the POSB from Queen Victoria Street to Blythe Road was completed in 1903.

It its heyday, thousands of Civil Servants worked on the ledgers, as small savers throughout the UK opened accounts at their local Post Offices. Bank books were sent to HQ to have the annual interest 'made up' (added). There were no computers back then, although mechanical adding machines were operated with much dexterity by their users. By the early 1970s, main operations of the POSB had

My GPO Family: Trilogy Edition

transferred to Glasgow and Blythe House became a huge storage warehouse for the overflow collections of organisations such as the Victoria and Albert Museum. The building has featured in films requiring historic government office settings.

I paid a fleeting visit to Blythe House in 2010 to take some external shots and to marvel at this time capsule of a GPO building dating back more than a century. Sadly, I didn't have an invite to explore inside, but I could imagine the endless corridors and vast rooms once filled with writing tables. The thousands of clerks quietly and orderly checking the nation's savings; another testament to the great organisation that was the Post Office.

Visit to Debden Postal Store (September 2012)

As a member of the Post Office Vehicle Club (POVC) I was invited to its 50th year anniversary display at Debden postal store. The store contains a wide selection of postal related items under the care of the British Postal Museum and Archive (BPMA). Cars, vans and motorbikes which were used to deliver the post, as well as motive units from the defunct *Mail Rail* (Post Office Railway 1927 -2003), are stored together with numerous pillar boxes 'through the ages'. A mix of telecom and postal vehicles attended the rally which was a static display in the rear car park. A unique entrant was SLO 24 - a red single decker bus, which once used to relay test match telegrams (via teleprinters) to the overseas circuits during the Australian cricket tour of 1956!

"Built on a Commer chassis, the office was designed by the Telegraph and Engineering branches of the Post Office External Telecommunications Executive and the Engineering Department. Engineers of the Telephone Manager's staff at Brighton installed the wiring in the works (Harrington of Hove) where the van was built. The vehicle is 27 ft. 6 in. long and weighs six tons. The

aluminium coach body is finished in Post Office red with gold anodised metal fittings and gold lettering."
Wow, that was a sight and it was wonderful that so many vehicles are in preservation to tell the story of the GPO.

Post in the 21st Century

As far back as 2004 the 'second post' house deliveries had been abolished in favour of a single, usually later, delivery per day. These tended to be of varying times and a 08:30 hrs delivery was becoming a thing of the past. The once short wait to see if the postman was coming to my house could last up to 16:30 hrs! This was only apparent when I was off from work, but it seemed that the once dependable and regular postal service was in decline.

In 2006 Royal Mail lost its monopoly which meant that competitors could transport mail on their own networks and then pass it to Royal Mail for the 'final-mile' delivery to the customer! Over the years a whole new range of franking appeared on envelopes, such as *TNT Post*, but latterly with the addition of *Delivered by Royal Mail*. What a farce that Royal Mail was expected to deliver a competitors' post for them, and probably at a discounted rate! Both other privatised firms and government departments increasingly sought to reduce costs and they too switched to alternate collection and delivery options for their post.

In 2012 the Post Office (counter's business) was demerged from Royal Mail Group and Royal Mail was privatised in 2013. Declining volumes of letters and the need to become more efficient resulted in reduced collections from pillar boxes and the closure of

My GPO Family: Trilogy Edition

many smaller delivery and sorting offices.

In my local newspaper a reader reported that the traditional 'red elastic band', with which bundles of letters were held together, had been replaced by a brown biodegradable type. The point being that it was no longer worthwhile to retrieve any which often trailed behind an errant postie on the pavements. On some ParcelForce vehicles, stickers declared 'turning red vans green' (by having lower carbon emissions). Times were certainly changing.

Take a Letter (May 2015)

There was once a letter service run by the GPO,
And you could time your watch by them and know if it was slow!

Everything was well-ordered and the post was rarely late,
But nowadays the situation's different and they tend to make you wait!

Letters in pillar boxes were collected throughout the day,
Now you check the panel and it doesn't really say?

The last collection from this box will be at 9 am!
I had to stop and read it several times again.

What do they do the rest of the working day,
When e-mail has taken most of the letter post away?

The red vans still race frantically up and down the street,
And sometimes on your travels a postman you will meet.

Going Postal

The parcel post is very good, they start early in the day,
Though other carriers are available, it's compulsory to say!
The new working regime was known as 'Collection on Delivery' as the postman delivering the daily post would also be responsible for emptying the boxes. Vans whizzing around just to empty boxes was a thing of the past.

Traditionally, the postman or postwoman would have been sighted riding or scooting along on a regulation issue GPO bicycle.

Nowadays OPGs (Other Postal Grades – the non-gender title) are more familiarly seen with red 'prams' (that's what my father would have called them) chained to lampposts. They are High Capacity Trolleys (HCTs) which are wheeled from Delivery Offices (DOs) and eliminate the need for the postman to carry a heavy post bag.

Chris Hogan of the Post Office Vehicle Club writes

"Essentially OPGs deliver to residences and SMEs by one of three methods:"

1.   Singleton vans on traditional rural routes

2.   Shared vans for 'walks' more than a mile from the DO crewed by two OPGs. They are issued with golf trolleys to be used on individual loops with more than a handful of letters. They are not greatly used, OPGs prefer to use bags over shoulders as it saves time and allows an early finish.

3.   Walks close to DOs should be done by HCTs. Normally within walking distance (one mile) but there is evidence that shared vans are replacing some of these walks even though they are close to DOs. The electric versions E-HCTs intended for hilly areas weren't a success and have generally been replaced by HCTs or

My GPO Family: Trilogy Edition

shared vans.

The combination of the withdrawal of 'Mail by Rail' and the additional Delivery Methods (DM) vans has led to the bulk of mail being transported by road. To me it seems a backward step to have so many competing vans vying for space on our already crowded roads, as the volume of goods delivered to individual homes increases as internet shopping becomes more the norm. Perhaps a new universal carrier will emerge in the future?

Modernising Post Office Counters

These changed little over the years as they needed to be secure from would-be robbers. In the larger Post Offices, separate queues at each window (staffed position) was the norm until, circa 1993, when (what my dad called 'pig pens') a single zigzag queue became commonplace. Enclosed by posts and straps, the 'pen' organised customers into one long queue feeding into all of the available positions. With the advance of recording- technology the now familiar *Cashier number 3 please* announcements together with a numbered display advised a waiting customer the location of the next free cashier!

The *Cashier number 3 please* queuing system was invented by, and is the voice of Terry Green who operates *Qmatic*.

This concept of being 'told' where to go was slightly irritating, but also rather endearing as the voice sounded so upbeat. If standing in the queue for a long period it was also somewhat repetitive to hear exactly the same intonations announced so many times. As with the 'music on hold' for phone systems, it would be refreshing for the voices to change at least occasionally!

Going Postal

The self-service aspect of 21st century life asserted itself upon the Post Office with the introduction of *Post and Go* machines from October 2008. These allowed weighing of items and the ability to purchase a printed stamp/label with the correct postage via a debit or credit card. Stamp vending was not a new concept, but the overall design of the service made it useful addition to busy main Post Offices. I do like customer service rather than self-service, though I had used 'self-checkouts' in a couple of stores. I hadn't yet seen any *Post and Go* machines locally. Of course, all of this technology continues to pave the way for staff reductions as costs and competition escalate.

By about 2011, in some Crown offices the 'pig pen' concept was updated. The single queue had gone and instead of having to stand, seating was provided. Upon arrival, you touched a screen to choose which counter service you required, cash, parcels, foreign currency, etc., and a numbered ticket was issued. You then had the choice of sitting to wait for your number to be announced, or you could multi-task and browse the shop area. This appeared to require greater concentration as there was no perception of 'moving up the queue' as the physical line was no more! This was quite a 'step-change'; it wasn't a proper way to queue! The boundaries between accessibility and security were beginning to merge as well. The more 'open plan' type counters displayed a polite notice requesting customers not to lean forward into the cashier's space! In the modern world, change happens more frequently and after decades of 'normality', new ideas can seem radical.

From August 2015, NS & I (National Savings and Investments) announced that Premium Bonds would no longer be on sale at Post Office branches and that this was the last of their products to be withdrawn from the counter's business. I remembered back to coach trips with my parents where we would pop into a local Post

My GPO Family: Trilogy Edition

Office and were able to buy a small denomination bond over the counter and have it date stamped with the locality. This was a fun way to buy more bonds and as a keepsake for the places we'd visited. National Savings had not been 'part of the Post Office' since 1969, so this long association of products had continued far beyond expectations. It was however, just another indication that a once valued business had moved away from the Post Office as, like many other companies, it increasingly does the majority of its transactions on-line.

Later in August, BBC 2 screened *Signed, Sealed, Delivered - Inside the Post Office*, which was a three-part documentary about the impact of the Post Office's 'Network Transformation' plans. Quite simply, 'Transformation' removed the subsidy from many offices requiring them to be more commercial by increasing sales to survive, or be hived off into a local shop if judged to no longer be a viable stand-alone business. The Post Office management clearly supported the Postmasters (financially and morally) to enable them to change within the terms of the new agreements, but it seemed that the concept of a Public Service was almost at an end as the Government adopted a free-market approach with reduced support for previous monopoly suppliers.

I was much saddened by this programme as it was obvious that many decades of expert knowledge of serving the public were being swept away and replaced by an emerging self-service culture which would have to compete with other providers or close. Tony Benn's once great vision of a Public Service Post Office providing post, telephone and banking in a co-ordinated, efficient, and above all, trustworthy manner had finally died. On balance, as the Post Office continued to lose subsidy, the Transformation plan was probably its best chance for the business to continue in the short term.

Going Postal

During my GPO career I'd witnessed the Government sell off virtually every department of the Post Office and had watched as it struggled to ensure that private enterprise continued to deliver the expected quality services, fairly to all, at a minimum cost. Regulation had become ever more problematic, tariffs more complex, and as firms vied for a competitive edge, prices had increased, jobs had been cut and service had only been provided where it was profitable to do so. The issues were complex as the world expected more flexibility and choice than it ever had in the past. Self-service could be quicker, but for the less able who needed assistance, it was a never-ending spiral of continually having to spend more, to get the level of help which they needed. Service jobs, although somewhat mundane, had maintained livelihoods for hundreds of thousands of families over many decades of GPO work. A once great organisation had almost been obliterated during a single generation.

By mid-October 2015 all of the Government's shares in Royal Mail had been sold, except a token 1% holding which was finally given away to employees. Effectively, the only part of the original GPO which had not been privatised was the business familiarly known as 'Post Office Counters'. The counter's business had been affected by direct competition from other parcel carriers, the Internet and direct trading by TV Licensing, National Savings, the DSS, and generally advancing technology. And with limited support from Royal Mail and the Government, its days may be numbered?

The GPO Family

Also in October 2015, BBC 4 screened *The Post Office and Me* featuring Alan Johnson MP, who in 1968 had worked as a postman in London and had later been General Secretary of the Union of

My GPO Family: Trilogy Edition

Communication Workers (UCW). The programme was a splendid retrospective of the organisation and it too highlighted the fate of *Mail Rail* and the TPOs. It included a wonderful quote from Alan at the end:

"When I left the Post Office, I didn't just leave a job. It felt like leaving a family, corny as it sounds."

Note: The Union of Post Office Workers (UPW) was the recognised union when Alan worked as a postman. The UPW changed its name to the Union of Communication Workers (UCW) in 1980 and then merged with the Post Office Engineering Union (POEU) in 1995 to form the Communication Workers Union (CWU).

WH Smith

In spite of providing a good service, the future of some long-established crown Post Offices, in their current form, wasn't guaranteed…

The Post Office today announced a new 10-year agreement with WH Smith to relocate more Post Office branches into the UK retailer's modernised stores, keeping services on high streets throughout the country and bringing further investment for customers.
[Extract from Post Office press release 13 April 2016]

Outlet 3: College Years

As a child, I can recall walking along the top of the low wall alongside the Southend College of Technology in the London Road. In later years, I looked up at the fairly open internal staircase, framed by large glass windows and thought that I wouldn't particularly like to use it. By September 1976, I was walking those stairs on a daily basis! Both the education and the stair climbing was to stand me in good stead for my future years…

The Southend College of Technology (London Road Annexe) opened in 1957 and was styled in the manner of a public utility building, set well back from the road, save for a curved protrusion which formed part of the library. With its metal-framed single-glazed windows, so typical of the period, together with dark blue cladding panels, it could easily have been mistaken for a police station.

College was a more relaxed and adult environment in which to learn and they also had a working UAX (Unit Automatic Exchange) which supplemented the official Post Office PABX (Private Automatic Branch Exchange). Mr White ran the courses for the Day Release students of Post Office Telecommunications, so a chat with him was always interesting, although we both had our own classes to attend, so our meetings were infrequent. Many of the lecturers had quite unique, somewhat quirky personalities, though this balanced out the ones who were slightly more formal in their attitude and teachings. Overall, it was an engaging place to be.

For each year at college I completed one mandatory project. Not surprisingly, my first-year pre-Dip (Ordinary National Diploma) project (1976/77) started with a 15-page report entitled *A short account on the routing of telephone calls in Great Britain*. As part

My GPO Family: Trilogy Edition

of this study I managed to arrange another visit to Southend Telephone Exchange, and here's that section of my report…

Visit to Southend-on-Sea ATE (Automatic Telephone Exchange)

This took place on Wednesday 30 November 1977 at 2 pm and was arranged by kind permission of the Public Relations Officer of Telephone House.

First of all I was shown round the engineering section of the exchange by an engineer who briefly explained to me the workings of the exchange with references to: Local Calls; STD Calls and ISD calls.

All of the lines coming into the exchange, after rising from the basement (which I did not see) were terminated on the Main Distribution Frame (MDF) and connected via fuses before being fed to the switching equipment. This equipment was not contained on just one floor, but several and was not arranged in a strictly orderly fashion, but sited where most convenient for connecting up. However, all of the equipment racks were numbered and charts were provided to enable tracing of calls (especially 999) to take place.

To describe the whole visit in detail would take too long, therefore the following are points that may be of particular interest.

The power supply for the whole exchange is provided by a cable of 11,000 volts from the National Grid and is stepped down, transformed and rectified to about 46 volts. Such a large cable is needed due to the high demand for current at the exchange, which was 1300 amps at 46 volts at that particular time. The exchange

College Years

does have some batteries (e.g. accumulators) which are approx. 4 feet high by 2 feet square, but these are only used to supplement the power unit in that they provide smoothing (e.g. reduce humming and similar faults).

In an emergency (e.g. a power cut) the power supply fails and the batteries can only provide power at the normal rate for about 15 minutes. To overcome this a diesel engine, worked by a compressor, is used, which automatically starts up if the power is cut, and operates a generator. (I was not able to see this as the particular room was kept locked due to the high voltages involved).

Situated in various parts of the exchange were recorded announcement machines; simply a loop of magnetic tape and a replay machine. One of these was connected to Eastern Electricity's old head office telephone number (the Board has recently moved from Southend to Rayleigh) to inform subscribers of the new number. Announcement machines were also available for replay to engineering staff, working on a faulty telephone line, to advise them of a particular fault. However, the machine was not working at that particular time).

Several testing machines were connected to the equipment; any faults being printed out in code on a ticket, by machine. Meters (i.e. counters) are connected to many junction routes of the exchange to record the number of junctions being used or the amount of traffic (e.g. calls) waiting for a junction to be available. Most faults that occur in the exchange are indicated by coloured lamps arranged on a large panel in the gangways (space between racks). A PA (Public Address) system is provided to call engineers to a certain part of the exchange or possibly to ask them to trace a call. This system is necessary because a few hundred selectors (mechanical selectors at that) make a fair amount of noise! In several places notices were

My GPO Family: Trilogy Edition

displayed advising other engineers not to adjust certain equipment as traffic recording was in process. In other parts of the exchange, testing switchboards, operated by engineering staff, were seen. These either received, subscribers' reports of faulty lines or similar, or calls from engineers working on subscribers' lines outside the exchange and needing technical advice or a line tested.

Two important machines were the tariff machines used to vary the pulses applied to the subscribers' meters, generating a large number of pulses at the period of Peak Rate calls, and a small number of pulses at the period of Cheap Rate calls. The machines were motor driven, operating a number of make/break contacts. One machine was in use, the other was a standby. The contacts are susceptible to dust, but the engineer assured me that they are more likely to miss a pulse rather than give an extra one, thus being favourable to the subscriber and not the Post Office.

The ringing machine for the exchange was again motor driven and had a standby. It provides all of the ringing current (for the exchange) which is supplied to subscribers' bells. The familiar ring-ring, ring-ring, and the associated tones are all generated within the machine by moving coils. In very modern or up to date exchanges the ringing is generated by electronic means.

Some trunk calls or routes from the exchange are signalled not by impulses along a line, but by tones of various pitches, which are less prone to distortion or misinterpretation by equipment. E.g. a machine might only detect five pulses, when in fact six were transmitted. The engineer stated that in the past, university students (in particular) had been known to whistle down the 'phone line to either get a long-distance call free, or to try and confuse the equipment. To overcome this, any voice transmission (during the setting up of such a call) coming from a subscriber's line is 'cut up'

College Years

or stopped completely by special equipment.

At about 3.15 pm, I was shown round the Switchroom (i.e. the room where the main switchboard was located) by an operator. There are three main boards, viz: General board, Directory Enquiry board and Service switchboard. The first board deals with most 100 dialled calls to the operator, as well as 999 calls. The second board is obvious. The Service switchboard deals with calls by Post Office staff who can be directly linked (usually free of charge) to the switchboard for Telephone House or other places or departments of the Post Office.

One special panel in the Switchroom is used for the transfer of numbers (e.g. doctors' telephone numbers). Doctors can 'phone the operator who, by depressing or releasing a certain button, can transfer that doctor's number to another line. This is useful for a doctor who is always travelling from one place to another.

Free lines from the exchange are indicated by 6-volt lamps, thus an operator setting up a call for a subscriber knows where to plug the line into. As a line becomes engaged (an outgoing line) the associated lamp goes out.

Operators in the exchange do not dial calls for subscribers using mechanical dials (as on most telephones) but on electronic keysenders. These are units approx. 6 cm by 10 cm, consisting of 10 or more pushbuttons numbered 0 to 9 (via 1) plus an extra button for cancelling. The units are electronic and are really push-button type phones. However, the units transmit impulses at the normal rate so that the mechanical selectors in the exchange have time to operate. If the exchange was of the electronic design, the keysenders could transmit pulses at a much faster rate.

My GPO Family: Trilogy Edition

The visit finished at approx. 4.15 pm and was extremely interesting, although it was difficult to absorb all of the information given as there was so much to see. Nevertheless, it did show the complexity of the telephone system and a typical exchange.

Mr Sampson, college lecturer marked this report and wrote…

"An excellent report. I am impressed by the concise report of this visit which is well produced and shows that you observed a great deal of the work that goes on."

Postscript (April 2015)

The above report was a visit to a Strowger exchange where all of the connections between the mechanical selectors were hard wired, meaning that it was labour intensive to both reconfigure and maintain. The switchboards had to be located close to the equipment for easy access to the junctions and for optimum transmission standards. The operators physically connected 'assistance' calls by plugs and sockets and flexibility in call loadings were also manually wired.

These days, the subscribers' lines still terminate on an MDF but split off to Test Access Matrix frames, solid state microchip switches, routers, servers, modems and fibre optic junctions. Operator assistance staff are located in remote offices (warehouse-sized spaces) and nearly all re-configurations of routes, loadings and numbering can be changed by firmware or software updates in the programming. A single engineer might find it difficult to identify all of the different 'black boxes' of equipment in a modern exchange. And there is no longer a local office to telephone and arrange a visit.

College Years

Second and Third Year Projects

For year-one of my OND proper (1977-78), I decided to investigate more fully the telephone service in Great Britain and thus my project was *Research, Design and Construction of a Switching Unit to be used with Two Standard Post Office Telephones*. The design didn't have to be solid-state, so I opted to use PO 3000-type relays. Mr White helped me to understand the importance of the 'ring-trip' and 'transmission bridge' relays, which were essential to switch from ringing current to speech. I had wanted to use a power transistor to generate the ringing current, but developing a suitable design and sourcing new components proved too time consuming for the weekly project slot schedule. I did however use a couple of (the then very new) NE555V integrated circuits to generate the timed pulses for ring tone. The completed unit worked well, although the ringing current was 50 Hz rather than the recommended 25 Hz, as a unit to split the frequency would have added to the complexity and cost. There was no budget for these projects; we had to finance them ourselves. I achieved a marking of 93% for this second-year project!

My love of trains and telephones came together when I spotted an advert in the local paper (appropriately the *Yellow Advertiser*) 'Buzby comes to Southend'. So, on Thursday 20 July 1978, mum and I went down to platform 4, Southend Central railway station and boarded a 'train to nowhere' – *The Buzby Special*! The windows were blanked out and in place of the seats, on either side, were displays of telephones and business equipment. We came out with 'goody-bags' of Buzby coasters, a push-out paper Buzby hat, and lots of telephone brochures. It was however to be almost another year before we placed an order for a home telephone line.

My GPO Family: Trilogy Edition

In the meantime, year two of my OND (1978/79) was a follow-on project to my two-telephone switching unit...*Design and Construction of a Telephone Switching System for up to Ten Telephones*. This was rather more ambitious, as it was to use miniature uniselectors which required a multitude of complex wiring! The aims of the project had to be defined precisely to gain approval to proceed. Here is the write-up...

This project will be a general continuation from the previous one which was the Research, Design and Construction of a Switching Unit to be used with Two Standard Post Office Telephones.

The new switching unit will be capable of connecting together any two 'phones from a maximum of ten. The switching will be controlled by dial impulses from the telephones.

The main theme throughout will be 'investigation into the Telephone Service in Great Britain', which will be achieved by designing and constructing the said unit. It is hoped that in doing this the problems involved in providing a communications service, such as that of the Post Office, will to some extent be illustrated. Only the elementary concepts will be dealt with, as switching techniques can become very complex and therefore would be beyond the scope of this project.

Most of the switching will be carried out with relays as a lot of research into their applications was done in the previous project. To use modern switching components e.g. transistors or integrated circuits would again be beyond the scope of this project. Some of these components will be used however for the generation of tones and for timing; e.g. dial tone and ringing pulses.

College Years

It is thought that only two 'phones will be able to be connected together at one time, since for any more, the circuits would be more complex, but this will be investigated fully. The ringing circuit of the previous unit was only just satisfactory and if possible, a better circuit will be devised.

The completed unit will be suitable for use in a large home as an internal telephone system.

North Wales

A field trip was part of the syllabus for the OND, so in the summer of 1978 our class headed off in the college minibus, plus a hired one. I have a photo of me sitting on top of the minibus roof, packing the luggage! Our main visit was to Ffestiniog Power Station, which had been one of the first pumped storage schemes in the UK, back in 1963. We had wanted to see the new installation at Dinorwig, but they had already started water-testing the tunnels, so it was too late. A highlight of our visit to Stwlan Dam was driving up the winding road which had featured in an episode of *The Persuaders* TV series! All was quiet along the walkway at the top of the dam wall; the latent force of water acting below wasn't apparent, though the tidal flow was of course contained and channelled in underground pipes. The vast pump house standing on its hollow supporting legs didn't look out of place in the rugged mountain landscape, and with a misty haze hanging in the air, it was picturesque, but it also had an eerie calmness.

Later in the afternoon, downstream, in the turbine hall, the scale of the operation wasn't so obvious, as all that could be seen was the

My GPO Family: Trilogy Edition

top of the rotating shafts of each high-speed turbine. We climbed down a staircase or two and inspected one of the turning shafts; it was noisy, but not especially impressive.

Another visit was to the slate mines and quarry at Lllechwedd. This featured a little train ride into the darkness of the mine and as the narrow-gauge carriages rattled along I wondered if this was such a good idea! We stepped off into one of the enormous caverns which was dimly illuminated by electric lighting. The guide then momentarily switched off the main lights to demonstrate just how dark it was with only a single candle that the men would have used right up until the 1950s! That was a memorable tour.

Project Finals

My final year project continued…
GPO relays and uniselectors were sourced from *Southend Electronics* whom I had visited many times in the past. Circuit elements for the Type 4 uniselectors were obtained from Standard Telephones and Cables. Upon application, GEC (General Electric Company) was kind enough to send me the multi-way bases (sockets) for the Type 4 miniature uniselectors that were essential to the project.

Everything was mounted on a sturdy blockboard base, with the numerous relay sets screwed and bolted firmly in place. I think the board was about two and a half feet square, so it was quite heavy once filled with relay cans! I knew the project would take more hours to complete than those available in college time, so I intended to carry out the bulk of the work during my spare time! The college allowed me to 'work from home' during the normal

College Years

allotted 'project time' each week, as the board could only be transported by car and we did not own one. This was quite a privileged exception to the rules, so my lecturer for the topic visited my home one week to check on progress, and he was satisfied with my assurances that the project would be completed to schedule! It was fun building this project at home as I could also listen to *Capital Radio* which was in its heyday.

The matrix for the miniature uniselectors was achieved by soldering over 100 x 0.5mm plate-wires (solid-core wire) onto the tags, and the wiring was then teased out onto two 50-way connection strips. As was once common practice for telecom wiring, I used a single colour of green for the whole switch wiring. This formed quite a bulky mass and the economy of using a single colour wire was offset by the difficulty of tracing the connections! I didn't attempt to construct the power units for this project, and the testing at home used transformers and power leads from my growing collection of Post Office kit. When I did a demo at college, I borrowed three of the department's units for the 50V d.c., 75V a.c., and 9V d.c.

I think my project was second overall, but all of the equipment and notes were held by the college until well after the final exam results had been moderated and signed off, as the project was a key part of getting a pass in the whole Diploma. I remember the winner had built a 'white line follower' which was an electronic box that could move along the floor.

Going on the Phone

With the prospect of leaving college and not having secured a job

My GPO Family: Trilogy Edition

with the Post Office, I was prepared to 'sit it out' until something equally appealing came along. In the meantime, it made sense to get connected to the telephone at home, so that I could receive calls of job offers!

Mum and I went off down to Telephone House and then were directed across the driveway to Metropolitan House, as the Sales Bureau was in the adjacent building! We expressed our preference for an ivory wallphone, and not shared service, and were told we would get an appointment about six weeks later.

On Friday 22 June 1979, to our surprise, the Post Office engineer knocked on our door to install the line. The Ax 7000, confirming the appointment, was delivered the following week, with a postmark of the 25th!

Ax 7000 - *'Acknowledgement of Application' – 'This is a formal acknowledgement of your application for the telecommunication service specified in the schedule below and in the continuation sheet(s) attached (if any).'*

At my dad's request, the main phone was installed in our large kitchen. He didn't want to take calls in a cold hall or have us be disturbed if we were in the lounge watching television. Extension phones were extra rental, but it didn't take long to run additional cabling to my bedroom, as the line was intended for my use too! Since I was about seven, we'd always had telephones in our house, but never before connected to the outside world!!

The novelty of having a working telephone at home was great as it meant I could ring up Dial-A-Disc and listen to the latest pop records, albeit in a much-reduced bandwidth of sound. Of course, it

College Years

wasn't so much the content, but more the fact that you could call up a record at all! *"This is the Post Office Dial-A-Disc Service"* the well-spoken lady on the recording said. *"Here is Boogie Wonderland, by Earth Wind and Fire."* [1979] Not 'til after 6 pm though, when Cheap Rate calls applied!

At the time I finished college, Post Office Telecommunications was not recruiting engineers, but they did need CAs (Clerical Assistants) in their Southend office…

The author in Southend AMC (1973)

My GPO Family: Trilogy Edition

```
A H McVitty         Southend-on-Sea      45 Victoria Avenue        Date
General Manager     Telephone Area       SOUTHEND-ON-SEA
                                         SS2 6BA                   14 September 1979
hrb                                      Telephone  44622          In any reply please quote
                                         Southend-on-Sea
Post Office                              (STD Code 0702)           P1. 2. 3
Telecommunications                       Telex 99279               Your reference
                                         (GM SD G)

Mr J Chenery                             Giro a/c 304 0003
```

Dear Mr Chenery

I now confirm that we should like to commence work as a Clerical Assistant at the above address on Monday 17 September 1979.

Would you please report initially to the Doorkeeper at the above address at 9.00am on that date and ask for Miss Jackson, Personnel Branch P1.2.3.

Contracts will follow shortly.

                                      Yours sincerely

                                      M. Chambers

                                      MRS M CHAMBERS
                                      Personnel Supervisor

Job offer letter (1979)

Outlet 4: Traffic

At the time I finished college, Post Office Telecommunications was not recruiting engineers, but they did need CAs (Clerical Assistants) in their Southend office...

Playing the 'GPO game' was going to get real! Earlier game playing had been as simple as following clues in the *I-Spy* booklet, *On the Pavement*, for sightings of telephone kiosks, telegraph poles, and green cabinets; not to mention wiring-up an internal telephone system at home! I had a Kodak camera, but film and developing costs were beyond the scope of my pocket money, so I didn't have a portfolio of telecom photos. In any case, it wasn't so fashionable then to photograph everything in sight. A roll of 26 shots was considered more than adequate, and even then, films were saved for special occasions, such as holidays.

In reality, the world was still balanced on a knife-edge as the Cold War kept the UK on its guard. The work of the GPO played a vital part in supporting Government defence policies. While we slept safely, all kinds of covert activities were taking place.

Cold War (2015)

Growing up during the Cold War with the GPO at the helm
While the Government was organising...
the defence against the realm.

Secret underground bunkers and a network of communication links
Vulcan bombers in the air to see what Russia thinks!

My GPO Family: Trilogy Edition

John Barry scoring the James Bond films where…
Christmas trees are grown.
Espionage was all the rage while so little was known.

All the time the WB400 speaker was sounding tick, tick, tick.
The 4-minute warning could be over oh so quick!

Civil defence planning as the preference keys are thrown.
Only essential people can use the telephone.

Teleprinters whirring as the messages come through.
This time it's a practice and no harm will come to you.

Troubles in Northern Ireland continued and bomb warnings, or hoaxes, added to the sense of unease in the UK. It had been ten years since the Post Office had become a Public Corporation and Post Office Telecommunications was about to be split from the once fully-integrated postal side of the business. Many years of Civil Service culture and Government policy had shaped the organisation. The Post Office was a much-respected employer and 'GPO-trained' telephonists were in demand in commercial businesses.

The Post Office had enjoyed decades of stability with little change in technology or working practices. Electro-mechanical (Strowger) equipment had predominantly switched local calls in UK telephone exchanges since 1912; the premises may have expanded, the number of lines increased, and the number ranges lengthened, but essentially the system was reliable and steadfast. Operators in larger exchanges continued to connect calls which couldn't yet be connected automatically.

Traffic

Exchange premises were clean and tidy; the on-site staff kept them fully maintained and because the equipment was susceptible to dust, floors were polished and cleaning routines were regular. It was the engineers' domain and they guarded its integrity with relish. Wiring was skilfully laced-up and tied off with waxed string and everything was well-ordered and in its place. Equipment racks were sign-written and meticulously painted; record cards neatly filed; the GPO was a well-oiled machine that ran smoothly.

It was a revered organisation to enter, as were most large companies which had layer upon layers of hierarchy, and in this particular case, much history. In practice, Post Office Telecommunications had a waiting list of subscribers, and was thought to be a burden upon the Treasury. The fast-changing culture of the 1960s and 70s demanded more choice and responsiveness and the business was expected to provide it. Time hadn't completely stood still. The STD (Subscriber Trunk Dialling) network was virtually complete and Crossbar switches routed Transit calls. Electronic switches were already replacing local and main exchanges and the demand for international calls was rapidly increasing. The first System X exchange was about to go live.

Somewhat unaware of this background, it was nevertheless, with some awe and wonderment that I went to see if I might gain employment at my local Telephone Manager's Office. Having filled out the application forms, I still had little idea of exactly what a Clerical Assistant (CA) might do, but I turned up for the interview armed with my college telephone project folder, and proceeded to have a fairly informal chat with Maureen Chambers (from Personnel) and Andy Tubbs (from Traffic).

A few days later I received a telephone call from Miss Jackson confirming that I had the offer of a job, subject to the usual checks.

My GPO Family: Trilogy Edition

A follow-up letter asked me to report to Telephone House in mid-September 1979.

I can't remember how excited I was, as this wasn't an engineering job, just clerical work, but at least I'd be employed! At about the same time, the principle of my college offered me a job as a 'lab technician', to set-up experiments for lecturers and he added (not sure of the exact words) that I shouldn't waste my career by joining a company where I might spend hours sitting with old ladies doing their knitting. I realised that the Post Office job was likely to be less of a risk and certainly more secure, long term, so I politely declined his offer. Later it became obvious that a CA in the Post Office was a respected position and certainly on a par with telephonists' pay.

Charles (Charlie) Gadd (TTO) showed me around the building on my first day in Traffic and my boss was Tom Gartell, a TTS. Telecommunications Traffic Supervisor (TTS) was equivalent to a tier 1 manager. Telecommunications Traffic Officer (TTO) was roughly a C2/C3 as in later gradings.

Traffic was an unusual name for a department and it encompassed an odd mix of grades and work. It wasn't an engineering job, though it helped to know all of the technical terms in order to solve complicated disputed accounts cases, or to plan call routing loadings. The Division covered Operational Planning (of lines) as well as Operator and Customer Services. Its remit covered everything that didn't fall neatly into Sales or Accounts or Engineering!

The Operator Services part dealt with staffing of telephone exchanges at a time when switchboard operators had to be located in or close to the equipment due to technical limitations of

Traffic

transmission and switching. Operator Services managed both the telephonists and calculated the expected call loadings for the 100, 191, and 192 numbers. The Customer Services part dealt with disputed telephone accounts where it was suspected that either the equipment was at fault, or that the customer was a devious toad, or just perhaps had been duped by his or her children's use of the phone. Cases were usually referred from TAG (Telephone Accounts Group).

Traffic followed close routines, tried and tested methods of working, because it had always been done that way. One had to be methodical and accurate, though you could have fun and chat as long as the work got done. Traffic was very much the Civic Service of the telephone world, ensconced in discipline, abbreviations and processes.

As a CA, I could do work for anyone in our office, if the other CAs were fully occupied or absent. This was usually to take urgent typing to the Pool or to go to the Print Room for a photocopy of a document. A lot of short memos were handwritten as this was an age before computers or e-mail! Alf Manning, Andy Tubbs and Charles did staffing for Basildon AMC. Tom, Keith Ward and George (Magyar) Miller did staffing for Chelmsford AMC. George must have been part Hungarian to get that nickname. Arthur Cox, Joyce Bryant and Jacki Boother did staffing for Southend AMC. Mary was the other CA, an older lady who had once worked on manual switchboards, and who first trained me in office work. George, Charles and Jacki worked predominantly on Disputed Account cases for their respective areas.

Cases required meter readings every few days so that the subscriber's usage could be checked. It was my task to ring the relevant exchange and obtain the meter readings. For UAXs (Unit

My GPO Family: Trilogy Edition

Automatic Exchanges) the engineers only visited infrequently, so it was difficult to get readings for these customers. Upon ringing some exchanges, a voice said, "I'm only the cleaner, but if you tell me which meter you want reading, I'll get it for you!" I never fully worked that out; in some cases, it may have been the engineers having a lark, as getting meter readings was quite tedious. Indeed, if you rang at the wrong time (tea break) you'd either get no reply, or be told to ring back. For the small exchanges, of say 400 customers, the meters were in a single bank and it was quite possible for the cleaner to work out which ones to read. I'd learnt that cleaners in any company had 'access all areas' and were always a force with which to be reckoned! At other exchanges, a rota engineer would visit five or six buildings, and if you called him at the right moment, he'd ring you back from each exchange with the ones you wanted.

There was no itemisation of calls, so if the TTO wanted to check if a certain number was being dialled repeatedly, then a PMC (Printer, Meter Check) had to be connected to the line. Post Office nomenclature, particularly equipment, stated the item e.g. a printer, followed by its use, e.g. for meter checking. Hence the abbreviation PMC. However, in clerical terms it was a MCP, Meter-Check Printer. Throughout my career, different parts of the business had varying terms and abbreviations for the same items. Exchange name abbreviations followed this pattern, so there were Traffic codes, Engineering codes and Operator codes, all slightly different! PMC connections often took a week to arrange as a form had to be sent off, so disputed cases could take a long time to resolve. Filing the papers of closed cases was a job for the CAs. One of the more laborious tasks! The PMC machines printed the numbers dialled onto a paper tape. It also recorded the number of meter pulses, and the start and end time of the call. The tapes were supposed to be sent to Exchange Clerical for processing, but many of them found

Traffic

their way to my desk, especially the ones where the tape had slipped and overprinted. I became quite an expert at working out the call charges and guessing the numbers which had been dialled!

The TTOs who worked on the actual cases had to make a judgement whether to maintain the charge, do an adjustment if the bill was wrong, or offer a goodwill waiver to resolve the case more quickly. Charles used to tease George for writing in his letters, "In the interests of good customer relations", as George seemed to offer a lot of 'goodwill waivers'. Charles had dealt with too many customers who he'd 'caught-out' and proved that a family member was using the phone.

Instances of any real problems were rare, as faulty (mechanical) meters tended to under-record. Occasionally, faults were found of PUBO (Picking Up Busy Outlets) on Strowger exchanges, due to worn or dirty contacts. For this reason, all disputed cases had a copy of the customer's fault history record card included in the papers and it was another one of my tasks to send off, or ring up, for these. A form 401/A was used to request a copy of the fault card, which was an A700. (TI E13 A0022 refers). At home we'd had a recent fault on our line, so I sent off for a copy of our card to see what had occurred. The fault report was I/C OK (incoming calls OK). No O/G (outgoing). The fault clear (resolution) was that contacts 21 and 22 on the line relay (LR) were C and A (cleaned and adjusted). The clear code was 1. In all work areas there were special codes to be used and learnt!

Going to work was an adventure for me in the 1980s; I was always looking forward to learn something new, or help-out where I could. As soon as my clock radio alarm started playing the jingle *'Mike Smith, with Capital Breakfast Show'*, I leapt out of bed to get ready for my day with Post Office Telecommunications.

My GPO Family: Trilogy Edition

[Capital Radio (194 and 95.8 FM) was one of the first 'commercial' radio stations which were set up in the 1970s with a licence to broadcast adverts. This was a novelty at the time, though today we are saturated with advertising. Capital had its pulse on the London scene with a mix of well-known DJs, Graham Dene, Michael Aspel, Kenny Everett, Dave Cash (Cash on Delivery), Pat Sharp, Nicky Horne, and a whole host of others. The jingles were catchy and happening; it was a lively station.]

Wow, such excitement, I could never be late, though with the 'Flexitime Agreement' you could, 'subject to the needs of the Department', vary your start and finish times by several hours from the norm. I was usually at work by 08:15 which meant I could finish roughly the same time as I did for college, no later than 16:45. Our grades worked a 37-hour week (7 hours 24 minutes per day), which many years later was reduced to 36 hours (7 hours 12 minutes per day).

We recorded our daily start and finish times (and lunch breaks) on our individual flexisheets which were held on a team basis. There were also 'Leave cards' showing our holiday entitlements which our TTS held. Additionally, there was the Attendance Book for the whole floor where everyone was 'marked in' daily. Iris Manning had the task of wandering the offices and checking that everyone was present. Everywhere was regimented and well-ordered.

New entrants to Post Office Telecommunications had an Induction Course to learn about the rules, regulations and the organisation, as well as the work of other Departments. Almost six months after I had begun work, I received a memo via my manager…

Traffic

Basic Induction and Methods of Work Course

Would you please arrange for: Mr J Chenery to report to the Clerical Training Room, 4th Floor, GMO at: 1.30 pm on Wednesday 5.3.80 to attend the above mentioned course.

Duration of the course will be approximately 2.5 working days. Would you please ensure they bring their cup and flexisheet with them.

Area Clerical Training Officer.

I think this was two sessions BIC (Basic Induction Course) and MOW (Methods of Work) combined. The courses were held irregularly when sufficient new entrants were available to benefit from them. Another CA on the course was Trisha Allard (Lester) who I was to work with (on and off) through the years, until we both eventually 'retired' from the same office. Trisha retired at a young age because (as she told colleagues) she had started with BT when she was five years old.

Such was the constancy of my GPO family!

Tom, Alf and Arthur were Exchange Superintendents which gave them overall responsibility for all of the telephone operators in their exchanges. When I began work, the auto-manual boards where operators connected calls were being rationalised and the obsolescent bridge-control board at Winstanley Way, Basildon was soon to close. Alf drove me out there one day and we met the Day Supervisor, Terry Houben, who had once worked with my dad (I think on the Southend Board). It was a quiet exchange, everyone was very polite; that was the nature of switchrooms and clerical duties then; a well-ordered and much disciplined, respectful culture. Winstanley Way was an industrial unit and the bridge-control board would have been installed when Basildon was still a New Town. When the GSC (Group Switching Centre) and local auto exchange at Long Riding was built (in the late 1960s) there should have been provision for a new switchroom, but it just never happened. Here's an overview of how manual call answering had changed since 1980.

Exchange Staffing

In the days of manually connected telephone calls, the operators had to answer the subscribers within a measured interval, known as the TTA (Time To Answer). In later years this became the PCA (Percentage of Calls Answered) in a given period. Targets were set for both measures and (in GPO days) supervisors encouraged staff to 'take the lights', meaning to quickly answer a call which was illuminated by a glowing lamp on the switchboard. Calls were made and answered by plugging a cord into a socket and throwing a switch. Standards in the GPO were high and both operators and supervisors were renowned for their professionalism and adherence to duty. Staff were public servants and were expected to be polite and efficient at all times. In early days, supervisors stood in the switchrooms watching over their staff, ready to intervene if procedures weren't being followed. Years later, the supervisor had his or her own desk, although regular 'Obs' (observations, listening in) to calls were carried out remotely to ensure that standards were being maintained. Operators had set breaks and could request a toilet visit by plugging up a 'loo line' which allowed them to be away from their position for a short time.

Fast forward 50 years to the Call Centres of modern times. PCA is important though CHT (Call Handling Time) is required to be

Traffic

short, so that a much-reduced number of staff can deal with a high volume of calls in a short period. Calls are recorded (for training purposes) and the log-on time in each computer system is monitored too. Breaks are timed to the minute and concentration needs to be high to enable the operator to deal with complex customer queries without reversion to another team.

I had a lot of energy in those days and used to run (with little hesitation) up the seven floors from the first to the eighth to take urgent memos to the Typing Pool. It was great fun! One Christmas our room clubbed together and got me a gift card endorsed, 'For your flights to the upper floors'.

Exchange Visits

Peter Spanton and Alan Houssart were new TTOs and part of their learning was to visit a number of exchanges and meet the engineers. I tagged on to several of their trips; it was probably when I was studying OTS1. We went to Bas Main, Laindon and Canewdon to see different types of equipment. I always enjoyed entering an apparatus room and hearing the switches almost continuously stepping and clearing down. Exchanges were the engineers' domain, with spotless floors, well-routined switches and miles of intricately tied-off cables. Alive with the sound of calls originating and terminating; the meters ticking up revenue for the Post Office. The lifeblood of the Company and the heart of the local community in touch with one another.

Stats Duty

A year or so later and a re-org had me 'transferred' to the 'large

My GPO Family: Trilogy Edition

office' with Bill Wisbey, Beth Bedford, and manager Betty Keeps. I took over Eve Allen's CA duty and she trained me and we remained friends for all her time in BT. Another CA joined at this time…Brenda Bowyer, and she too 'followed' me around as the divisions changed throughout the years! This was a 'stats duty', with monthly returns, so it had its busy periods, but was quite varied and gave me more experience of the running of the telephone service. The Call Count meters in the main exchange had to be read monthly and there was a whole A4 ledger in which to write down the readings! An engineer would ring me and call out the readings, almost without stopping, for all the meters. There were about a 100 or more, and they were 5 or 6 digits! The ledger was typical of the era, a buff hard cover book imprinted S.O. (Stationery Office) supplied for the public service. The SO was the government supplies office from whence all items were sourced.

The cost of coinbox vandalism was calculated by the number of panes of glass replaced, doors mended and mechanisms changed. Another task was updating the Service Switchboard VIF (Visible Index File) inserts, every time that there was a change to duties in the Internal Telephone Directory. A VIF was a tabbed look-up file attached to the keyshelf of the main office switchboard and was referred to by the operators who connected the public to our extensions. The updating involved sending the new details to Typing Pool, checking the entries and forwarding them on to the exchange. Occasionally, by the time the records came back from typing, another amendment was required. Office work required meticulous attention to detail, and was very labour intensive, for even the most-simple record change.

The RIS (Recorded Information Services) services, particularly the cricket, was another set of meter readings to calculate when Test Matches were played. For one of the Centres, the meters had to be

Traffic

manually switched (by the telephonists) from Dial-A-Disc to Test Match as the number one-six (16) was used for both services. Well, either the equipment didn't operate or they forgot to switch it, but we often had no readings and had to estimate the number of calls! We had a new HOD (Head of Division) Trevor Greenwood join us and I was chosen to draw (62!) graphs of the TIP plans and how the Area was performing. TIP was the Telecom Improvement Plans, forming part of the Quality of Service report. This was quite high profile and I later worked with Trevor's wife, Anne Greenwood, but that's another chapter!

Bill was a real character and sometimes would answer internal phone calls with the tag line, "*Wishey Washey Laundry*"! He was responsible for testing of circuits for the Cold War EMSS (Emergency Manual Switching System) which would operate in the event of a nuclear attack or major civil unrest. Bill was often out of the office playing practice war games! I didn't take much notice of what was in reality a very real possibility at that time. It was quite thrilling working for Post Office Telecommunications as you knew that secretive stuff went on, but unless you were directly involved then you didn't ask questions. Traffic Div. carried out lots of peculiar functions, unknown to other groups. There was stocking up of civil emergency places and testing of teleprinter installations. A new defence co-ordinator was tasked with writing up the use of preference switching on Strowger exchanges. On provision, Sub's lines were normally allocated Preference Cat 3 – the lowest preference. Cat 1 customers would retain outgoing service during most emergencies. I think in the hurricane of 1987 they may have been used as faulty lines and junctions began affecting grade of service. Another concern was the susceptibility of the emerging TXE4 (electronic) exchanges to the possibility of failure due to (EMP) electromagnetic pulse radiation from a nuclear blast, thus Strowger expedients may have been retained for longer than

My GPO Family: Trilogy Edition

otherwise necessary. Practice exercises for war situations took place at regular intervals, though no one knew what would actually happen in a real emergency or how effective the plans might be.

Traffic Officers could improve themselves and enhance their chances of promotion by taking an internal correspondence course, OTS1 (Operational Telecommunications Systems). As I was keen to learn the inner workings of telephone exchanges, I enrolled for the course and spent many hours studying the likes of 'Trombone working', 'Metering Over Junctions' and learning about 'Contiguous Charge Groups'. I reached a good enough standard to sit the exam, but didn't quite have enough practice of trunking diagrams to pass. The OTS1 was a great overview of all of the switching kit in the Post Office and remained a useful reference source.

Post Office Telecommunications was about to be renamed British Telecom (although still) - *Part of the Post Office* (for a while). By 1981 the liberalisation of the telecom market led to the launch of the PST (Plug, Socket, Telephone) system, which replaced hard-wired home phones with ones that could be unplugged and moved from room to room. This was already possible with the existing Plan 4 extension arrangement, but the new PST system was designed to have a lower fault rate liability as everything was wired in parallel and thus new sockets could be added without complicated rewiring.

British Telecom was experimenting with how the new sockets would be offered to the customers. It was always illegal for anyone other than a British Telecom engineer to convert a hard-wired line to the new socket system, or to directly connect extension sockets (before NTE5), but a memo was circulated asking for 50 volunteers to rewire their own home phone. Several kits were to be available;

Traffic

a master socket and a replacement dial telephone (for those with a block terminal existing); two extension sockets (for those who already had a master socket). I rang the contact number and they said I could take part in the trial and that they would get back to me. After I returned from lunch, it was apparent that all the socket kits had been allocated and I'd missed out because I was not at my desk when they rang back. I was really disappointed as I was so looking forward to taking part. I rang and complained to the manager, Peter Pratt, who then 'found' another kit so that I could join in, after all!

'British Telecom SOC-KIT Front End Conversion Kit – This kit enables customers to convert their existing telephone connexion to a plug and socket system. This Kit can only be used with telephones fitted with the new British Telecom plug. It replaces any existing method of connexion. Not suitable for shared service telephones lines.'

Peter was to be my manager in future years, but that too is another story. The trial was otherwise well-organised and ANs (Advice Notes) were issued so that our installation records reflected the changes which we had made. Gallup visited afterwards for feedback on how easy the kit was to use and I said to the lady that 'SOC-KIT' was such a memorable name!

Throughout my BT career, I tried to be an early adopter of new ideas and services. My managers would often give me new procedures to try out first, as they knew I would be receptive to them and not make a fuss. They trusted me to make the most of anything new and to give my honest opinion.

The Post Office had an A-Panel scheme whereby if a CA achieved good markings on their annual reviews they would be added to the

My GPO Family: Trilogy Edition

list of people suitable for promotion to CO (Clerical Officer). As none of the functions of Traffic required COs (they were all TTOs or higher), I had the consideration of being promoted to possibly Sales or Accounts. On an earlier appraisement with my manager, Betty Keeps, she had identified that I had a preference for work at the heart of the business: *"He would prefer to work in an area which is close to the Business...An area such as Wages or Personnel is not sufficient involvement."* Thus, it transpired that I was destined for Sales.

During my first interview with John Manning (Area Sales Manager) I have a vague recollection that he drew a comparison between selling shoes in a shop and telephone products. BT didn't have *Phoneshops* in that period, so he asked how customers might find out about our products? The answer was DLs (Descriptive Leaflets) which we could post out. I found out later that there was an extensive range of literature available. This had only been an informal interview; the senior panellist filled the one vacant position in October 1982, and the following year's A-Panel was soon to be prepared.

The very stable Post Office organisation had begun to change and adapt to a new commercial world unlike any it had known previously.

In the Day (2015)

In the days of Public Service there was the GPO,
And if you wanted a phone put on, it's where you had to go!

A visit to the bureau, the Sales lady at her desk,
Writing out the details with oh so much finesse!

Traffic

A shared line or exclusive, there wasn't any choice?
A piece of wire to talk down and make heard your voice.

A waiting list of connections, equipment or line plant.
A wayleave for the wiring, permission yet to grant.

A new four-digit number to tell all of your friends.
After six and at weekends, on that you could depend!

An engineer climbing steadily up the pole,
And another doing jointing, sitting in a hole!

The operator service, politely answering your call,
And a bill through your letter box, accounting for it all.

From May 1980, British Telecom was the name of the new corporation which ran the telephones part of the Post Office. The outdated Civil Service attitudes and rules had to be changed, but it was a slow process. The unofficial finish time on Fridays was 15:45 as non-customer facing groups finished up for the week. Changes were expected to be ratified with the Unions, who had many members and much influence. For Maundy Thursday, it was almost compulsory to take the half-day annual leave entitlement on the actual day. It didn't matter too much if departments were closed on semi-public holidays. I remember a memo being circulated suggesting that staff be encouraged not to take their leave on that day, but to defer it to a later date, so that there might be sufficient cover across the groups. This made sense, although it was contrary to the long-established rule of taking official holidays at the time they were due, and not letting them accrue. In future, hours of business were going to be dictated by market forces and this was just the beginning of the transition.

My GPO Family: Trilogy Edition

> Buzby says:
>
> "Make someone happy with a 'phone call"

Further information about charges for all telecommunications services may be obtained from your Telephone Area Sales Office.

Leaflet PH 2028 (12/76)

"It's so cheap to phone your friends after 6 and at weekends."
Call charges slogan (1969)

Sales

Outlet 5: Sales CO

"Authority has been given for the undermentioned officers to be placed on the 1983 Grade 'A' Panel for promotion to Clerical Officer."

The 'notice to staff' read like a legal document. It had to be carefully worded as it originated from Personnel Division; it couldn't be open to misinterpretation. It was a proclamation of intent and if anyone had been left off the list, then they'd better appeal, and fast! The 'A' Panel was for any CA, Shorthand Typist, Audio Typist or Typist with two years long term service to be considered suitable for promotion.

My name was correctly on the 'list' for the second year, as officers were usually taken off in seniority order as vacancies became available. John Manning had interviewed me once before, and now it was just a formality to join one of his teams. I don't think there was a particular choice in the matter! Many years later, when John Manning retired from BT, I received the paperwork to issue the AN (Advice Note) for his presentation telephone and an extra socket for his home. He was quite a humble, proud man and he told me he didn't need another extension socket as his house wasn't a big mansion.

Sales was challenging. It was somewhat removed from the quiet backwater of slowly moving 'Traffic'. It too had its age-old processes and procedures and some of the managers were very 'old school'. I had to prove myself and adapt to a faster environment where targets for workflow were more strictly measured, expectations higher, and competition for attention, greater!

My GPO Family: Trilogy Edition

Initial training was with Tony Cooke and I remember he showed us around the equipment in the Sales Bureau and handed us a full set of ANs (Advice Notes), so we could study how the different copies were filled out. Desk training was with Elsie Smith who went through all the standard abbreviations and Sales terms, while we wrote longhand notes, in time honoured fashion, into an A4 SO (Stationery Office) book. We had a whole A5 ring binder of practice ANs and a few live ones as we became more familiar with the correct wording and layout, and took real work from our colleagues.

John Tyrer's team was almost exclusively male, and a mix of different ages, temperaments, and experience. John made you wait and stand quietly at his desk if he was busy and woe betide if you interrupted him at the wrong moment. He'd give you a look of distain and make you come back later, and it was always difficult to judge the right opportunity to get up from one's desk and be bold enough to approach him. The team members were friendlier, though they had their own workloads to handle and had adopted their own techniques of balancing phone calls with the all-important AN issue. John Tyrer was strict, but he knew what he wanted from his team, and after all, this was a working environment! He once said to me, if I was ever to get the chance to do 'public speaking' to take up the opportunity. Most of the managers throughout my career had good advice to impart at various times, though I always had to continue and do things the way that I understood them, for to deviate would be unthinkable! Everything was considered and I always took note of what was said; their influence didn't fall on deaf ears, though a slow, long learning curve always suited me better.

I learnt the hard way that it was all very well to answer the phone quickly and to please the customer, but unless the orders got issued

Sales

I was not going to get any awards! These were fun times and anyone on the team who spoke with conviction and authority could charm the difficult customers. Ian was particularly good at this and it was a standing joke that if anyone had a problem, just tell them to ask for the 'General Manager, Ian Reid'. At this time it was not policy to give one's name when answering the phone. It was encouraged, but left to our discretion. We were third floor Sales and the drinks vending machine was located on the fifth. We took it in turns to collect the money and return with a tray of drinks for the team, as phones had to be covered at all times. It was fun trying to remember who had tea or coffee, with or without sugar. Later on, we had filter coffee clubs with the pot on an adjacent table.

On promotion to CO, my starting pay was calculated and paid too high, as the pay progression was slower for younger staff. I should have been on 'mark-time' pay in the new grade. This took several months to sort out, though I fought my corner and only had to repay half of the total, for which I was allowed to repay in instalments. This did little for my self-esteem, while at the same time, our senior manager (Sales Office Manager) decided that my work output was not sufficient. I had coaching and assistance from my colleagues and eventually became knowledgeable enough to strike the optimum balance between getting my work done and helping the customer. Although we didn't have selling targets, we were expected to perform our duties proficiently. A substantive CO on our team failed to maintain a sufficient standard and was demoted to CA. There was no mistaking the pressure, but working smarter, not harder was the key to staying on top of it all. Brenda Bowyer and Eve Allen, CAs who I had worked with in Traffic, had been promoted at about the same time and they, being rather more 'world savvy' were performing better.

My GPO Family: Trilogy Edition

"The job comes with a desk." [quote from JK Rowling's *The Casual Vacancy*.]

Wow, I remember getting my first 'own' desk at work, exclusive to the duty I was doing. I owned the GPO, it was mine, I belonged there. I had to make it work, it was my survival, my passion, my destiny. It empowered me, within the boundaries of my work. I built up my knowledge to be authoritative and confident and bathed in its divinity and uniqueness.

Oh yes, I was still enjoying having my own desk and being responsible for an allocated group of subscribers. If you wanted telephone service in that particular area, I was the person to call!! I took pride in answering the telephone quickly and being as helpful as I could. Those who let the phone ring for longer may have had the edge on productivity.

Desk layouts were always controversial; some people stacked rows of folders, or trays in front of them so as to not look at the opposite desk, or person! Part of this was out of necessity for more book space. Later desks had a separately fitted top section for in/out trays and books, such that you needed to stand up to view the rest of the office. Like fashion, this followed a trend over my many years of working. It varied according to team organisation rules, office policy and/or senior manager recommendation.

In our team of territorial sales, we each dealt with our own dedicated telephone exchanges; all the stops/starts/new provides/conversions, everything within the remit of Residential customers. Once I worked on a split duty (alphabetically) for Brentwood Main with Lorraine Waymont. She had a wonderful saying to lighten the mood, *"Come on, John. Pull yourself to pieces!"* Lorraine went off on maternity leave and it was not until

Sales

many years later that I caught up with her on her retirement day, actually in BT Brentwood! Great times.

Customers would ring via the Service switchboard which originally had a five-digit telephone number. The operator on the Board in Southend Telephone Exchange would refer to the Visible Index File (VIF) to connect the caller to the appropriate territorial sales duty. The calls terminated (typically) on a ten-way Key and Lamp Unit, causing a coloured light to flash against the associated line. If the key was fully down on the unit, then the bell in the telephone would also ring. The three positions of the key were: flash, hold or ring. The control relays for the Key and Lamp units were located in a shallow wall cupboard behind our bank of desks. The mains plug was pulled at the end of the day and if not reconnected on the following morning one could hear the line relays clicking away in the cupboard, but no lights would flash (and thus no callers were answered) until the power was reconnected!

"Telephone Sales – How may I help you?" was the usual salutation, although in later years you had to include your name. For existing subscribers, rental details could be quickly checked by finding their Customer Rental Record (CRR) card which was filed numerically in the desk well of each duty. If you answered a call for another member of your team, you'd have to run round to their desk in order to locate the number range of the matching card. I made a point of asking for the telephone number as soon as possible, so that I could extract the CRR card from the well and thus have all the details to hand.

Background: Subscriber's rental details were originally recorded manually on an A3016 card which was held and updated by TAG (Telephone Accounts Group). CRR cards produced and printed by computer were introduced into Sales in 1976 to replace the A3016.

My GPO Family: Trilogy Edition

Data from closed ANs was written (by a DPCO) onto keyforms which were sent daily to the computer centre where operators keyed the information onto magnetic tape. The tape was run on an ICL System 4-70 computer to produce updated CR cards, which the Sales CA would file, usually weekly.

[Reference: JT Greenwood *Eleven million records at a glance* - Post Office Telecommunications Journal Spring 1973.]

While the customer was still thinking what they wanted, it was possible to flick through the numerically filed (CR) cards and extract the particular installation record and say, "Yes, Mr Smith, I can see you've got a Plan 1A and an extension bell." And Mr Smith would remark, "Oh, that was quick, are you using a computer?" Then of course, when MOH (Mechanisation of Order Handling) did come in and CRR was loaded on, it was: "Can you hold on, my screen is stuck?!"

Apparatus, Facility and Service (AFS) codes were allocated to every single product which could be rented (or sold) from British Telecom. Handwritten ANs used simple letters such as Ex/L for Exchange Line, but upon closing, I think the DPCO would have used the AFS code EL24 on the keyform to feed into CRR. With the introduction of MOH, all issuing staff had to learn the AFS codes to type directly on each order. A rather thick book of all the current AFS codes was published from time to time as new products and services were launched. It was always slightly frustrating that MOH held a list of AFS codes in order to generate the correct plain language description, but that one couldn't interrogate the file to learn the code to type in the first place!

Whenever a group of customers were moving house at the same time, usually on a Friday, it was like playing *Happy Families* and

Sales

Patience all rolled into one! You'd have so many CR cards laid out on the desk so you could issue to 'stop' all the items of the installations. A clipboard of 'buffs' (already stopped lines) and a wodge of hand-written memos from team colleagues who had scribbled down orders from other customers on the same exchange. And you'd have to match the 'incoming and outgoing' tenants. And of course, they all wanted to take their numbers to their new addresses, didn't they? But there were some requests from the incoming tenants where the outgoing tenants hadn't phoned us with their requirements! The limitations of the process didn't allow a new customer to 'take over' an existing line before the removing customer had notified us. Invariably you'd be waiting for two or more people in the chain to get in contact, then you'd have to be proactive and go ringing them for details. You'd rush to get all of the ANs issued and then the unthinkable... the date would change and the jobs would have to be cancelled and re-issued another time. The exchange engineers were very good at sorting out these problems and keeping continuity of service for the customers and a lot of extra work went on outside of Sales to make it happen.

If two customers were effectively 'swapping houses' we could issue a 'Tran B' to transfer the records of each line into the new owner's name, and it would only require a meter reading to enable a clean split of the bills. If any renumber or additional work was required, then follow-on AN had to be issued and all AN numbers cross referred. It was often safer to issue 'stops and starts,' though if the dates didn't match then one of the customers may have lost service for a day. This was true if a stop order had been issued and the start order went missing. We relied heavily on the exchange to match all stop/start orders for continuity of service. On one occasion, the work involved several renumbers and when I rang the engineer (Tony Nesnas) to expedite the job, all he wanted was the bar-pairs. He had to re-jumper the MDF (Main Distribution Frame)

My GPO Family: Trilogy Edition

to do the renumbers, but the bar-pairs were on the routing records and nothing to do with Sales. I suspect that Tony didn't have the actual AN to hand, such was the helpfulness of some engineers who went out of their way to assist us with urgent work.

We used to get letters from customers who were moving house, requesting us to read their meter at midnight on a certain date, and we would smile and think they might be lucky if the engineer was even able to visit the exchange sometime that week to complete the job. This was especially pertinent to the very small unattended exchanges. At the time I left Sales, the latest release of CSS (Customer Service System) actually made you input a time (on the order) that the meter reading should be captured. The interface to the OMC (Operations and Maintenance Centre) processed the requests (every 15 minutes or so) to automatically 'stop' or 'start' the line and to record the meter reading. Wow, so requesting a time for moving house was finally not so silly!

The wording on the ANs was very precise as it was the authority for the engineers to carry out the work and for the AN coding team to update the computer records, and ultimately produce a correct bill. The nomenclature was memorable to everyone who had issued a few thousand or so ANs!

AN Talk (2015)

Take advice and note this well
Just be careful how you spell!

If you want to start a line new,
Just write SN and the engineer will do!

Sales

SC is a stop-cease, a TOS or OCB,
Depending on the policy.

SCR is a stop and renumber on removal,
With of course the customer's approval!

You can SNR (start new and renumber)
If the sub wants to keep his number.

New (N) is brand new, a whole provide,
With or without the wiring inside.

A new removal (NR) the number persists,
But just not where it used to exist.

Cease (C) is where it all does end,
On that one you can depend!

But on a CR (cease removal) the number's
Kept to sub's approval.

Discon/Recon a socket too.
A PST line for you.

I made steady progress on the team and eventually I was writing over 100 ANs per week (the team average varied around the 90 mark). Most orders required an 'acknowledgement letter', which was a handwritten form (Ax 7000) confirming the appointment and charges.

Ax 7000 (rev 8/81) – *'Telecommunication service is provided under the applicable provisions of the British Telecommunications Act 1981 and any schemes from time to time in force under that Act*

My GPO Family: Trilogy Edition

(a copy of which provisions may be seen at any British Telecom Area Office).'

I soon became proficient at scribbling the addresses on those too.

I'm a Small Mag Bell! (Circa 1984)

[First published in Telecom Heritage Issue 11 Summer 1989]

Telephone operators working in AMCs (Automanual Centres) would often perform clerical work on a rota basis with the Exchange Clerk (EC). A proportion of this work involved updating the T68 record cards (cards of subscribers' name and address info. filed in telephone number order) from the ANs (Advice Notes) issued by Sales, and obtaining meter readings for TAG (Telephone Accounts Groups).

The Exchange Clerk was also responsible for arranging 'urgent' Stops and Starts for Sales, as well as TOS (Temporary Out of Service) requests from TAG. 'Stops' created a final record for an outgoing tenant (subscriber) and 'Starts' created a new record for the incoming tenant (subscriber).

In the 1980s, the workplace was still very formal and full names were rarely given. Work requests which were 'rung over' to the EC were endorsed by a telephone number to ring back on, and the person's initials.

On this particular occasion, as a Sales CO (Clerical Officer), I rang the EC and the conversation concluded...

"...and I'm JC, and you are...?"

"I'm a Small Mag Bell."

Sales

"You're what?!"

"S.M.B." The EC lady explained... *"My initials are SMB, but can easily be misheard over the telephone. I was reading the ANs one day and saw in the text, 'Provide Small Mag. Bell' and so I decided to use that instead of spelling out my initials."*

I thought this was very appropriate and from then on, whenever I needed to contact SMB, I would ring the EC number and ask,

"May I speak to 'Small Mag. Bell'?" Most times, they knew who I meant!

Note: A Small Mag. Bell, is a magneto (a.c. alternating current) bell which as a 'Bellset 50C' was used as an internal extension bell on customer's premises.

Territorial Team Working

It took time to understand the processes of how other divisions worked as we were all usually too busy to visit them and find out. It always made a big difference if you knew the name of a friendly CO or manager who was receptive to helping you achieve what you required, within the remit of one's job.

Orders for new lines were written on *blue skins* – an A4 cardboard pro forma. These were given to the CA who would ring over the addresses to the Router to locate the correct serving exchange and DP (Distribution Point, i.e. telegraph pole), from his line plant records. Later in the day, the Router would ring the details back to the CA, who would in turn pass the *blue skin* to us for issuing. In some of the more rural areas, there seemed to be an abundance of dwellings known as *Rose Cottage* and requests for service at these

My GPO Family: Trilogy Edition

properties had to be forwarded to the Survey Officer to visit the site and confirm the routing to be used. Occasionally, the wrong serving exchange was quoted and thus the customer's telephone number had to be changed. It was for this reason that subscribers were requested not to have any number cards/stationery printed until the service was actually working!

The Routers tended to know most of the DPs on their patch off by heart; some of them had been doing the job for so long! We had good support from the engineers, though it was always wise to be straight with them and not keep asking for favours all of the time. Charlie Richardson, the exchange engineer would usually accept urgent requests over the phone on the promise of the AN number. If a job was being updated, he always used to say, "I must have a red amendment for that change." The IC (Installation Control) did their best to schedule extra appointments to get the work completed. I rather think they relished the overtime when it was available! Ironically, Saturday appointments, which customers found most convenient, could only be offered when overtime was in place. Once we had cleared a backlog of work then only the normal hours during Monday to Friday were offered.

New lines usually went in within a fortnight and existing lines could sometimes be 'started' the next day. There were exceptions for new housing estates where the infrastructure hadn't yet been completed and also in localities where demand was higher than forecast, and the capacity of the original cables had been exhausted.

New cables schemes could take months to plan and implement, but a system known as *1 + 1 Carrier* had been developed in the 1970s to allow a limited shortage of lineplant (wires, cables and poles) to be overcome. Also referred to as *WB 900* (Wideband 900), the system used a single pair of wires to give exclusive (not shared)

Sales

service for two customers. Interestingly, the technique used modems and filters (much like today's broadband) so that the dialling and speech for the *Carrier* customer was sent at a higher frequency than the *Audio* customer. The system ran into problems in the 1980s as customers wanted to use computer modems which conflicted with the signalling of the *Carrier* circuits! Unlike normal Shared Service lines, the *1 + 1 Carrier* was not publicised as being any type of inferior service, although recipients of the additional equipment and power boxes must have wondered just what the engineers were installing. A later version, DACS (Digital Access Carrier System) was compatible with lines used for faxes and some modems, but such expedients were always a bugbear for anyone expecting a truly exclusive line.

We faced no end of difficulties in providing what was a basic telephone service! The ivory wallphone could not be obtained for love nor money. I think Stores (local stock rooms) could only obtain refurbished ones. However, the quality of telephones which had passed through British Telecom's refurbishment process was better than new. Customers wanted wall telephones and we couldn't supply them. In Sales, we rarely got to hear about how any of our ANs weren't fulfilled, as the Installation Controls and field engineers handled most of the flack, and sorted out failed appointments and 'out of stock' telephones! The engineers sometimes fitted whatever phone was in supply, with a promise to return at a later date to swap the phone for the one which had been originally ordered. The A864 form and process dealt with any 'departures from the AN' (changes to the order). The new *Statesman* and *Viscount* (press-button) telephones were ideal for wall mounting, but so often the separate wall bracket (in matching colours) was not available! The stores may have been in stock at the time the AN was struck, but had run out by the time the order was due.

My GPO Family: Trilogy Edition

Each team had an Appointment Book in which to schedule a date for the engineer to visit the customer's premises to install a new line or convert to the new socket plan. Even back then, we were able to offer morning or afternoon visits as well as a 'first call', and occasionally Saturdays too! If we arranged eight appointments for the morning and they were all for new provides (lines), the engineers could be busy all day and never get to the afternoon appointments. So it was that Quota Units were introduced and each job had a numerical value. The more complex the work, the higher the number of units allocated. The Book was a ring binder with loose leaf pages and it jostled for position on the team as we later retrieved it to add the AN numbers for every job. Appointment dates also had to be coded onto the AN using the 'Chinese aka Working Day' calendar (A4230). Saturdays and Sundays (when worked) were coded as for the following Monday.

When a customer moved home, their line was 'Stopped and OCB'd'. The 'stop' was an instruction to read the meter and produce a final account. The OCB was to make the line 'Outgoing Calls Barred', the idea being that Sales could ring an incoming tenant and easily sell the service to them, but they wouldn't be able to make outgoing calls until they had applied to 'takeover' the line. This did not deter some people who were quite happy to have incoming calls only and not pay any rental. After a number of months, 'stopped' lines were added to a Bulk Recovery AN, for the engineers to pull out the jumpers and release the phone number(s) and lineplant for re-use elsewhere. Bulk recoveries were a low priority activity for the engineers and it was sometimes up to six months later that the jumpers were pulled, usually on a Friday afternoon. At this late-hour the householder would ring us and demand to know why they couldn't receive calls anymore. By this time the CR card may have been destroyed and there would be no record of telephone service ever existing at their address. And they

Sales

weren't happy when quoted the full connection charge to have 'their' line restored, most likely with a different number too!! In these rare cases, a 'new provide' AN was always issued with the note 'apps in situ'. After a quick call to number allocation, I was usually able to secure the original number. Another call to the Router and the lineplant records and bar-pair were retrieved, so that the exchange engineer could re-jumper the line. A final call to Installation Control to book an early appointment in case all of the above failed, and I almost had a happy customer! We worked hard to sort out these little problems and as we knew the people on the other teams, they supported us well. These were the days when much could still be accomplished on goodwill, as long as we followed up the request with the official paperwork, i.e. the AN. Our process was soon strengthened by making all stopped lines TOS instead of OCB. In Strowger exchanges, OCB was carried out by putting a paper sleeve on a contact of the subscriber's K relay. TOS was done by moving the position of a black plug on the IDF (Intermediate Distribution Frame) block.

Third parties used to call and enquire of stopped lines for potential incoming tenants. I recall that on a few occasions when *Hilbery Chaplin* (estate agents) rang, I mistakenly thought it was something to do with the local vicarage! Another regular caller was Mr Thain of Ford Motor Company who used to arrange telephone service for company employees. This was a special agreement that Fords was billed for the service, although the lines were residential. Again, over the years the processes were tightened so that we performed credit vetting for new customers and additional checks for existing ones. A 'Homemovers' process had us faxing off details of customers to gaining areas outside of our Telephone Area. It was usually better to offer the FreeFone number and suggest they discuss it directly!

My GPO Family: Trilogy Edition

Our *Sales Handbook* listed all of the important prices as taken from the TIs, though we always had a wodge of telexes, memos, and BTHQ Circulars advising us of new products and changes to existing ones. Apart from set charges for providing extension sockets, there was a special rate for complex work. If customers were having the barge board of their property replaced they usually needed the external lead-in/dropwire temporarily moved and reinstated. *Cost of Works*, later known as *Timescale* charges, were (in 1981) £19.50 for the first half an hour's labour, and then £4.50 for every subsequent quarter hour or part. I used to read out the details very matter-of-factly and then wait for the exasperation from the customer! Most then wanted an estimate as to how long their job might take, and we were able to send the survey officer out to meet these requests, as there was no way we could price them from the comfort of our office. In several cases the survey officer completed the work at the same time he did the estimate, I think for a nominal call out fee. It certainly saved us some hassle and helped with customer satisfaction.

Our CAs, Lorraine Lyons and Laura Huggins did all the filing of Office Whites, CR Cards and Dead Papers. They also sent out DLs (Descriptive Leaflets) and a list of charges. Office Whites were our file copy of ANs that we had issued and were the only way to check details of a job, as we didn't have computers! With an issue rate of approximately 90 ANs per team member, per week, the books of Office Whites quickly filled a lot of cabinet space.

Advice Notes (ANs)

Historically, ANs were written on a proforma and sent to the Typing Pool who then produced a seven-copy note using carbons on a non-electric typewriter. The copies were returned to the Sales Office for checking and sending out to the various departments. By

Sales

1955 an eight-copy AN pack was in use. From about 1963 a Sales CO prepared a hectograph master...

'After removing the protective tissue a Clerical Officer adds the variable details to the master, using a ball-point pen over a hard, smooth surface, and printing the important details.'

[*Spirit duplication saves time and money* – Post Office Telecommunications Journal Summer 1963.]

The master copy was then run-off on a spirit duplicator (*Banda* machine) to produce the required number of copies for circulation. A Directory Copy was once separately produced, but over the years this was included in the eventual nine-copy set of ANs.

From my time in Sales I recall being allocated a 200 pack of master-copy ANs in a number range for which I had to sign, for audit purposes. The protective tissue was always carefully slid into the bin, for if I screwed it up, then my hand was covered in black carbon ink! A hard-plastic board with two pegs located the AN in the correct position to record onto an 'edge punched card' which for a while was used to collect statistics. If an AN was spoilt then two diagonal lines with the words 'cancelled' had to be drawn, and it still went for duplication as every AN had to be accounted for. The 'pack-type' of F, X, T or M was marked so that the duplicating duty knew how many copies of each AN had to be run off. Not all ANs went to every group. This was occasionally a problem if the work required all groups to be involved, but the AN issuer didn't mark it as a 'full pack'! [See the chapter about MOH for later AN developments.]

Blank packs of ANs were held on the *Banda* duty for running off the necessary copies from the master. As with everything in the

My GPO Family: Trilogy Edition

organisation, these too were allocated numbers:

M-Pack A4206, T-Pack A4207, X-Pack A4208, F-Pack A4210.

Additionally, *Prestel* was issued on a V-Pack (4 copy) AN.

Transforming Sales

As British Telecom prepared to be floated on the Stock Market (1984), the implications of becoming a Public Limited Company (plc) had a wide-ranging effect on the day to day workings of the business.

Up until then telephone service was connected upon 'application' either by a 'phone call to sales staff or the completion of an A4000 (Application for Telecommunication Service). Service was supplied under a 'Scheme' which was authorised by the Government.

As a 'plc', service had to be supplied under contract law. A new form, the AX8345 became the *Customer order for Equipment hire and Network service,* and this was soon incorporated to include the Consumer Credit Act 1974 (and subsequent revisions). Our manager Eileen Goodchild helped us through this period with a 'notes and procedures' pack. Eileen was firm, but fair, and ran a tight ship.

Office processes were about to be transformed as a Sales Office computer system, MOH (Mechanisation of Order Handing), was to be introduced into Southend Area…

Outlet 6: Mechanisation of Order Handling

Oh, the number of happy and sometimes tedious hours spent playing with MOH, which arrived in Southend Sales Office during 1984.

MOH was designed to computerise the complete order handling process from when the order was taken, through installation or delivery by the engineers and finally closed into the billing system. These early days of computing found us staring at 'dumb' CRT (Cathode Ray Tube) green display screens working to a local 'mini' processor (Ferranti PT7) which could operate no more than 16 terminals. In turn, this accessed an ICL mainframe at a remote centre, via PWs (Private Wires).

MOH was planned to be rolled out in four stages as both the equipment and software was developed. Stage 1 was a 'clean *Banda* system' in that ANs (Advice Notes) were typed into the local computer and then multiple copies of the AN were printed, in place of hand-written notes and spirit duplication. I can't remember what was special about Stage 2, it may have simply been printing of an acknowledgement letter. Stage 3 allowed interrogation of issued ANs via a remote Mainframe and later software gave access to on-line CRR (Customer Rental Records). Stage 4 was the electronic transmission of ANs to the Exchanges and Installation Controls. Southend never implemented the last stage as by then CSS was imminent. Finally, MOH DS (Decision Support) was a stats package for managers.

MOH brought a massive change into the Sales Office. For many, it was the first encounter with a computer...and typing. Of course, some of the girls had learnt to type at college, or in earlier jobs, but everyone needed training on how to use the system. Staff were

My GPO Family: Trilogy Edition

trained in small groups and then a new VDU (Visual Display Unit) was added to the system. It wasn't a sudden change-over. I had my two days training on 23 and 24 May 1984. MOH was menu-driven, mainly by tabbing through the fields on screen and keying a few important characters, such as C (cease) or P (provide) and finally hitting *SEND* to complete the order.

Initially it was to be one VDU between two (people), as it was expected some of the team would always be answering phones. Of course, if you were talking to a customer on the phone you would want access to CRR, so it wasn't too long before everyone had a dedicated screen. And eventually extra screens were added so that several could be left logged onto CRR. It was possible to switch between issuing an AN and CRR, but work in progress was lost until a later software update allowed you to save and recall. Invariably there were glitches which froze the screen while switching; the tedium of future computing was being learnt!!

The MOH keyboard was unique as it had a built-in *badge reader*. A plastic key (with cut notches) was inserted into the reader and this provided the authentication to use the system. There were no passwords to remember! Different coloured *badges* allowed various job functions to be performed. Green was for training, beige was for issuing, black for supervisory functions and so on.

The early days of MOH had lots of downtime as the local PT7s froze, or the remote links dropped out, or the loading on the mainframe became too great. Such was the expected disruption that a buzzer and red warning light was installed on each floor to warn when the system was unavailable. This alarm was made up of GPO power units, red '999' switchboard lamps, and miniature lever keys, all readily available kit! The managers didn't always have time to stop and sort out the problems with MOH, but the COs and

MOH

COMMOs couldn't get on with their work when the system was down. In Res Sales, a memo was circulated asking for a CO to help with system resets and to check the stock of fanfold stationery during the day, to ensure ANs got promptly printed, as many orders were time sensitive.

A few days later, another handwritten memo stated.

'John Chenery will be the Site Officer for MOH with effect from 12/02/1985.'

This was quite a responsibility, but was also great fun! Peter Pratt my new manager oversaw the operation, but otherwise I had a free hand to shut the system down and reset it when there was a fault. Our set-up at Southend had seven PT7s, each with at least 10 users. A PT7 was two large boxes (front face approx. 400 mm square) one stacked above the other. The top unit showed the polling status, the bottom contained a 'tape streamer' which accepted a tape (like VHS) to allow software to be loaded, or a system dump to be carried out. With hindsight, most faults were probably software glitches, the system would lock up or stop polling (sending data to the computer centre). It could have been the PT7 software, or the modem, or even the remote end which stopped the polling. A reset of a PT7 only took a few minutes, but anyone with a half-typed AN would lose it and potentially this was 15 users every time. The 16th terminal was reserved to carry out system commands. I filled out a pink A4 fault sheet and these were sent to the MOH User Support, although I don't remember any solutions being passed back. However, MOH had a dedicated development and testing group, so the system was constantly being improved and that meant new software had to be loaded into the local processor every few months.

My GPO Family: Trilogy Edition

Branding

A newsletter acclaimed: *"MOH the age of the electronic Advice Note."* MOH was the most extensive Sales and Installation computer system yet to be rolled out and to 'sell it' to British Telecom users there were branded key-rings, ties, LCD clocks, user guides, and stickers to assist in system config marking. Today there would have been mouse mats, but MOH was keyboard driven; the GUI (Graphical User Interface) was another decade away! I proudly wore my MOH tie on most working days.

MOH was a long time in development and deployment. Both the kit and the software had to be constantly redefined, as the requirements of the business evolved, with the marketplace and the regulator. A new national system which was destined to integrate and replace these early attempts at computerisation was only a few years away… the Coming Soon System* (CSS) was on the horizon!! By March 1986 the first CSS customer order had already been processed in Thameswey District, and the nationwide roll-out was gathering pace. *Nickname.

The Computer Room

MOH was very much a DIY system as the processors were stood on some redundant metal desk tops. The windows were not to be opened, because a wall-mounted air con system kept the environment at the right temperature. I assume we didn't have the landlord's permission for the unit, as the water discharge was into a plastic drum on the floor! This needed emptying at intervals and we used to ask one of the stronger lads to move it for us. One day the air con unit went wrong and the temperature in the room was getting rather warm, so I had to squeeze round the back of the desks, pull the blinds up, and struggle to open the stuck windows! I

MOH

think when the unit was repaired it was reconfigured to condense on the outside wall. The PT7 processors had dust filters and periodically I took them home to be washed! The room was locked overnight to prevent tampering as the system was essential to the operation of the whole Sales Office. I had a separate key; it was like my own executive office, although there was no space to do any work other than monitor the comm links and printers!

Shiny multi-coloured wall charts displayed a representative diagram showing the configuration of each PT7. At the back of the desks, on which the PT7s were stacked, a multitude of cables snaked around the room, to the daisy-chain wiring of the VDU links and the impressive modem cabinet (wardrobe) which connected the private wires to the remote mainframe computer centre.

Loading Software

This had to be done when the system was not in use, either early morning or evening, with all of the users logged off. You couldn't really stop users logging on, so a handwritten note was circulated to every team manager requesting their staff not to use MOH until advised. The tapes would arrive by post a few days in advance and you hoped they were going to run through without any problems. With seven processors and only two copies of the tape, it took a while to complete the task. Later software releases required a dump of the current system to extract partial files before loading the new software and then adding the local files back. The tapes for one release failed and I spent a long evening ringing the support team to obtain system command codes to allow the patch to work. There was no 'downloading' of software over the line at that stage of development. I could have had 60 very angry users the next morning if the patches hadn't worked and the Sales Office would have quickly reached a backlog of orders! There was the option of loading back the tapes of a previous release, but as the mainframe systems carried out more functions, they were upgraded at the same time and may not have continued to work if the local software was out of date. It was a big responsibility and the manager trusted me to do it proficiently without close supervision.

Paper Trouble

Space was severely limited in the Computer Room and the boxes of ANs (Advice Notes) and Contracts, when placed in front of the printers, made walking through the room quite tricky. If we kicked a box accidentally out of alignment, then the paper feed would catch and jam. To prevent this, when a new box was opened, I cut the flaps off the box. Also, when a box was almost empty, we carefully lifted the fan-fold paper out completely and removed the box. Such were the tips for smooth running of the *Newbury* line printers.

A full box of ANs contained 400 five-part carbons, which were perforated to give ten copies of each AN, once split out by Peter's CAs: Jean Griffin, Gill Slade, June Brown and Jill Barrett. The girls all wore aprons and gloves while separating and teasing out the individual AN-copies; it was a very messy and time-consuming process and not much quicker than the *Banda* system. When the office was busy and a large batch of ANs had printed, then the decollator and burster machines were used to separate out the pack copies, though they still needed to be sorted by hand afterwards!

Each AN printed ten copies as standard, but the extra copies had to be discarded to match the pack type that the issuing officer had designated:

MOH

F was Full pack
X was eXtra copy buff
T was Transfer copy
M was Miscellaneous copy

The ten MOH copies were:

Engineering Buff Copy and Directory Copy
Blue Copy and Stats Copy
Yellow Copy and Accounts Information Copy
Progress Copy and Exchange White Copy
Red Copy and Office Copy

The old *Banda* spirit duplication process enabled only the pack types which were required to be run off, whereas MOH printed a full pack every time.

A single delivery from the manufacturer was 40,000 forms! Usually our manager was busy so I had to run downstairs and tell the lorry driver into which store room we wanted the 100 boxes unloaded! We had our fair share of paper problems. A new batch of paper kept jamming in the printers. I called out the Rep from the suppliers *Kenrick and Jefferson* and he visited and discussed the adjustment of the printers and I think we then got another delivery of paper which was less prone to misfeeding. I had to carry the boxes of paper from the cabinets in the main office to the computer room and for one batch I noticed that some of the boxes weren't quite so heavy? I later found that some had a piece of foam packing in the bottom which meant the number of forms were short. As British Telecom was charged for hundreds of boxes of forms per Telephone Area, I flagged this issue to David Porter in HQ and I believe we got a substantial refund. I worked really hard to ensure that MOH ran properly in our Area.

My GPO Family: Trilogy Edition

Comm Links

The VDUs were connected to the PT7 via two-core screened cabling on a 'daisy chain' (or loop) to several ports. Each VDU had a D-connector and lead which then terminated on a jack 96; the same as the old-style Plan 4 telephones! The system must have been designed to use up obsolescent British Telecom stock. Every VDU had a 'sub-address' to identify it on the chain, but if its battery back-up failed, then the address reverted to a default which usually clashed with another user and so locked them out of the system. Resetting the sub-address was a quick fix, but often the VDU died again overnight if it was left powered off. Later firmware fixed the sub-address problem, but was too late to be of benefit to us.

At first the PWs terminated on Case 200s with separate modem boxes per circuit, but then one day, John Greenstreet arrived with a wardrobe-sized glass-doored cabinet and the modems were changed to plug in card types. We had dial-up standby circuits too, so the whole set-up looked rather complex! Most times it either functioned or it didn't! I don't recall the standby circuits being particularly useful, I think they were prone to dropping out. We had line faults on a couple of PWs and our managers had to get involved to expedite their repair. Remote VDU links to the Chelmsford and Southend shops were rarely satisfactory as they would lose sync with the system and get locked out.

When Closing Duty were due to move to an adjacent building the comms guys were going to provide ten or more remote modem links back to our PT7s. That might have meant me spending all my days resetting modems, so I put together a proposal for them to take a complete processor with them, rather than having numerous links spread across our remaining PT7s. So, they took one of *our* PT7s

MOH

back to Telephone House and the comms guys there had to look after it! Closing Duty transactions took a lot of processor power and they complained that by connecting the whole team onto one PT7 it was too much load. It was just as likely that a single comms link couldn't handle the traffic, as closing meant recalling an open AN from the distant database and then adding and amending details. Either way, the case was made for an additional PT7, which they successfully got; I don't think we gave any more of ours away!

Other Systems

My 'MOH empire' was confined to Sales. However, Billing used the BEST (Billing Enquiry System for TAG) application which also ran on PT7s. On one occasion that I visited TAG, I noticed that their PT7 was in the main office; they were a little more casual in running their computers and it was the team manager who dealt with any faults. I don't think they had a tape streamer, so the set-up wasn't quite so complex. Divisions in British Telecom were very insular and generally staff had neither the time nor the inclination to discover the daily workings of other groups. Older terminals in TAG gave access to rental records via TOLD (Telecommunications on Line Data) on *Cossor* CD 3005 VDUs through GENFAC. Multi-user, multi-processor systems (MUMPS) were available for managers' communications at Area board level, but otherwise normal office memos still circulated by hand.

MADCs

Multi-Area Data Centres provided the mainframe computing power for a group of Telephone Areas. MADCs were big, spacious rooms which housed ICL or later IBM mainframes, together with scores of 'washing machine sized' stand-alone disc drives, each with a

My GPO Family: Trilogy Edition

capacity of just 200 Mb! Typical processor memory was 2 Mb, this being adequate for the applications. When you compare the data transmission rate from the PT7 over a line speed of just 9.6 kb/s it gives you the perspective that today a complete MADC could run on a desktop PC over a single broadband connection!! Back in 1985 however, computer centres were phenomenal places, almost beyond comprehension. MADCs cost hundreds of thousands of pounds to set up and were a major investment in early computing.

For a while it was a novelty typing ANs on a keyboard and then watching the screen messages flash up: *Transmission in progress* (sent from PT7); *Spooling in progress* (sent from mainframe). Then the system would lock up and die! As more Telephone Areas introduced MOH, the demand for mainframe capacity increased and new centres had to be built to handle the loads. Consequently, it wasn't surprising that our first MADC was as far away as Portsmouth Computer Centre. Cardiff held the load until a new facility in Cambridge was ready, all happening during 1985. Cambridge Computer Centre was equipped with an ICL 2900-series VM (Virtual Machine), which was state of the art. I never visited either Portsmouth or Cardiff, but I did drive up to Cambridge on several occasions to sit in on the monthly support meetings. These were opportunities for managers to check progress of future software enhancements and to flag up unresolved problems.

Looking after MOH

When I attended a Site Officers' course in Bournemouth, I found the other Areas tended to have managers sorting out system problems. The facilitator wanted someone to demo issuing an AN, and everyone was astounded at how fast I could whizz through the screens! It was great fun! With the help of MOH Support in

MOH

London and Cardiff, I became quite an expert in running the system as, apart from Peter Pratt, our sales team managers didn't wish to be involved in the daily running of computers; they just wanted them to function so that their staff could get the work done!

When I first took on the Site Officer role it was envisaged that it would be a full-time task and that I would do ad hoc work for the manager too. In practice, it occupied far less of my time and over several years I worked part-time territorial and leave relief on every Res and Stats team across the office. I got to know everyone in Sales, although sometimes there was contention between answering my phone, serving my customers, or fixing the system!

The Basildon team under Maureen Minto covered Grays, Stanford le Hope, Laindon, Bas Main, Vange and Tilbury. Maureen was strict and there was no unnecessary chatter, but there was a good atmosphere and everyone shared the work and took messages and orders for each other's duties. Some of the team were a little younger than me, but they still organised their work proficiently and it was a pleasure to cover for them. Working on Tilbury duty included 'Ships in Dock' which used a range of reserved numbers with a coinbox which could be 'stopped' or 'started' at a moment's notice. There were stories of ships sailing away with the coinboxes as they couldn't always wait for an engineer to turn up. The Installation Control dealt with the consequences of this and it was rarely a problem for Sales, other than to issue an 'abortive charges' AN. As for the billing... we never got involved with that!!

Terry Hopper was my MOH manager for a while before Tony Cooke agreed to take on the role and transferred me to his team. Throughout, I carried on my Site Officer role and often 'educated' the managers in what had to be done! In September 1986 the CARD Service (Customer Apparatus and Rental Display) was

My GPO Family: Trilogy Edition

about to be implemented and Tony wrote, *"I am arranging for John Chenery to visit each level 1 to discuss the implications so that managers can inform and train their own staff."*

As there weren't always MOH problems to sort out, and if others didn't submit work for me to do, then by default I was hustled off to cover duties where people were on leave for a week. By design, some of the duties which I covered were already onerous, without the added pressure of dealing with any major MOH downtime for other teams. The management wanted it both ways and it wasn't always easy to strike the right balance of covering a full duty while trying to ignore MOH problems which in turn affected my own output! It was part of what I called 'playing the GPO game'. Both sides knew it, but let the status quo prevail.

On CARD there was the facility to type freeform notes against an installation. We used one page to record the availability of telephones and wall brackets for the issuing teams. The info was gathered from Cullinet Stores programme which CA Paul Tyler used to update. Paul was an endearing chap who often smoked. He had a jovial sense of humour, though there was always something a little odd about him, which people couldn't quite figure. It was many years later that Paul came to work on our team and his slightly quirky behaviour was finally explained. Our use of the stores matrix didn't really help, as although items were in stock at the time of issuing the orders, the actual picking usually took place sometime later, when stock levels had changed!

I worked a few weekends overtime in the cause of MOH. One time the Sales Office was due a new carpet and this meant clearing the room completely. The floor held three teams, so it was a big job. Accommodation services were on hand to move the furniture. By then I think we had a Computer Group on site who could assist

MOH

with moves, but perhaps they weren't available the weekend that we chose? MOH terminals had a mains power lead, and the comms lead terminated on a socket. Although we already had desks made of MDF (rather modern for the time), they weren't wire-managed; wiring was strung or taped up in an ad-hoc manner. Anyway, Computer Group allowed us to go ahead with the move and promised to attend on a future date to tidy up the wiring. It was 'all hands on deck' with a couple of managers and a few other volunteers to unplug and untangle the masses of cables, and separate from the general detritus, as the desks were lifted onto trolleys and wheeled away! We worked late into Friday evening to clear the room, as the carpet fitters began to scrape the old carpet off the floor. Putting everything back on the following day wasn't quite so easy. Some screens needed extension leads for the power cables to reach, and each VDU needed the 'sub-address' changing to match the link into which it was plugged. The phones were *Statesman*, but a few sockets had been wrongly marked so it took some fiddling about to get everything working correctly. Staff had been asked to label their phones, trays and screens if they wanted to see them again, with the option of arriving early on Monday to re-arrange their desktops as they preferred. Dealing with people's quirks was never easy! The new carpet was a close-weave, plain orange, which was thin but hard-wearing. There is an offcut under my chair as I sit and type these words!

As MOH software development progressed the PT7 processors were upgraded with extra storage running OSC245 on IT166s.

Team reorganisations occurred periodically and I was moved onto Sue Rothon's team with responsibility for Shoeburyness, Rochford and Canewdon. I think by this time MOH was operating as well as it ever could and I was able to concentrate on running a normal sales duty with fewer distractions. Ron Hoar took on the MOH

My GPO Family: Trilogy Edition

manager role and occasionally he used to 'borrow' me to advise on system problems. Southend was White Area Working. This meant that 'provide' orders didn't have to be sent to the Router; the DP number could be read out of a line plant book which was kept on the team. If there was a cross in the book, then the order went for survey and an appointment could not be made straight away.

This was my final year playing with MOH as I was told that the dedicated computer teams would take over all responsibilities once the replacement system came on-line in the New Year (1989). I'd really enjoyed faulting MOH's quirks, so a few years earlier I'd applied for SDPO (Senior Data Processing Officer) in Network Control at Southend, but there was only one post, which went to the candidate with an engineering background. For another opportunity in Colchester, I passed the Berger Computer Operator Aptitude Test, but didn't get selected for interview. I was destined to remain in Southend, and that suited me well.

Contract Letters

One of the advantages of MOH was that it offered automatic printing of the acknowledgement letters/contracts for the customer. No more form writing for us! Though of course, there were other minor problems with which to contend. If you wanted the notes to the customer to be printed on the contract, they had to be typed in the correct field on the electronic order. There were other anomalies such as rentals printing on the wrong side of the contract. Equipment hire, telephone rental printed on the left, while the line rental (network) printed on the right. It was a huge form, almost A3 sized! Printed contracts were originally distributed to the issuing team(s) to be checked and enveloped, but this sorting of forms was time consuming for the CAs, so central despatch was later the norm. Every time an order was amended, it generated another contract, so on occasions that the customer rang back to change their order the same day, they would end up receiving multiple contracts and be thoroughly confused! Previously, customers hadn't taken much notice of their paperwork, but now if we misspelt a name or an address, they promptly sent the contract back with all of the corrections. Suddenly we were drowning in returned forms! Minor amendments to customer details could be carried out by completing a keyform and sending it to the data processing team (Closing Duty), but some changes required a new AN to be issued. The changing of British Telecom to a Plc status had generated a lot of extra paperwork.

The Final Run

Towards the end of MOH there were approximately 8000 terminals connected nationwide. Finally, we made up and I typed a dummy AN, which was printed in Southend Area on 22 December 1988.

"This is the last MOH Advice Note. Lay MOH to rest with honour. Let CSS give birth painlessly. Happy Xmas and A Prosperous New Year from the now redundant AN Distribution Team."

I think a few more live ANs may have been printed after that, but CSS the Customer Service System was finally going on-line in the New Year!

MOH Girls (2016)

The MOH girls run the files when full
And watch the paper so it doesn't pull.

They have ribbons in the printer and black in their hair...
While they tease the paper so it doesn't tear!

My GPO Family: Trilogy Edition

With gloves and aprons they sort away
All throughout the working day.

M, F, X and T, sealed in pouches
And dispatched by three (pm).

And when they've finished they Rest In Peace (RIP)
MOH is such a beast!

MOH Computer Room (circa 1986)

Outlet 7: TAG Telephone Accounts Group

The Telephone Accounts Group(s) (TAG), first introduced in 1954, dealt with the accurate production of telephone bills, the collection of payments and any customer queries. I never worked on an actual TAG duty, although in later years I carried out similar job functions in other roles. Some of my 'GPO Family' have helped me with contributions to this section.

On the few occasions that I had visited the Account Groups, it was apparent that they had once been the very epitome of the Civil Service-like organisation of the Post Office. The rows and rows of metal-topped desks and matching drawer pedestals, together with tall, *elephant grey*-coloured filing cabinets filled with shelves of A4 ring binders all gave the impression that little had changed for many years. The tarnished plastic of the coat hangers on the rack, and lino floor coverings, harkened back to another age. Attempts to brighten up some work areas had resulted in garish Seventies-style paint colours of orange backed cabinets, that actually were well-matched with the yellow and orange (PO issue) chair covers. Change was overdue and was to be brought about by the full-computerisation of the billing processes. In reality, this was to take several decades as both the technology and the once steadfast Post Office became a very different company.

TAG groups were organised by Exchange and Number Range, spread across the Telephone Area, so that there was an even balance of workload for every duty. Working practices were matched to the exchange technology of the era that was electro-mechanical meters of 4, 5 or 6-digits, which recorded one unit or more for each call made. Each unit bought a period of time and call charges were calculated by the number of units used during a given tariff period of Peak, Standard or Cheap rate.

My GPO Family: Trilogy Edition

Historically, telephone bills were rendered quarterly, but this changed to half-yearly in 1939, at the start of war. They didn't revert to quarterly until the introduction of STD (Subscriber Trunk Dialling) which was progressively rolled out from 1958. STD bills were produced in the Telephone Managers' Offices on large multi-key specialist typewriters, using NCR (No Carbon Required) formatted paper. As MATS (Mechanical Accounting for Telephone Service) processing of ticketed operator calls was introduced, bill production was transferred to regional centres. Billing was the culmination of meter readings, operator ticketed calls (MATS), rental, and any closed Sales orders. The processing of these activities was continually revised as newer and ever faster sorting and coding machines were invented. The handling of ticketed calls was more important at the start of STD, as so many calls were still connected by the operator.

While the MATS units predominantly handled the processing of telephone tickets, by mechanical means, the Post Office had plans for a National Data Processing Service (NDPS) using state of the art computers. The Kensington Computer Centre had been set up in 1964 for Telephone Billing (TB) Stages 1 and 2, using LEO III machines and these were upgraded to LEO 326s by 1965. In practice the Post Office work remained separate, but one can imagine how these ideas led the way for National Giro to be established a few years later.

Accounting for Calls

From about 1968, the photographing of meters in the exchanges was a routine task, using a mains-powered flash camera, fitted with a large hood. The hood rested over a group of 100 meters to capture many readings on a single photograph. Photographers could be night telephonists (on day overtime), clerical grades, or engineers.

"When a female camera operator is employed, she should be advised to wear flat-heeled shoes."

The films were developed and sent to the Area Office to be read on a light-box. The individual meter readings were transcribed onto keyforms which were then sent to a Data Conversion Centre (DCC) for transfer to punched cards for input into the billing system.

TB Stage 3, using the LEO 326s, created a magnetic tape file of customer details which were sourced from TMOs (Telephone Managers' Offices) and MATS records. In 1973, ISOCC (Input System for Operator Controlled Calls) superseded the MATS tickets as TB Stage 5. By the mid-1970s the Telecommunications On Line Data (TOLD) network allowed inputting and validation of meter readings via horrendously large 'black-box' *Cossor* VDU terminals in the TMOs.

TOLD

TOLD used ICL System 4 or 2960 series mainframe computers. Initial TOLD applications were, Billing Payments, Billing Amendments and Interrogation, Billing Meter Readings, and NIS (Number Information Services – Directory compilation). The roll-out to all Areas was a gradual process and as CAs tended to do the data inputting, it wasn't always obvious that computerisation of the TAG duties was creeping in.

Dawn Wigley writes...

"I left in 1981 and at that point (in TAG) we had no computer terminals on our desks. I remember being taken down to the

My GPO Family: Trilogy Edition

basement to see the new mainframe computer, but the only real evidence of activity (and change) were the billing printouts that were produced each quarter and then further printouts for reminders, and finally a printout for those that still hadn't paid to potentially be cut off. There were still manual exchanges too with a card filed away in banks of drawers for every manually recorded call made."

Yve Collins, who joined in 1985, writes...

"We had an old type of computer, the films came in, and were loaded onto a fiche reader. I viewed the film and input the readings to a computer that sent the data to the mainframe to produce the customers' bills. I remember manually inputting the meter readings, oh heavens, Roxwell was the most hated, not easy to read, and all over the place! You used to have to input each film twice so any anomalies showed up, then try and find out what was correct. It used to take hours and your eyes would be out on stalks."

"I got so used to it, didn't look at the number keypad, used to read the film and type the numbers straight in, but the computer used to make this loud noise if I tried to enter too many digits into a cell. And it all had to be done the same day the films came in! Once, I was on my own doing the inputting, had been at it for several hours, my eyes were getting really tired, and I must have nodded off. My head hit the keyboard, which set off an alarm which immediately woke me up!"

MILO

Brian Henwood recalls his time as Meter Input Liaison Officer during the 1990s, as the exchange modernisation programme was gaining momentum.

TAG

"I was MILO for the old Southend Telephone Area reporting to a manager in Colchester. I was responsible for planning and organising the meter photography for the customer bills on the old Strowger and Crossbar (mechanical) exchanges."
[Reed relay types, namely TXE2 and TXE4 had electronic meter stores and TXE4 was later enhanced to allow itemised billing.]

"The meters were filmed by ex-jumper runners if I remember correctly. They would have to physically drop the films off at the GMO (General Manager's Office). Once received they were taken to *Photo Visual* near Hamlet Court Road who we had a contract with to get them developed within 24 hours. They would then be collected by myself or one of the Billing agency CAs (I had a team of two or three working mostly to me)."

"Once developed I needed to check each film on the Zeiss-Jenna viewers (big battleship-grey things); we had to make sure all meters had been filmed, and were readable, and label them up and prep them for input. They then had to be input ASAP into the system by manually inputting each 1000 number range into CSS (Customer Service System). At this time, I could call on all the billing CAs to get this work done on time, or anyone else who was free, myself included. Really mind numbing and eye straining!"

"The films were usually kept for a few years (can't remember how many exactly) before being destroyed by the hi-tech method of physically cutting them up with a pair of scissors into the general waste bin! If you had a lot to do, people would quickly get fed up of the constant 'snip, snip, snip' of the scissors."

"In a similar manner I also was responsible for the billing side of the exchange modernisation process. When an exchange was due to

My GPO Family: Trilogy Edition

switch to digital, all the meters needed to be read to provide a 'final' meter reading on the old equipment. The same process was then followed as for the cyclic readings."

"When billing was functionalised [territorial TAG groups disbanded] the MILO role had shrunk to such a degree that they only needed one person in Colchester for the whole of East Anglia District so I ended up on the new Invoice Control team which eventually became the CFB Onebill team."

Accounting for Rental

Subscriber's rental details were originally recorded manually on A3016 cards which were held and updated by TAG. I assume that Sales had to refer to TAG for every AN (Advice Notes) that they issued, although many installations would have only had a single hard-wired telephone, lacking the complexities of multiple socket products of the post-privatisation era. Requests to TAG for PARS were sent on an A4017 form. In 1973, CRR (Customer Rental Record) cards were destined to replace the A3016s, albeit the new computer printed cards were to be held by Sales.

* It is thought that PARS was Proforma of Apparatus and Rental Services. Others suggest it was an abbreviation of 'particulars'.

CRR

CRR was designed to give Sales up-to-date details of products and services, which their customers rented, to enable the CO to deal efficiently with requests for additional apparatus or removals. Bulk printing of replacement cards at each tariff revision was a simple process, although the careful filing of thousands of cards in the office was to become a tedious and low priority task for busy CAs.

TAG

Staff publicity leaflets of the time embraced the forthcoming system.

"Remember, CRR will make work easier and not more complicated."

[Quote from leaflet *The fact is - work would become more and more difficult without CRR.* July 1972]

However, a new design of bill with specially produced printouts was also under consideration for TAG. Previous records of bills were held on 19-inch wide paper listings which were unwieldly to handle. It wasn't until 1982 that trials of GENFAC allowed TAG and DP (Data Processing) teams to access an Area's CRR on line. I recall this being possible on the *Cossor* VDUs operating via TOLD links.

NBS (New Billing System)

NBS was first introduced in Middlesbrough in February 1977, primarily to run on ICL 2970 computers as the LEO 326s could no longer cope with the volume and complexity of telephone billing (TB5). The last of the 49 Areas, Sheffield was converted in 1980. NBS was designed to integrate with CRR, ISOCC and TOLD.

The customer bills had a modern look and TAG summaries were now small enough to file in handy-size ring binders.

Yve remembered using several coloured binders...

"Yellow, green and blue ring binders on a carousel, but there must have been another colour for four quarters? Two-hole, but only about half A5 in depth – yes, about 3 inches deep, but about as long

My GPO Family: Trilogy Edition

as an A5. The binder was about an inch deeper than the sheets."

"Every new bill run you had to take out the old pages and put in the new ones, all the notes were written on the paper sheets. They had the quarter, date, and tel. number on it, underneath the bill breakdown, very simplistic, rental, usage, VAT and total, on the right was the name and address. When a payment was rung in you noted the sheet for that account, and rang the late payers."

The 1977 NBS booklet illustrates five coloured binders, which appear to be black, lime green, orange, white, and yellow. The extra folder many have been for reports such as follow-up action lists.

The two main sub-systems for NBS were TRAM and BPF:

TRAM: Ticket, Rental, Advice Note, Meter Reading.

BPF: Billing Production, Payments, Follow-up.

Later computer applications followed this trend of having a number of sub-systems dedicated to specific processes, each with their own buzz-word acronyms.

In Sales, CRR was available via MOH (Mechanisation of Order Handling) menus on the Ferranti PT7 controllers. Closing Duty had access to BEST (Billing Enquiry Service for TAG). Other Ferranti controllers in TAG offered TOPS (TAG Office Products Service). TABS (Telephone Account Billing System) was proposed as the name of an interim billing system before CSS.

My GPO Family spans a long timeline. Colleagues who started work in TAG eventually moved to 'Billing' as duties became more functionalised and the Telephone Area structure gradually changed beyond recognition. More than a few people moved away as promotion or families led them to seek opportunities in other towns. Those whom remained in the Area became the most able to adapt to an ever-evolving computerisation of their work.

MCAT Onebill

Just outside of TAG in MCAT (Major Customer Accounts Team), Southend GMO (General Manager's Office) was proving the Onebill (1982) concept. All of the UK bills for a particular firm were diverted into Southend and loaded onto a small business computer. A summary and bill total were provided, effectively presenting a single bill which could be settled quickly by Direct Debit. This process was further developed and later became a national system.

Andrew Herbert recalls...

"Onebill ran on an early computer which had a processor unit and a separate disc drive. The software was written by a specialist group within British Telecom."

"TOLD access was via a dumb terminal using different coloured keys in the badge reader for the authority level required. A yellow key allowed PIF (Payment Input Facility). Another coloured key was used by the supervisor to release batched meter readings to Billing."

CACTUS

From October 1981, Southend also pioneered the payment of Residential bills by Access or Barclaycard (early credit cards). Credit Card Control and Transaction Update System (CACTUS)

My GPO Family: Trilogy Edition

was run by Julie Wren and Jean Wilson under the supervision of Diane Upton. A side office was utilised because it was essential that the processing of card details was kept secure.

Eventually, the taking of credit card payments became far more routine and new processes were built into the billing systems to handle them more easily. In later years their use was discouraged by local policies, surcharges imposed by the Card companies, and a more general idea of not encouraging debtors to effectively transfer their payment problem to another company!

MAG

Tucked away on the first floor of Telephone House, the Miscellaneous Accounts Group (circa 1980) dealt with spare lines, Telex, Ship to Shore, Private Wire billing, Call Offices (Public Payphones) and Credit Cards (Chargecards). I had occasion to visit the team when I was distributing CPSA union literature, such as *Red Tape* and circulars, at the time I was on the committee. The Civil Service connections of Post Office Telecommunications lingered on for a few years more.

References

Post Office Telecommunications Journals:
Charging for STD Calls by HA Longley - Winter 1959.
Telephone Accounting Developments by AM Jones - Winter 1960.
The Computer Centre in Kensington by HG Robson - Spring 1965.
The National Data Processing Plan by CR Smith - Winter 1967.
Producing Telephone Bills by Computer by LK Hinton - Autumn 1968.
Eleven million records at a glance by JT Greenwood - Spring 1973.

TAG

Now it can be TOLD by LV Reinger - Winter 1975/76.
A new bill is on the way by AG Martin - Summer 1976.

Other literature:

PH 1851 (8/73) *ISOCC how it affects TAG.*
PH 2023 1977 *New Billing System.*
Meter Photography report 1967/8.
CPSA Annual Reports 1981/2 (Posts and Telecommunications Group).
LINK CPSA Newspaper April 1982.

NBS leaflet PH 2023 (1977)

My GPO Family: Trilogy Edition

*Redesign Sales Office QIT winners (1990/1)
Julie, John, Eileen, Laura and Elizabeth*

Outlet 8: CSS Customer Service System

CSS was developed to deliver the *Front Office* concept whereby a receptionist could confidently deal with straightforward Sales, Billing and Fault enquiries at first point of contact. Until then there had been a multitude of local and national computer systems such as MOH (Mechanisation of Order Handling), BEST (Billing Enquiry System for TAG), LLIS (Local Lines Interim System), and various RSC (Repair Service Centre) remote testing facilities.

CSS was to be the most extensive computer system introduced across British Telecom to date. The first CSS customer order was issued in Thameswey District in March 1986, but planning had been years in the process. In East Anglia District the new DISU (District Information System Unit) in Colchester, had been topped-out in late 1984 at a cost of £1.6 million. A completely new network build was required, and in every Telephone Area hundreds of (dumb) terminals had to be supplied and individually cabled to each cluster controller.

Southend

CSS training started in September 1988 and was a week's course with Laura Huggins and Sheralee Deboick, learning how to create and interrogate orders. The fictitious database of Ringford, Ringshire drove us all mad as the number of inhabitants in the town was rather limited, so there were lots of repeat orders for the same customers! In the weeks that followed, we issued many practice orders as key CSS transactions required an exact sequence to correctly generate the required activities for the jobs to proceed. Much like MOH, CSS was still menu-driven by keyboard tabbing, but its versatility was the hundreds of powerful mnemonic commands, such as ECO (Enter Customer Order), to call-up

My GPO Family: Trilogy Edition

subsequent actions. A typical job might have included twenty separate commands and we learnt them (and many others) all by rote. I don't think CSS crashed in the same way as MOH, but there was the dreaded ABEND (ABnormal END) screen when a transaction failed to ledger.

The last MOH Sales orders were issued just before Christmas 1988 and CSS in Southend Area finally went live on New Year's Day 1989. We were all encouraged to work that Sunday to catch up with the backlog of orders and to test the system before Monday! It must have been the one time when nearly the whole office turned up to do overtime!

150

Under CSS working, territorial duties were to end as everyone would have access to the whole District database, and in theory be able to type orders for any locality within. A new switch in place of our direct line telephones gave us our first ACD (Automatic Call Distribution) system where we signed on with an agent ID and took calls directly into our (Madonna style) headsets! Callers rang 150 and the service operator simply asked if they wanted Sales or Billing, and the next available agent took the call. One's earpiece would give a single bleep and the customer was straight into your head! Customer service etiquette demanded that everyone answered their calls with the correct salutation and their name. This became a problem if the caller then wanted to speak to the same person again, as DDI (Direct Dial In) to extensions wasn't a *Front Office* concept. This tended to take away the satisfaction and convenience of having duties which were territorially based. Agent's 'idle time', 'wrap-up time', and 'call handling time' were now all under scrutiny. The age of the Call Centre had truly arrived!

ACD

Our ACD (Automatic Call Distribution) switch was from a third-party supplier. It was OK for transferring calls within the office, but if you tried to transfer a caller to a distant sales office, invariably the call got lost in the system, or simply dropped out. It caused quite a few repeat calls. It was most likely the interface between the ACD and the external lines, causing the problem, but despite several attempts at monitoring the situation, no one ever admitted that perhaps it simply didn't work! It was very frustrating to follow the correct transfer procedure only for the call to be lost. A colleague wrote a rather derogatory ditty, which circulated in one of our area magazines. The first line was quite memorable, "ACD is a load of balls, cos you don't get no effin calls". I can't recall the other lines except, "You hear the bleep from far away, by the time you answer the caller's not there to say."

CSS Process

CSS brought with it 'address matching' so that every address that was input had to be validated against the PAF (Postal Address File) which was supplied by the Post Office. Exceptions were new housing estates which often only had plot numbers, let alone postcodes! CSS generated lots of manager reports so that every issuing error was highlighted. As well as unmatched addresses, it flagged up orders which hadn't been progressed (no ECDD) or had the directory entry omitted (EASDR). In hindsight, these could probably have been sent back in a queue to the issuer, but instead a separate 'Case Team' was set up to deal with all anomalies. This was functional working where users didn't deviate from their designated tasks. The main sales teams were now a single answering suite which was not designed for making outgoing calls. However, there was a rota for one person on the suite to chase jobs

My GPO Family: Trilogy Edition

on behalf of customers who raised queries directly. On the occasions that I took on this role, I naturally had to ring the engineers, or other departments to get jobs completed, and also to ring the customers back, but I was often then told that I had made too many outgoing calls, which looked bad on the stats. If I was to be accountable by always giving my name, then I also wanted the flexibility to chase up any problems on my own behalf. And the job satisfaction of not being able to 'own' a problem was, for me, diminishing.

There was a Sales Bureau (desk) in the foyer of Telephone House for customers to place orders, but when the first *Phoneshop* opened in Southend High Street, Doreen Tate was displaced to the Stats team. Conversely, as the shop became inundated with returned rental phones, Doreen took on the role to update CSS. Doreen was out of touch with issuing, so I spent some hours over occasional days helping her understand the 'office records only' orders which were required. Doreen's husband, Ken was trained up to operate the new machine which folded and enveloped the CSS customer contracts. Ken had the patience to watch each operation of the machine and to pause it if there was a problem, although it was intended to be an automatic process; whenever Ken had a day off, the relief CA(s) always managed to get it jammed!

Ken also kept an eye on the contract printers which, to screen-off the noise, were in a side room. The printers were numbered S CON (Southend Contracts) 1 to 4; Ken always made me smile by calling them scons or scones! There was a 'print queue' which I could interrogate from my screen, so if the number of contracts waiting to print was building up I would wander upstairs in my tea break, to check. This was always a good opportunity to join Ken for a friendly chat in his 'office', away from the babble of the crowd. If nothing had printed, one of us could then call the Computer Centre to restart the SCON in question; then of course it would churn out several hours-worth of prints!

CSS Support

CSS was not without its teething troubles, so my site officer role continued and I completed a half-day course at Brentwood TE, for an overview of the network, the new VDUs, and cluster controllers. By this stage it was somewhat 'hands off', with problems being reported and passed to specialist teams to deal. I did manage to get a couple of visits to the DISU which was running an IBM 3081 and later the IBM 3090 with 20 Gigabytes storage and support for 1000 terminals. The DISU filled a large area; the era of true personal computing was still several years away!

Gill Cotter, our Level 2 had supported us during the MOH to CSS transition years. Her priority had always been the smooth running of the Sales Office, but she mostly listened to my suggestions of how to manage some of the day to day problems of the systems! In February 1989 she moved on, but not without a good parting word to us all...

"I would like to take this opportunity of thanking you on a personal basis for your hard work during the time I have known you and for the team spirit created by all during the past four years."

Eileen's Team

By about 1989 I had come full circle and was back on the Chelmsford team which was headed by Eileen Goodchild. I think by then we fielded calls for all areas and I was certainly familiar with all of the exchanges. Eileen was a stickler for the processes, but if one worked hard, she was fair.

My GPO Family: Trilogy Edition

TQM (Total Quality Management) was being introduced into British Telecom. Everything was getting more formal. Processes had to be followed, new instructions written and behaviours modified. The more liberal time directly after privatisation was giving way to a more regulated regime, rather like the GPO era! I took part in two QIPs (Quality Improvement Plans).

The first was Tony Cooke's DPA (Departmental Process Analysis) *Speedy and Professional Response to Customers Telephone Calls*. Also on the team were: Dot Downs, Sylvia Day and June Barker. This dragged on for many months with brainstorming sessions and questionnaires being sent out to both internal and external customers. We didn't have the resources to allow a very extensive study, and frankly didn't have the authority to make any major changes to the existing call handling set-up. It was an interesting exercise, but somewhat futile.

My second QIT (Quality Improvement Team) event, and rather more productive, was Eileen's *Redesign Sales Office Layout*, with Laura Sheppard, Elizabeth Chantilly, and Julie Melvin. The project involved the re-arrangement of desks, computer terminals and telephones and that was another weekend's overtime with us doing much of the work! We proudly won the 1990/1991 East Anglia District Quality Award for 'Teamwork' for our QIT.

Visit to BT Centre 1991

At the launch of BT's new identity, 'the listening, speaking piper', tickets were offered to visit BT Centre and learn about the brand and the vision for the company. I managed to secure a place on this prestigious event, which I think was held over several days to allow plenty of staff to visit. I travelled up to London and entered the revered BT Centre for the first time. I think there was a brief reception and then everyone started queuing to ascend a staircase, which at the time I felt either led to heaven, or quite possibly the executioner's scaffold!!

BT Today (staff newspaper) April 1991 *'...walked up a winding staircase into the specially-constructed auditorium'.*

The event was being televised, so the lighting was extra bright. I didn't feel that this was a very relaxed environment and I was relieved when we were able to descend back down! The platform had been cleverly built in the huge atrium space and must have cost many thousands of pounds to stage. Memorable for the wrong reasons, but I was pleased that I had the chance to be there.

With everything well-ordered and running smoothly it was time for *Project Sovereign* to bite. The new BT was looking for efficiency savings and was shedding layers of management. It was also studying the optimum sizes for call centres and decided that the accommodation in Southend, spread over two buildings and many floors simply wasn't viable. We were given the option of relocating to Colchester or applying for a different job function within Southend. I helped with the wind-down of work on our team until the prospect of securing a new position was looking rather unlikely.

Jumpering

Of all the engineering jobs, jumper running had somehow survived the revolution of the analogue to digital equipment conversion, with little noticeable change. All lines still had to be jumpered between the MDF blocks, and in some exchanges, wires had to be soldered using the large soldering irons which conveniently plugged into the 50V jacks on each rack. Even this appeared to be a dying art, as 'punch-down' blocks were becoming commonplace.

My GPO Family: Trilogy Edition

Nonetheless, I spent a day or two job shadowing Tony Nesnas and Dimitri in my local exchanges. [More than 20 years later I bumped into Dimitri as he was exiting an exchange. I was pleasantly surprised that he recognised me and we shared a few moments of recollections.]

Tony showed me how to count the tags on the blocks and thus locate the correct bar-pairs. Jumpers had to be run with enough slack for tracing purposes, although if an engineer was under pressure to get to the next job, and a jumper was cut slightly short, there wasn't always time to redo it! Some frames were impossibly jam packed, especially if ceased lines had not been recovered!

The smart way to work on ANs was to check all of the associated ones and ignore the ghost numbers created by Sales. For example, two customers who were swapping homes and numbers might only need the bar-pairs changed, whereas the ANs may have included two batches of 'stop and renumber' instructions. At another exchange, Dimitri let me have a practice at wire-wrapping (on a spare block) with an electric gun. That was fun!

I observed that jumpering was a singleton job which provided little contact with others and with the prospect of more blocks being pre-wired (less work), it didn't especially appeal to me as solving my long-term career problem. Note: These days jumpering is more complex as lines are run through broadband back-hauls and test access matrices. I assume that with customers changing supplier more often, the daily jumper 'churn' is as intensive as ever!

I held out for another office job and didn't have too long to wait for my next change of job title.

Southend TAO

Outlet 9: Southend Telephone Area

Post Office Organisation

The structuring of the Post Office has always been a complex matter, no doubt partly due to its size, and also for the number of different services and functions which it once provided. Adapting to meet changing customer needs was a constant challenge, and perhaps the Post Office did this the best? As a player in the GPO game, it often seemed (to me) that as one transformation had been achieved, it was time to start on the next!

A full account of all the organisational changes is beyond the scope and time of this current publication, suffice to show that, like fashion, the same ideas wax and wane over the years…

Provision of Telephone Service was vested in the Post Office Engineering Department (POED) with other divisions playing a secondary role, as without the physical infrastructure, there is simply no business.

In the 1930s the POED was responsible for 15 Engineering Districts, under the control of the Engineer-in-Chief, in London, with local Sectional Engineers employing the front-line engineering staff.

In a GPO, *Green Paper*-type publication (The Post Office Engineering Department) it lists the activities and responsibilities of the POED as:

- Lines
- Trunk Lines

My GPO Family: Trilogy Edition

- Repeater Stations
- Automatic Exchanges
- Testing of Materials
- Telegraphs
- Postal Services (including the Post Office Railway)
- Submarine Cables
- Radio
- Research

Regionalisation

As the demand for telephone and postal services increased, a centrally organised District structure was too far removed from the daily tasks of providing that service. A Regional structure was recommended by the Gardiner Committee.

Two experimental regions were set up in 1936:
- Scottish Region
- North Eastern Region (9 March)

The London Postal Region (LPR) was formed from the London Postal Service and Surveyor Home District.

The London Telecommunications Region (LTR) was created from the London Telephone Service on 26 October. The six other provincial regions were set up between 1939-1940.

Green Paper No.34 Post Office Regionalisation:

'*The appointment of a Telephone Manager equipped with the necessary powers effectively, under the Regional Director, the day-to-day control of all telephone questions arising in his area...*'

Southend TAO

'...*We hope in this way to attain the elasticity and responsiveness to public demands.*'

Telephone Areas

Between 1935 and 1940 the Telephone Area structure was established. This devolved much of the admin from Telephone Districts and combined local engineering activities from Sectional Engineers into a number of self-contained units with responsibility for smaller geographical areas.

Thus, Telephone Area Offices (TAOs) headed by a Telephone Manager (TM) were created. Noticeably, van fleets began to display the lettering 'Post Office Telephones' together with the designation 'Telephone Manager' and the 'Area'.

The first Telephone Area (TA), Bradford was created on 16 December 1935. Further TAs in Scotland and North East England were established during 1936, and the remainder progressively until Reading TA on 11 March 1940.

Southend Telephone Area

Was established on 11 July 1938.
"*The Southend-on-Sea Telephone Area is one of the smallest in the Kingdom, covering an area of 400 square miles and having 37,012 telephone subscribers. Known as 'Sunny Southend' the Headquarters town takes its name from the fact that it is situated at the south end of the ancient parish of Prittlewell, which contains the famous Priory founded in A.D.1100.*"

[Extract from *Post Office Telecommunications Journal* February-April 1954.]

My GPO Family: Trilogy Edition

As part of the town centre re-development of the 1960s, Southend's TMO (Telephone Manager's Office) was relocated from Strand Arcade, Warrior Square to a brand-new building at 45 Victoria Avenue. This road was to become the hub of all office work in Southend until the end of the century, although the total scheme required the demolition of many grand residential dwellings in the process. The TMO however was built on an otherwise unused piece of land, as a report from the Government's developmental department states...

Southend T.M.O. Site (1951)

Structural Engineering Section, Ministry of Works:

"A vacant site in Victoria Avenue, Southend, is under consideration for the proposed erection of a Telephone Manager's Office. The site, which is indicated on the attached plan dated 9.3.51, includes the location of an alleged old gravel pit, now filled."

Built on the site of former gravel workings, Telephone House, Southend on Sea, was of an unusual design having steps up to the front entrance, a long ramp from the back door and a large loading bay platform for deliveries. A first-floor office was suspended over the driveway and the land (west) to Baxter Avenue dropped off quite sharply.

North of the TMO site was Clark's College, which was soon to be displaced by the DHSS (1961) – Department of Health and Social Security. It is thought that part of the TMO site had been used (at least since 1939) as an allotment. From the mid-1960s Metropolitan House (extension) was built to the south of the TMO. I have vague memories of walking around a small raised garden which today is the down ramp to Thamesgate House car park. Such was the

Southend TAO

growth in telephones during the 60s that the TMO also rented space in other buildings along the Avenue.

My Telephone Area

In the late 1960s I marvelled at the Post Office organization. I studied any new leaflet in detail to see what wonders it beheld!

A 1969 GPO leaflet displayed a map and proclaimed:

*'This is **Your** Telephone Area... 590 square miles...66 telephone exchanges and 167,000 telephones, as well as 962 public telephone kiosks.'*

My Telephone Area? We weren't actually 'on the phone', but it all sounded very impressive!

My father's work was contained with the Southend TE, so there was never any opportunity, or reason, to visit the TMO, at least not just yet...

During the 1970s, the area office was organised as four divisions of Clerical (C), Engineering (E), Sales (S) and Traffic (T). Sub-divisions, duty references, and names of groups and departments changed many, many times over the following years.

Southend GMO

The Telephone Manager's Office became the GMO (General Manager's Office) in 1973. Logically, it was no longer necessary to differentiate between Telephone and Postal managers as they were now separate businesses, but it may also have been that the TM title didn't convey the fact that the manager had responsibility for the whole area and not just the telephone products.

My GPO Family: Trilogy Edition

However, as services were provided within a geographical area, the more familiar name of Telephone Area Office (TAO) was often used.

Chris Hogan of the Post Office Vehicle Club (POVC) has been researching the organisational changes of the Post Office structure...

The announcement to split the eight Great British provincial regions into postal and telecommunications was made on 31st August 1967 and implementation was 8th January 1968.

Although Home Counties Region (HCR) was split to Eastern Region (ER) and South Eastern Region (SER) in 1965, this was purely geographical as the region had become too big to manage from London.

The first region to split was London and the last was Northern Ireland. The others were split during 1968

After the split, the former Home Counties Region had become:

- *Eastern Postal Region (EPR) and South Eastern Postal Region (SEPR)*
- *Eastern Telecommunications Region (ETR) and South Eastern Telecommunications Region (SETR)*

Northern Ireland remained a combined region until November 1980 in the run-up to the demerger of British Telecom from the Post Office. HQ functions followed.

The POVC records the Motor Transport function splitting in 1968 and this meant the later F registration blocks were exclusively either Royal Mail or Post Office Telephones.

Southend TAO

We believe that the change of title from 'TELEPHONE MANAGER' to 'GENERAL MANAGER' took place in 1973. The 1974 contract year vehicles were delivered without the familiar TELEPHONE MANAGER lettering on the cab doors underneath POST OFFICE TELEPHONES. Earlier vehicles started to lose the lettering but without any consistency.

This is reiterated in the telephone directory *green pages* of the era, with earlier editions suggesting subscribers contact their Telephone Manager for more details. Editions circa 1974 advise contact to be made with the General Manager in the Telephone Area Office (TAO).

My Era

When I joined Post Office Telecommunications on 17 September 1979, all work for the Southend Telephone Area was centred on the General Manager's Office (GMO) at 45 Victoria Avenue, Southend on Sea, SS2 6BA. This local headquarters had control of engineers, telephonists, clerical workers, mechanics, typists, canteen staff, cleaners, stores and supplies. It was everything needed to supply, service and bill all aspects of the public telephone service, in our locality. It was quite a sprawling operation: Nine floors of people in Telephone House, and five floors in the adjacent building, Metropolitan House. Stock Road was the local stores and vehicle workshop while the Main Telephone Exchange accommodated the telephonists and more clerical staff, plus enough on-site engineers to keep it all in perfect running order. Additionally, each telephone exchange throughout the area had a dedicated number of staff, for the day to day operation and maintenance.

My GPO Family: Trilogy Edition

In the Office

The organisation was steeped in tradition, respectability and reliability. It may not have been the most efficient business, but it was an instantly recognisable public service and was the one I found most fascinating. It was so well-ordered. Everything had a detailed description and there was a process to follow for any activity.

In the foyer of Telephone House there was a bill payment counter and a doorkeeper who controlled access to the other floors. Registry on the second floor sorted incoming and outgoing mail for the building and its post boys (and girls?) still worked for the postal side of the business. At this time the Postal and Telecom businesses were both controlled by the Post Office. The post boys did morning and afternoon deliveries and collections to every post point (trays) in all rooms. Memos, letters, newsletters, periodicals and notifications to other offices within the building were all circulated in this manner. Trolleys were used, and a separate one was kept under the stairs on the first-floor as there was no lift access. It was a very unusual building! Bundles of papers had to be carried down the stairs from the second-floor Registry.

Memos were usually handwritten on a sheet of plain A4 paper, which had a hole pre-punched in the top left corner. An A5 circulation slip was attached to the memo with a metal-ended tag. A short red tag for just a few papers, or a longer yellow tag for a whole bundle. Extra-long tags could be used for really lengthy screeds. Metal, single-hole punches were provided to aid tagging of papers. Brown or blue 'skins' were A4 cards with pre-printed headers between which to sandwich a bundle of particular case papers. Some staff used pins instead of tags. Others stapled the papers together. For papers that had been circulated to many

Southend TAO

groups, and returned with more comments, it was common to find the bundle had grown with the addition of extra tags, staples and pins! A CA's 'toolkit' included a staple extractor and a small box of linen 'reinforcing washers' to repair the holes which had become ripped by too tight a tag! Tag misuse was rife!

Papers were placed in one of the many *Out* trays, to be collected by the post boy. *Personal* or *In Confidence* memos were placed in a buff envelope and sealed with a gummed label, which had to be moistened by tongue or by one of the round plastic 'water trays with sponge' usually found on CAs desks. Memos took a long time to circulate, especially those placed in the tray of anyone on annual or sick leave. This was especially true of cash collections for colleagues' birthdays and much panic ensued when the card or money envelope could not be located!

For important memos or letters, work could be sent to the Typing Pool from whence it would be returned a day or two later. A 'required by date' was written on the typing card to prioritise jobs. As a CA, many times I ran from the first to eighth floor with an urgent typing request from my TTS (Telecoms Traffic Superintendent). Any typing errors could be sent back and corrected while you waited. Corrections were *Snopaked* or *Errorexed* with typing fluid, then overtyped. The shorthand typist, Rosette would accept dictated letters over the 'phone and these would usually be ready for collection a few hours later.

Smoking was allowed in most offices and public places, so anyone could freely 'light-up' in the building. The middle Traffic office was particularly bad as the team dealt with service complaints, so they tended to quickly get stressed and frequently needed a fag! Though of course it was mostly habit. It's hard to imagine how we tolerated it. Male toilets were on one floor and female on the next.

My GPO Family: Trilogy Edition

Two lifts served the building, although there was no lift access to the first floor, which was a non-standard layout of corridors and stairs. An opening to one of the lifts was made some years later, and you had to choose the correct lift if you wanted to exit on the first floor!

On the second floor, 'Addressograph' had the facility to print (via metal plates) rolls of gummed labels, typically with the name and address of each Telephone Exchange, as correspondence to other buildings in the area was frequent. Mail was sorted in Registry and couriered to other buildings by a dedicated Royal Mail van, if the volume of post warranted it. Some internal post may have routed via the local Royal Mail centre in town, but it was only in later years that postage had to be charged, when the Telecom business split from the Post Office.

The fifth floor had a conference room at one end and then either side of the long corridor were the HODs (Heads of Division) offices (also carpeted). At the opposite end was the GMs (General Manager's) office. About halfway along was the TI (Telecom Instructions) Library which contained a bookcase of about 100 or more A4 ring binders. Iris Manning, our 'long standing' CA explained *"One must never run on this floor and must keep very quiet as it's the managers' floor."* Invariably, the managers tended to leave their doors open, unless they wanted privacy.

Metropolitan House

Met House was a bit of a rabbit warren of British Telecom offices spread over many floors and levels. It was possible to enter the north side of the building, access the centre extension, and finally exit on the south side, all without going through another tenant's area. As a CA it was always quite an adventure walking through

Southend TAO

another department's work area to deliver an important memo or visit a colleague.

The Sales Bureau, for new telephone connections, was in this building in the 1970s. The bureau moved back to Telephone House foyer in the 1980s, until it was superseded by the *British Telecom Shop* in Southend High Street. By then, the Business Equipment Centre (BEC) occupied a large area of the fourth floor of Met House.

Met House was completely refurbished in the late 1980s and was renamed Thamesgate House. As the common areas were accessed by the public, we were issued with keys to the locked toilets. This was the closest I ever got to having my own executive washroom! For a year or two, I also paid to use a numbered car parking bay; it wasn't too harsh a life.

Southend Main

Southend Main was built circa 1929, at the time that the Linked Numbering Scheme (LNS) and multi-exchange area for the town was being developed. The *1141 code* SMU is very simply the Southend Main Underground (cable) which linked it to distant centres. The third floor housed the AMC (Auto-Manual Centre) at which many hundreds of operators (day and night staff combined) once connected a majority of the calls, in the days before STD was in widespread use.

The street numbering of 221 London Road is a misnomer as today the exchange entrance is via North Road. Access to the original premises was down an alleyway between 219 and 223 London Road. Thus, my earliest memory is of waiting at the end, in the yard, while my father popped in to check his rota duties for the

My GPO Family: Trilogy Edition

week. One of the big green mobile exchange trailers was parked up in a corner. I didn't realise it at the time, for I knew very little about telephones, but this was an expedient as demand for service was exceeding the capacity of the equipment in the main building.

Southend Main was four storeys plus the basement, but another floor was added (possibly in the 1960s) and then a new building, doubling the area, was added in 1974. In the car park a small two-storey pre-fab (used as offices and training) was known as the *Wendy House*! As a youngster, I would ride my *Pavemaster* bicycle to the exchange to meet my father on the Sunday mornings that he'd done a through-night. We didn't own a car, so there was little chance of missing him on his way home, except on the occasions that a colleague gave him a lift home.

Stock Road

On the outskirts of the town the TEC (Telephone Engineering Centre) was the car park for all the local telephone vans. As the road name implies, this was a mini-industrial estate of builder's merchants, timber supplies, light engineering works, printers, etc. The TEC held the telephone stock and supplies for the Area, as well as being home to Routing and Records, and the Motor Transport Workshop. Engineers on duty parked their own car on site and took out a telecom van for the day. Overnight the compound was full of rows and rows of *Golden Yellow* British Telecom vans!

British Telecom Phoneshop

The first new-style British Telecom shop (in the UK) opened in Southend on Sea High Street on 3 January 1985, selling a wide range of telephones, business equipment and telephone accessories.

Southend TAO

The new shop was an extension of the existing chain of 53 phoneshops, most of which had been located in department stores or in local telephone area offices.

BT stalwarts Karen and Nigel were ensconced at *94 High* along with other very personable colleagues, with whom I regularly spoke to on the phone, when I was responsible for a geographical Sales duty. At that time, I rarely encountered customers in person, as I was desk-based, whereas the shop staff literally had the customers constantly 'in their faces'!

Anglian Costal District

In 1984 with the onset of the 'Coming Soon System*' (CSS!), as it was jovially known, the long-established Telephone Area hierarchy was to be superseded by a District structure. * Nickname.

Liverpool and Manchester Districts became operational on 1 October 1984. Outside of London, 24 Districts were to replace the existing 50 Telephone Areas.

Dedicated Computer Centres (for CSS) were to be provided in every District as economies of scale under the new organisation would make them viable. Additionally, with the rollout of System X and Y exchanges gathering pace, the days of comparatively small AMCs (Auto-Manual Centres) handling manually connected calls, on obsolescent technology were numbered!

With larger centres and new technology, the geographical distances between offices handling calls or processing orders was no longer a handicap to efficiency. Anglian Coastal District (ACD) encompassing Southend was formed on 1 April 1985, but by April

My GPO Family: Trilogy Edition

1987 it had merged with Mid-Anglia District (MAD) to form the larger East Anglia District (EAD).

Functional working was displacing the geographical organisation as the concept of serving the customer by locally-based staff was no longer so important. As a place of work, Telephone House, Southend closed during 1999, although area working had disappeared long before.

This was just an outline description of parts of the organisation of the Area. You had to have worked in it to fully appreciate the complexity of the rules, regulations and daily working practices.

Perhaps you did?

Buzby promoting Post Office Telecommunications (c1977)

Outlet 10: Office Machinery

This evolved over the years from being just one or two items in an office full of pens, paper and filing cabinets, right through to screen-based working and even more paper! It gets harder to remember all of the variants of automation across the many jobs which were performed, though some will be described in greater detail. As with all helpers, the machines often conspired to test us to our limits.

Telephone House, Southend

Our typical office of the early 1980s had a Typing Pool of maybe six female typists, plus a shorthand typist, as well as a Telex machine, all overseen by the Superintendent of Typists. Work was usually distributed in large foolscap-sized envelopes, circulated via Registry (internal post). Urgent requests could be placed in person by visiting the Pool, or dictated by telephone to the shorthand typist. There is reference that a *Stenorette* (tape) dictating machine was available, but I don't recall seeing one in my time. Letters were normally produced on headed paper for the top copy, but just a flimsy for the under copy. Spirit duplication was used for running off copies of ANs (Advice Notes) using a carbon master copy. Circulation slips and local forms could be produced by having a stencil cut from a typed draft on the Electronic Stencil Cutter!

Trips to the pool were a lesson in diplomacy, pleading for another 'urgent' memo for my TTS. Occasionally, there was a typo on these rush jobs which meant a second run up the stairs, a check of the typist's initials, and a wait while they finished their current work to do the correction. A root through the *Out* tray ensured that any other completed jobs for my office could be distributed on my return journey.

My GPO Family: Trilogy Edition

Photocopiers weren't commonplace, so a visit to the Print Room was often essential; you handed the operator the original and they ran off the copy for you. Very small, wet-toner machines (*Infotech*) soon began to appear in the corner of several offices. The copies produced were poor quality compared to the much later laser drum machines. The innovation of machines on every floor saved the CAs much running about! At this time, memos were still handwritten on paper and the standard issue (approx. A5-sized) *HMSO Duplicate Book,* with carbon paper, was widely used. Stationery was strictly controlled and filled a whole side room, which was securely locked when the duty officer (CA) wasn't in attendance!

Office Furniture

Traditionally, office furniture was ordered under contract, in bulk, following the age-old manufacturing and supplies procurement of the Government and Post Office. A typical Civil Service office may have used the same suppliers, commonly the Ministry of Works.

My father purchased a surplus wooden desk from the Telephone Exchange in the 1960s and appropriately I'm sitting at it to write this book! The supply code is FTA 22/LOPL. [Table, Committee, 4ft. 0 in. x 2ft. 6in.]

GPO codes were often a puzzle. A *Furniture and Fittings* EI, A3110 implies that FTA was Furniture, TAble. I asked Ernie Coggins (ex of Post Office Factories) who said that these were *Rate Book* codes. One of his colleagues suggested that the LOPL suffix is 'Local Office Portable' because the table has detachable legs, and the 'L' could be Linoleum - referring to the brown inlaid section of the table-top which is more than likely Linoleum cork.

Office Machinery

Wooden desks and lockers in Telephone Exchanges gave way to pressed steel types, although the old switchboards with their wooden panels remained in use as long as the equipment was still functioning. After many years of remaining untouched, Telephone Managers' Offices (TMOs) gradually updated their furniture. As computerisation replaced many paper records, so filing became less important and cable management more so.

The Traffic Office

The term *traffic* referred to the occupancy of telephone lines over a given period. And *Traffic Division* calculated such loadings and the staffing of operators to handle telephone calls. In the early 1980s about 12 people worked in our particular office. This was a typical 'Civil Service/Government' room with lots of metal filing cabinets, roll-front cupboards and tarnished metal-framed coat racks. There was lino or an equivalent covering on the floor. Metal pedestal drawer units had a top board added to form the desks, so changing room layouts was impractical. Telephones were direct line 706 (dial) types or the later 746s terminating on 10-way Key and Lamp Units. Plastic *In, Out,* and *Pending* trays were supported by plastic-covered wire frames, which could be used as a desk division to partially 'hide' from one's neighbour opposite! The larger desks had one complete panel forming the desktop for two people. Venetian blinds covered the windows. The walls were plastered and emulsioned. Fluorescent lights were controlled by a bank of switches just inside the door.

The chairs were a formed tubular frame in a sort of s-shape which gave them a natural springiness. Seat covers and backs were floral patterns of yellow/orange or mauve/blue. It was often joked that the CAs were only allowed chairs without arms, but higher grades had

My GPO Family: Trilogy Edition

chairs with arms! Of course, if you were sitting next to someone to train them, or do filing, the armless chairs made it easier to move freely. Chair covers and tea towels were laundered by 'Accommodation', such was the wide range of services provided by them.

Much excitement followed, circa 1981, with the fitting of carpet in all offices. Previously, carpet was the luxury of the HODs (Heads of Division) on the fifth-floor. Kettles were kept out of the sight of 'Accommodation' (officers) as staff were expected to use the 'trolley service' which did the rounds once in the morning and afternoon. Trolley ladies were generally older females who would politely call out, in a sweetly voice, "Tea Time, trolley's here" as they carefully manoeuvred their trolley with large water urn into position. The best cakes were quickly sold, so it was advisable to get up promptly when you heard the wheels squeaking, or otherwise be friendly with the canteen staff.

The Service Switchboard

In the 1960s, company telephones were usually connected via a Private Branch eXchange (PBX) either manual (PMBX) or automatic (PABX). Typically, the staff would be allocated extension numbers off of the switchboard which would have a limited number of Direct Exchange Lines (DELs). A main telephone number might be published as (0702) 49401 (8 lines), indicating that eight simultaneous calls could be made to the company. The number of associated extension telephones could be just a few or many hundreds depending upon the calling patterns. Additional outgoing lines may have been unlisted, but the total number of lines would have been restricted on a cost basis. Calls from the main number could be transferred to a required extension via the on-site operator, or by dialling a code. Larger companies

Office Machinery

had DDI (Direct Dialling In) lines, so that an external caller could directly reach a given extension user without going via the operator.

Southend TMO was located close to the Main Exchange, so the usual PBX was deemed unnecessary. Post Office Telecommunications didn't (at that time) charge itself for telephone calls, so each officer could be provided with their own DEL! In the Main Exchange a suite of operator positions was dedicated to connecting 'service calls' from the public to the TMO and thus the Service Switchboard dealt with most of the incoming traffic. A few published numbers accepted the bulk of incoming calls, which were transferred to the users, by dialling the individual DELs. Customers could of course dial the user's DEL if the number was known to them. Calls between users and other departments were also made via the PSTN (Public Switched Telephone Network) whereas in other organisations calls were made between extension numbers. The TMO could also be reached by dialling 100 and asking for the Service Switchboard and the operator would then ask which department you wanted.

The list of extension ranges and duties were presented to the operator by a VIF (Visible Index File) which was basically pages of a paper flip file enclosed in plastic which could be quickly thumbed through; this was still some time before computer screens. As a CA in Traffic, I updated the information and had the pages sent to the Typing Pool whenever duty changes occurred.

The Sales Office

The Sales Office was open plan and had at least three teams of eight to ten people. Desks had metal pedestal units. Some desktops had 'card wells' in which the newly introduced CRR (Customer

My GPO Family: Trilogy Edition

Rental Records) cards could be filed, in telephone number order, and thus quickly accessed. The cards were approximately A5 landscape size.

With the advent of MOH (Mechanised Order Handling), circa 1984, new fibreboard desks, with metal legs were introduced. A slot-on top unit provided storage for books or folders, as well as privacy from one's opposite neighbour. Pedestal units were also of composite material and were now fitted with castors so that the units could be easily repositioned. The small VDUs (Visual Display Units) for MOH were initially placed on side desks, but as their functionality and use increased, were later placed at an angle on the main desks. In some circumstances, the top-units of the desk were removed so that the depth of the VDUs could be accommodated. There was one screen printer per team. We now had adjustable chairs with wheels. The seat covers were blue.

Telephones in the Sales Office terminated on 10-way Key and Lamp units for Residential and 20-way units for the larger Business teams. Many phones were 756s (press-button). All phones had direct exchange line numbers, so anyone could ring straight through to your desk, if they knew the number. At this time, Sales was organised into territorial duties, so COs (Clerical Officers) tended to deal mainly with their own patch.

Circa 1982 the Key and Lamp units were replaced by a Merlin switch, and brown MF *Statesman* telephones. These were a pleasure to use and served us well. The direct exchange lines were replaced by a main number 372000 and numerous extensions. Direct Dialling In (DDI) to individual phones was still possible, though not encouraged, as work areas began to be merged.

The Merlin switch had a new operator console, so calls were no

Office Machinery

longer connected on the old Service Switchboard suite. The 'Merlin Room' was supervised by Ellen Ives with operators Carole Young, Sandra Davis, Anne Sturley and a very young, Kerry Wood. All were very well-spoken and polite; it was still a rather strict regime.

Kerry writes, *"I was the youngest operator ever to have been invited to work in there. Ellen ruled that room. She was well respected and I remember being a teeny bit scared of her! She had a right dirty laugh! Anne had a very husky, sexy voice! Good times."*

The 'Merlin Girls' dealt professionally with calls to the Sales Office (and other offices) so that they were connected to the correct person. Anne sounded very earnest, like Fenella Fielding, when she connected a call to my extension, *"Mr Chenery, it's the Service Board, I have a call for you."*

With the introduction of CSS (Customer Service System) in 1988, the green-screen MOH VDUs were replaced with larger, colour VDUs on the existing desks. The Merlin switch remained for a few select phones, but the Sales Office installed an ACD (Automatic Call Distribution) system to handle calls on the new '150' number. COs now had headsets and once you were logged on, calls came straight into your ear with a single 'beep' and you were connected to the customer! Our managers could now see (on their turrets) if calls were waiting, and the pressure was on to finish calls in progress and answer another one! Idle, and 'wrap-up' time was measured, and outgoing calls were discouraged. 'Wrap-up' was a grace period after disconnecting a call, to finish typing the order or write notes, before being 'available' for the next call. The *Answering Suite* as it was now known, dealt with all straightforward orders. An 'off-line' *Case Team* handled correspondence and more convoluted orders. Southend's call centre

My GPO Family: Trilogy Edition

closed in 1991 before the CSS *Front Office* concept really took hold.

The Accounts Office

From about 1992 standalone PCs running *Windows 3.1* software began to be used for letter writing and local instructions. *Statesman* phones on the Merlin switch continued to be used. By 1995 the 'dumb' CSS VDUs were replaced by PCs running *Windows 95* with *Attachmate Extra* to enable links to mainframe systems. *Converse 250s* replaced the *Statesman* phones as they reached the end of their operational life. Meridian Switch phones gradually became the norm in all customer-facing groups.

Photocopier - Printers

During the era of 'Phil's team-member experts', I was assigned to look after the new photocopier. If I remember correctly this also doubled as a printer for the team's screen (VDU) prints. This was a floor-standing machine with multiple paper trays, top and side feeders and a hungry toner cartridge. It was a beast of a machine and I think the first I knew of it was when it arrived with my name on the delivery advice note! Jayne had ordered it for the whole floor, and volunteers to attend to such complex devices weren't often forthcoming! One afternoon I was told to expect the Training Officer from *Canon* who was going to give an overview of its operation. No one else had wanted to learn of this new device, so I stood in the middle of the office, for what seemed like an eternity (possibly an hour) while Rita the rep demo'd all of its functions. Single sided copies, double sided copies, collated and stapled. Doubled sided through the feeder or 'on the glass'; how to load the paper, change trays and read the meter. The rental agreement charged us for the number of copies through the machine. It all

Office Machinery

appeared straightforward and simple.

It didn't take too many weeks before the display demanded 'change toner'. The new toner was in a black plastic container, shaped like a box of washing power, but with a sliding lid to release the contents. To load the toner, the box had to be turned upside down and the lid slid along, like a magic trick. It seemed an accident waiting to happen! The instructions were just a number of arrows pointing in different directions.

I slotted the toner box into the photocopier in what I thought was the correct sequence and released the lid. As I then lifted the now empty box away from the machine, the very black toner powder cascaded out and spread all over the floor!! There was another sliding panel which I should have moved to allow the toner to drop into the copier. And remember, the copier was in the middle of the office for everyone to view. It was rather embarrassing, as I then had to get the hoover and pretend I was just cleaning the carpet. Luckily, the toner was very dry powder and it didn't spread too far! There was of course still the problem of having to get another box of toner and finish the job. I don't recall any repercussions from this incident other than the fact that I retained the task of looking after the beast!

Paper jams were another exciting task to sort out! The later machines actually showed on the display where the jam was located. There were all manner of levers and rollers to pull down, slide along or turn to enable all of the jammed paper to be extricated. The machine wouldn't restart until every lever, flap and door had been correctly repositioned. Worst case was when the paper got compacted in the rollers next to the drum and one time a new part had to be ordered. Another time the developer unit had to be replaced as it was time-expired. These were very clever

My GPO Family: Trilogy Edition

machines, but they took a lot of abuse in the office environment!

The day of the 'paperless office' was still far away, particularly as most accounting transactions needed a paper trail for audit purposes. With new software packages (DUs) coming on-line, it was possible to amend telephone bills and to print them locally on the correct-sized bill stationery. Thus, we soon had two *Newbill* printers in the office. These were as problematic as any other printer. There were two paper trays, one for the bill front and another for the statement pages. Luckily, Andy and Brian usually attended to these when there were serious jams. And I never ever attempted to replace the toner on them.

E-mail and Intranets

BT's internal e-mail and Intranet developed slowly and quietly from late 1994 and it took about four years to roll-out as the infrastructure was built up.

Office Automation (OA) in BT (also known as BOAT), had its roots in the electronic messaging systems of the 1980s with Telecom Gold Mailboxes for HQ staff. CSS had the functionality to send terminal messages to other users, but neither of these systems were designed for the structured mass communication within the company that the forthcoming POP3 (Point Of Presence) nodes were to offer.

A desktop icon (Netscape) allowed us to browse the World Wide Web and gradually BT's Intranet was filled with company-wide information. Wow, the internet was addictive! I looked up an episode guide of one of my favourite 1960s TV programmes and (over several tea breaks) printed off about a hundred pages of synopses. I had to remain disciplined and get on with my work, but

Office Machinery

a computer with internet access for home use was now top of my shopping list!

From late-1997 our team had *Outlook* access to individual e-mail accounts, at first linked to internal IDs, but soon part of the BT dot-com name hierarchy.

The introduction of e-mail brought about the greatest ever change in working practices, and the biggest ever burden of a never-ending stream of messages. Scholarly hobbyist internet pages in the late 1990s gave way to adverts, social media, business presence and widespread commercialism in later years!

As part of my development, I managed to arrange a morning out to Riverside House where Richard was responsible for updating the main Billing pages of BT's Intranet. Whilst this was an interesting visit, it wasn't as awesome as I'd imagined. Pages were uploaded and amended using pre-formed templates. The 'illusion' of a whole intranet of information, coordinated and indexed across hundreds of pages, was difficult to grasp. There was obviously a myriad of design and technical support staff behind the scenes.

The Exchange (1999)

Following our relocation from Telephone House, into Southend Main, our new floors (which were once redundant equipment areas) were fitted out with curved desks and Meridian Norstar phones throughout. The Meridian phones were the best I ever used as one could transfer or shuttle calls to any other destination with the confidence that the call wouldn't drop out.

Less popular were the lights that you could never turn off. Sensors in each unit detected movement in the room and switched the light

My GPO Family: Trilogy Edition

on to a pre-set level, which was often too bright! Just like a TV, there was a single remote control which could be used to permanently turn off a light or adjust the brightness. I think there was only one remote for the whole building, so it was never easy to borrow it for any length of time. On the occasions that I did Saturday overtime, if I was first on the floor, the pitch blackness of the room would slowly disappear as I walked the length of the office and more and more lights magically switched themselves on. Of course, with only part of the room occupied, the lights in the rest of the office would suddenly switch off as they timed themselves out due to no one moving about!

Workstations

Our photocopier contract was now with *Xerox* and that meant another session of learning how the beast worked. These machines were no longer a simple photocopier, but a complete *office workcentre*! Most of the time we only wanted a single screen print or a quick photocopy, but in our much larger office space it was a long trek to the dedicated printing corral. Double sided printing was possible if the correct tray was selected on the pop up screen menu. Toner changing wasn't too difficult; it was a push-in cylinder, but there was often a trail of powder remnants inside the machine. This was a modern laser printer, so messages such as 'change waste toner bottle' came as a surprise. Lo and behold, hidden away behind yet another drop-down flap was a plastic bottle full of liquid!

Office machinery never ceased to surprise us with its hidden features or unexpected operation.

Outlet 11: Billing One

In 1990, Sales and TAG began to merge as the CSS *Front Office* concept envisaged that simple enquiries would be resolved on first contact. Residential customers ringing 150 (one, five, oh) would be answered by a dual-skilled reception CO who would be knowledgeable of all products and processes. In East Anglia District, the optimum size of call centres dictated that Southend work should move to Colchester. This was part of the gradual elimination of Telephone Areas no longer serving their surrounding localities, and the centralisation of work functions to District level.

When a good performing team is disbanded it's like having a rug pulled from under one's feet. Balance is lost and you tend to fall flat on your face. Managers assure you that there will be someone to pick you up off the floor, but you've got to seek them out and present your best face to them!

I held on in Sales and assisted the migration of work and watched as my colleagues had interviews and took on new jobs in whatever divisions were viable for them. We had tours of other teams and I had hoped to join Invoice Production as my keen eye for errors and methodical approach would have been put to good use. A few colleagues opted for PW (Private Wire) Billing and I was to meet up with them again some years later! In the meantime, I was 'head hunted' by Jacq Norris who interviewed me and kindly offered me a job on her Credit Control team. Although this wasn't my ideal choice, I gratefully accepted as I had no desire to move out of Southend, or to leave BT.

Sales had been located 'across the driveway' in Thamesgate House, but now it was time to return to Telephone House and to get back in touch with the organisation and community, such that remained,

My GPO Family: Trilogy Edition

of the original Telephone Area from which I'd been separated since 1983. For all divisions in which I'd worked, they were always somewhat insular from the rest of the company, having their own ways of operating, but usually too busy to fully appreciate how the functions they performed affected other groups, and how any problems were interrelated. On balance, senior managers were aware, but each division had its day to day operating difficulties and there was little time for collaborative improvements with those of another work area.

Credit Control

Business Credit Control wasn't easy and I didn't know many people in Billing to help me. For quite a while I was a bit of an outsider who wasn't familiar with the processes nor the politics of refusing customers extra time to pay. Many of the team had worked TAG duties, so they knew all of the 'tricks' for handling the bill payers and calling their bluffs. We inherited aged debt for customers where the follow-up had been suspended and not resumed after queries had been resolved. Often, we weren't sure if there were still ongoing disputes with an account and a lot of time was spent chasing answers and not making much progress. One time I disconnected a particular line and was told to restore it as it was a high-profile customer. It was very hard distinguishing between those who were 'trying it on' and those who had genuine difficulties paying.

Disconnections were flagged for action once the follow-up of a given bill had reached a certain stage. A transaction on CSS (Customer Service System) sent a message to the engineers to physically carry out the TOS (Temporary Out of Service) in the exchange, though as Strowger equipment was replaced by TXE4, TXE2, System X and Y, the processes became fully automated

Billing One

with no engineer involvement. For a period, we had interim systems which could be accessed by stand-alone computer terminals and our CA, Barbara Carlyon input the requests for us. One terminal interfaced with the System X subsystem as the automated link between that and CSS was to be in a later software release. The TOSCA terminal interfaced with the TXE2 exchanges.

Missing payments, RD'd cheques, phone call action lists, suspended follow-up reports, and customers pleading for more time to pay meant that the time passed very quickly. *Return to Drawer* (RD) cheques were a real nuisance as the customer had to be sent a bill payment counterfoil to be able to pay cash at a Post Office. Invariably it was difficult to track if a payment had actually been made, as the Post Office was no longer part of our organisation. If the line was TOS'd the customer would ring up screaming about loss of business and thus further diminishing the hope of making a payment. The line would have to go back on, but then the payment may have been lost? Missing payments could take weeks to track down. The customers were very good at playing the game!

Our team was quite a mix of young and old and each had their own special personality and had to be approached with forethought. The young tended to be coy and prickly, while the older ladies were more 'clicky' and with their years of billing training didn't always understand why it took me so long to grasp the processes. I got a lot of teasing during those first years in Billing and although my easy-going sense of humour was a way to cope with the situation, this was my most trying and emotional period of work and some days it took all my concentration not to be distracted.

Autodialling and Arthur

We still had 'dumb' terminals giving us access to CSS and there

My GPO Family: Trilogy Edition

was a whole new set of Billing mnemonics for me to learn. Letters still had to be sent to the typing pool, but new technology was creeping in. New stand-alone PCs had the ability to access CSS and to 'power dial' from a list of customers which were downloaded daily. Liz, Jono, and I were among the chosen few to try out what was known as 'Autodialling'. If I remember correctly the screens would toggle between CSS and the debt list. At the press of a key the system dialled the highlighted number to the customer, so we could talk through our headsets, and see the associated record on screen. During the call, notes could be written back to CSS before the machine automatically dialled the next customer. If there was no answer, then the system generated a letter via the *Arthur Letter Printer*!

Arthur was one of our first laser printers which was linked to a package of pre-formatted letters held on CSS. Liz who looked after the printer simply loaded letter-headed paper into the trays and if all was well, it trundled out high quality prints. Occasionally, it didn't! Liz was a good colleague and worked well with Jono and I, though on some days she could be a little stressed. Quite often, *Arthur* took ages to churn out the letters which we had requested during the morning's autodialling session. It was usually a hold-up in the print queue which required 'kicking' from the Computer Centre to resolve.

CERS

As I remember, the Customer Enquiry Referral System (CERS) was an early method of sending queries to other departments by entering CSS *Issues* and terminal messages. This was soon upgraded to the full-blown CCH (Customer Contact Handling) package.

Billing One

Bill Handling

Being a Credit Controller meant requesting lots of copy bills, usually because the customer had misplaced the original. If you wanted to include a letter with the copy bill, the copy had to be printed in the normal batch runs at the Computer Print Centre and then diverted to the GMO (General Manager's Office) to be matched up. The arrival of two more specialist laser printers allowed us to RIP (Request Invoice Print) a copy bill and print it locally on the correct stationery. This was a marvellous innovation except when the paper jammed, the toner ran out, or the comm-link broke! Printers, in all their guises were the bane of my time in BT.

Software for producing amended bills was slow to be developed, but a rather earnest, young, freckle-faced Angela Goodrich introduced me to the MAGENTA bill utility programme.

"MAGENTA is a menu-driven system accessed via TSO (Time Share Option) upon which bill details can be typed to produce information in a Newbill format which can be printed locally and sent to the customer."

Enquiry and Support (1994-98)

By 1994 the Credit Control function had moved to another site and our team was disbanded. Some of us joined Invoice Control, though many of us remained at our desks and formed a new group for Telephony E & S (Enquiry and Support) Business Customers. The job of E & S was to explain complex bills to the customer and encourage them to pay, or if the bills were wrong to take the necessary actions to correct them. This was rarely a simple process and often involved Sales issuing additional orders, followed by manual credits on the account, and occasionally amended and

My GPO Family: Trilogy Edition

reprinted bills. Also, quite a bit of detective work to find out what had gone wrong and the best method to put it right. Again, there were new CSS transactions to memorise and quite a steep learning curve to become proficient!

Phil Dorman was now our manager. Phil's wife was Jane Gartell whose father Tom had been my boss when I first started with BT! Phil was a stickler for detail, some might say infuriatingly picky, and he gave few concessions. If you asked him to sign-off a letter he would make sure you'd thoroughly investigated the case before he acquiesced. He did get you thinking through all angles, though it drove everyone to annoyance at the additional time it took up! The majority of the time he was correct to do this, and he knew it. If you needed a sympathetic ear and had good reason to be asking, he was fair in his judgement, although perhaps he enjoyed being in a position of power, just a little too much! As with some of the older managers, you had to choose your moment to approach him carefully as his own activities usually took priority.

Rental and Call Charges

You'd think that quarterly rental for a telephone line would be simple to calculate and easy to explain. It rarely was, and it got progressively harder as privatisation approached and thereafter. In Sales Division (using the AFS codes) a line with a dial telephone had been an EL24; a single rental for both the service connection and the phone. As the regulations changed to allow customers to have 'lines only', the codes became an EL03 for the line and a UB01 for the dial telephone. Incidentally, an EL03 was a hardwired connection (before sockets), so in practice the UB01 could not be separated, but the rental still became two items on the bill.

Billing One

Customers converting to the PST (Plug Socket Telephone) system had to be discon'd and recon'd on the billing computer, so the resulting changes produced extra entries on the bill.

This was fine as far as Sales Division was concerned, but for Billing it refunded the quarterly rental for the EL03 from the date of the work, up to the end of the quarter period, and then re-charged rental for the EL08 for the same period. The charges effectively cancelled each other out, so the total bill for the line rental remained unchanged, but it still showed as 'broken period rental' on the statement. With VAT rounding, the old and new rentals may have differed by a penny, causing some customers to query their bill! For business customers with multiple lines and products a straightforward rearrangement to their telephone installation produced pages and pages of rental calculations.

Call charges were another matter. A product known as *Business Choices* gave discounted calls to telephone numbers which the customers opted into in advance. There were delays in processing the applications and problems with the discounts being automatically applied to the bills. It was a classic case of BT promoting a scheme for which the necessary processes were sadly not yet in place. From a Billing Officers' point of view, it was difficult to correct, as the customers had to prove that they had requested the discount scheme and that their application had been accepted. Billing was never well-placed to seek answers from either the Account Managers who had submitted the contracts, or Sales who processed the orders.

Winning Deal

BT regularly operated staff incentive schemes to improve sales and revenue streams. *Winning Deal* was Sales orientated, and as I now

My GPO Family: Trilogy Edition

worked in Billing, I was most surprised to be told that I had won £80 of vouchers as a result of a sales lead! My manager checked it several times and it was correct! In hindsight, I was often chatting to customers and referring them to their Account Managers if there was a query which wasn't proper to Billing. I think one customer had changed his Switch (Call Connect System) as a result of my referral. Wow, how good was that?!

As I continued to get to grips with how items were charged and billed, products and services were continuously changing.

Phonecards

There was an evolution of cashless payment ways to make a telephone call via the PSTN as the technologies and billing platforms improved.

The progression was roughly...

1. Credit Card Calls - Plastic card with an account number to charge calls originated anywhere to your own line – Had to be made via the operator.
2. Chargecard – the updated name, which included a pin number, so calls could be directly dialled.
3. CARDPHONE – A new public payphone which used pre-paid plastic cards inserted into the mechanism.
4. PHONECARD – the updated name for both the card and the mechanism.

   During this period, the use of store cards, credit cards and debit cards was also changing to allow more widespread use.

Billing One

Chargecard calls were processed via the CSDB (Cashless Services Data Base) with some help from the TIBS (Telecom Input Billing System) and CCI (Central Charge Inputs) to be included on a bill via CSS.

Service Calls

In those sober days of Post Office Telephones, there was a facility for 'Officers of the Post Office', who were perhaps working in a customer's premises, or away from their normal office, to dial 100 and ask for a Service Call to a local or trunk destination, to be connected without charge. [Engineers on duty would have dialled 151 to be connected to the test desk.] The only proviso for a trunk call was that the operator would ask, "May I have your name, rank and department please?" This was a perk of working for the Company, though any abuse of the privilege may have met with disciplinary action.

As British Telecom became more commercially aware, it encouraged each department to issue either *Chargecards* or *Phonecards* to staff who had a genuine requirement to make calls from external phones on official business; an operator's time was now more valuable to serving customers than maintaining the internal running of the organisation!

Invoicing

Bills produced on CSS initially couldn't easily be amended, although debit or credit transactions could be added to an account to make it balance, and a supplementary bill could be run to inform the customer of the adjustments. A billing utility, MAGENTA (an acronym without meaning) was used when the customer wanted to see an amended bill, correctly presented. The biggest bugbear of using amended bills was that the customer was supposed to return the original so that VAT could not be claimed twice. A standoff was often reached as the customer wouldn't pay the bill without receiving an amendment and they wouldn't return the original either. Credit Notes could be sent to effectively cancel an original bill, but then there was the age-old problem of customers claiming the credit against a different bill and underpaying their total remittance! A later DU (Development Unit) to CSS gave access to SuperMIX which was an integrated billing manipulation tool, but it wasn't very WYSIWYG and had a tendency to fail when the invoice was loaded back onto the system. Those staff who became expert users were very skilful. Complex MIXes could be passed to Invoice Control/Production.

The IC team members were rather good at helping us out with complex bill amendments and they'd offer to fix an invoice if we really couldn't get it to load back onto the system. Otherwise, they may have had the error reports landing on their desk to sort out a suppressed or rejected bill! But, generally they did know their stuff and a few of them worked long hours to provide work-arounds for us. Adjustments to bills were strictly audited, thus an A3060 form had to be completed for every monetary value that was amended. These were placed in our work folders for checking by the team Commo.

The Commercial Officer (Commo) grade had been introduced towards the end of my time in Sales. Business Sales groups were exclusively Commo grade officers led by a team manager. In Residential Sales, teams of Clerical Officers once led by a manager had a Commo leader added as a first line of command. For COs this meant that complex problems had first to be run past the Commo who might then have to seek authority from the manager to implement a process. It seemed a retrograde step to me as it

Billing One

distanced managers from the coal face and meant that I had to schmooze two people instead of just one!

Commos within E & S allowed quicker sign-off of work and stalwart personalities were, Angela Goodrich, Deb Webster, Mandie Longbottom and Lynne Fewtrell. Mandie wrote process documents for E & S and coached me in letter writing. Initially our word processor ran *Wordstar*, but later we had the luxury of *Word* on *Windows 3.1*.

Another of our younger team members, Jayne Tremlett trained us whenever major CSS DUs (Development Units) were released. Notable packages were SuperMix and Per Second Pricing. Jayne had trained us when we first joined Credit Control. She had an easy-going nature, was very enthusiastic and an excellent presenter. The majority of long-term Credit Controllers had opted to join Invoice Control so that they wouldn't have to be 'customer facing' again. The remainder of the team for E & S were a mix of ex-Sales and ex-TAG. Those who'd run TAG territorial duties were Jean Church, Sylvia Bearcroft and Shirley Knight. These were proud ladies who were billing experts, but were somewhat zealous of explaining their methods to less experienced colleagues. I think they'd been doing the work so long that it had become second nature to them. One had to persuade them that you'd really value their opinion on how to tackle a billing query.

CCH

CSS had introduced the Customer Contact Handling (CCH) sub-system and I was familiar with it from my work in Sales. In its simplest form, any contact with a customer generated an 'issue' which could either be closed immediately (as a record of the interaction) or left open for further action(s) to be taken. As we inherited a backlog of work on E & S, which was far greater than the clearing ability of the team, the number of 'open' issues got totally out of hand. Issues which were over a certain age progressed automatically to escalation, for a manager to review. It was a very complex system as the issues had varying target dates to be completed, dependent upon the initial categories, which were struck at the time the query was entered onto CSS. Queries awaiting replies from other departments aged in the same manner although the timescales were often beyond our control. It became embarrassing to own 'aged queries' even if the delays were in the hands of senior managers, or were caused due to backlogs of work in other groups. Issues had to be regularly urged and interim replies made to the customer, which in turn delayed the time available to actually solve the queries. We had been placed in an almost impossible position.

One Five Six (156)

Although we were inundated with CCH issues, our team members were well-versed in dealing with customer contacts. 156 had been set up to handle straightforward Business Billing enquiries, such as payments, postponed payments and explanations of bills. For more complex queries a CCH issue was generated and sent to another part of BT. Typically, E & S would have received a complex rental case, while poor payers were referred to the Collections Team, both functions on which I had worked. Currently 156 was also struggling to cope with the influx of calls. A new (156) team was shortly to be established in Southend, but temporary relief with the overflow calls at peak times was needed immediately. As most of our own work came by letter or CCH referral, our phones seldom rang; we were ideally placed to answer the 156 calls and were 'volunteered' to help!

Billing One

All the 'lucky' staff had a second telephone placed on their desks. This was a Meridian Norstar, which had a whole row of extra buttons, so you could 'log-on' to the call queue, take calls, transfer calls, hold calls, and make a second call, while holding the first. The phone also had an LCD screen, so you could view call progress and numbers entered. It was an 'all-singing and dancing' phone!! We had a half hour training on how to operate these phones and they were great, as you could transfer a held caller, with confidence, knowing that the call wasn't going to 'drop out'. Fantastic, but you had to remember the correct sequence of buttons to press!

We also had an additional 'profile' added to our computer log-ons, so we could access all the customer information. As we had to read the PC screen, type AND operate the phone too, we were issued with headsets that could be plugged into the side of our new phones.

Well, you can imagine the scene... Our manager tells us we HAVE to log-on NOW, and take the overflow calls, as the PCA is going down the toilet, and our senior managers are having a fit! We try to log-on, to the phone, but the ID codes are wrong. We can't find the right sockets to plug in our headsets. We take a call, but can't hear the caller. The database on our screens won't switch us to write the notes or an explanation of what the customer needs, and it's all taking far too long to get up to speed.
Forget it, we just might not have bothered!!

We did get to grips with the Meridian phones and they were actually the best ACD system that I'd ever used. By now the new 156 team had been formed from members of Southend's Directory Group and Exchange operators who had come into the CO grade. Our E & S Team was asked to floor walk for a week or two and

My GPO Family: Trilogy Edition

help the group gain confidence in their new customer facing roles. This was going to be the blind leading the blind, but I agreed to join the floor walkers and see what I could do. I knew my way around both CCH and CSS orders, so I was confident that I wouldn't be out of my depth.

I can't recall if I'd known any of the team previously, other than the manager whom I'd met during my MOH Site Officer role. I think there were two of us on the floor for the first day and we just hovered and waited for someone to put their hand up and call us over for help. If I was slightly nervous, well the newbies were too, so they readily took any help which was offered. A lot of the time they weren't sure how to create issues or check orders or what action to take next. For the most part we just had to talk it through with them and they were OK.

Some of the 156 team were a little shy, so they acted a bit silly, and we simply reassured them. Typically, Gisela Schwedt would pull a funny face or say, "Please Miss" to get our attention, but it didn't take too long before everyone was more at their ease. It was rather a fun experience helping and I also got to learn how billing queries were referred to E & S, so it was a useful exercise all round. A week or two later, our manager received a letter from Mo Woodey:

"...my main thanks and appreciation must go, however, to Rob, Debbie, John, Kath and Jonathan for helping us as floor walkers. Please thank them for me and tell them how much we have appreciated their help and patience. I don't think we could have succeeded without them."

[Myself, Rob Hickey, Debbie Webster, Kath Matthews, Jonathan Allen.]

That was a great achievement and we also got to know the team

Billing One

very well, which was good, as ultimately some of us would be working together in the future. For the meantime, we still had our own backlog of CCH issues to clear.

Phil wanted his team to develop and have individual roles, so at one point I became the ISDN (Integrated Services Digital Network) expert and had a folder full of literature and explanations of how the product worked and was billed. Documentation on new products were vital to us as we needed to understand them in order to resolve any billing problems. Phil enjoyed, with much glee, our monthly Team Talks and he took great pleasure in making sure every agenda point was discussed fully before he finally closed each session. The one time we finished early was when poor Jono was taken ill. Phil was a bit of a taskmaster, but with a soft heart if you caught him in the right mood! The Commos pretty much ran the team for him while he was out doing project work; it was always satisfying if we could get a letter pp'd by them without so much interrogation!

By 1998 we still had a backlog of CCH issues and it was decided to concentrate Business E & S at other sites. I think one-day Tom Boyle (senior manager) came and stood on his soapbox (almost literally as he wasn't very tall) and proclaimed he was bringing in some exciting and challenging work for us! As usual it meant learning a completely different system, but this was to stand us in good stead for many years.

My GPO Family: Trilogy Edition

British Telecom INPHONE tag (circa 1983)

"It doesn't cost much to keep in touch."
Call stimulation slogan (1981)

Outlet 12: Billing Two

My GPO Family included not only the people, but also the systems which I used daily. These too had their quirks to the point that some simple customer requests were almost impossible to fulfil. There was often a work-around to fix the problem, but the resulting, incomprehensible bills took much explaining. Technology often conspired to make the correction of a straightforward bill, quite complex. As the billed products continued to evolve the supporting platforms and processes became ever more complicated! Sometimes we were fighting a losing battle.

PCB

PWs or Private Wires were dedicated 'leased lines' which carried voice or data signals between two fixed sites. Low speed analogue circuits gave way to high speed digital ones as the technology and demand for the services developed.

Private Circuit Billing (PCB) was an existing Telephone Area function for the closing of datacomms orders and their subsequent billing. My colleagues Trisha Lester and Barbara Reeman had transferred to the group, from Sales, as early as 1992. In 1998, as we lost our Telephony E & S function, Southend took on PCB work for the whole of the South, which once again overloaded us with both debt and queries! I think initially we took on whole databases and I remember doing both the credit control and query work for the 8332 Area. The query work tended to take priority as customers wouldn't settle a bill which was in dispute! As we took on more databases the work was split so that dedicated credit controllers chased the debt, while the more patient members took on the query resolutions.

My GPO Family: Trilogy Edition

[In 1982 a trial of 'WIREBILL' used a small business computer to produce Private Service bills (Source: CPSA Annual Report). The datacomm's market was growing rapidly and a national computer system was going to be needed.]

Comparatively, PCB gave the appearance of being an ancient system, which was accessed via CICS (Customer Information Control System), although through the same computer terminals that we'd used for CSS. Just like CSS, you had to choose which database to log-on for the geographical area you required. PCB databases broadly took their numbering from the old Regions and Areas hierarchy of which Home Counties, Eastern Region had been formed way back in 1966. The Eastern Region databases were 6370 Oxford, 6371 Bedford, 6372 Cambridge, 6373 Colchester, 6374 Norwich and 6375 Southend. This numbering appeared to be similar to the earlier telephony CARD databases.

In October 1989 the District-wide CAPSS (Computer Automated Private Service System) had been introduced as the newest system linking sales orders with the circuit design engineers. It ran on 27 regional databases. In summary, PCB must have been a relatively new system, though it can't have been very long ago that hand-written ANs would have circulated and, upon completion, circuit details would have been manually typed into the PCB.

By the time we joined Private Circuit Billing, a new Sales system COSMOSS (Customer Orientated System for the Management Of Special Services) was already in use. COSMOSS orders automatically downloaded the circuit details into PCB.

[*COSMOSS-An Innovative Approach to System Development* Henri

Billing Two

Van der Stighelen. *British Telecommunications Engineering* April 1994.]

All customer interaction was centred on COSMOSS as being the up to date system holding both the circuit details and billing accounts. PCB was the back-end system which produced the bills. Historically, if a customer needed a particular circuit billed on a separate account this was created manually on PCB, but little thought was given to correct COSMOSS. I recall that each system ran independently for a while, but then the account number links between the two systems was fully activated. COSMOSS downloaded into the account number it held and produced a bill. If the circuit had been manually built on a different account number within PCB that also produced a bill.

Uniquely for Billing, our group had the ability to issue CA (Change Account) orders in COSMOSS to effectively move individual circuits between accounts. This also impacted the billing so that the rental was credited and debited accordingly depending upon the effective date used. This process couldn't move single payment (connection) charges; these had to be manually adjusted, suffice to say that the resulting interim bills became very messy!

Gradually, our dumb terminals were replaced by PCs running *Windows NT* (or equivalent), so we had the facilities to use *Word* or *Excel* in our daily work. All-hail the 'CBA Macro' which was developed by the COSMOSS support team, allowing us to generate 'Change Billing Account' orders automatically from an *Excel* list of circuit numbers. The macro file had to be pre-set with the parameters of the *Attachmate* COSMOSS session and it took much 'fiddling about' to finally get it to run on a new PC. It was well worth it because the effort involved in manually transferring (sometimes) hundreds of circuits would normally take days to issue, whereas the macro could complete the task in just several

My GPO Family: Trilogy Edition

hours. Needless to say, some circuits which were in a status of *Retro* on COSMOSS couldn't be automatically transferred as the full circuit details had not been available at the time of the conversion from the legacy CAPSS system. CAMSS (Computer Aided Maintenance of Special Services) sometimes held details of older circuits, so team members who had this profile were handy to know. Teamwork often paid off.

Some customers with many circuits preferred to have one bill per circuit, but they did not make this clear at the point of ordering. We had instances of Sales teams putting all new circuits on a single account number (which was the logical thing to do) and then the customer refused to pay until the circuits were split off into individual bills! Other customers required connection charges billed separately to rentals. We really did pander to our customers' demands and spent many long hours reformatting and rebilling charges. Private Circuits were high revenue products so it was usually a reasonable request to bill them as the customer dictated.

Working in BT (A 1990s Muse)

What is BT?
BT is me!
BT is you and what you do.
BT is us, don't make a fuss.
BT is alive, we're making it thrive!

Plug into a turret and the network that's BT is there for you to 'see' And hear, not to fear; log on and you become an integral component of the expert BT machine.

Instantly you can access the whole of the UK; and sense exactly what's happening today.

Billing Two

The information flowing, the constant knowing...
The Power behind the button!

You *ARE* BT, as perceived by the customer.
No one else, simply *YOU*, an individual representing the whole,
To produce a united goal.

You alone are the single most important resource in the company, an interactive, information-gathering, storage, retrieval, output unit with infinite processing capability, who is sometimes handicapped by being human!

BT was still changing and moving away from dedicated staff who knew their customers well, into a 'anyone can deal' and 'next in the queue' production line, as it continued to streamline its processes and staffing levels. This was fine in theory, but a simple omission of a discount flag by a Sales Issuing Commo would lead to an incorrectly billed product and ultimately an unpaid bill. Discount schemes were becoming ever more complex as BT strove to retain its competitive edge in an unforgiving marketplace. With the rate of change in the company it was difficult to track discount contracts. Often these were signed by Account Managers, issued by Sales Teams and the papers mislaid during one of many office moves. We wanted stability but too many forces were conspiring to hasten the rate of change and enforce a modern world upon an organisation steeped in the past. Larger customers used this as leverage not to pay their bills and in hindsight BT looked silly for not having robust processes in place.

The People

Sarina was quite a looker and she loved to joke around all day as

My GPO Family: Trilogy Edition

she mostly got on with her work. She was always pushing the boundaries of being naughty and trying to shock colleagues with her smart talk or her 'come hither' expressions! I usually tried my best not to be distracted by her, but sometimes it just wasn't possible…

A Profile of Pearl

Sar-ee-nah is really rather sweet,
She's one you'd like to meet, she dresses very neat.

Her make-up's quite discreet, with matching lips and nails,
And curly hair that flails.

Sometimes she speaks like a little girl.
'I want a *Twirl*! Where's Dolly? Do-ll-ieee.

Other times she's more refined,
With a calculating mind...

'If I pay my Council Tax in arrears, then here's to far more cheers.'
Rolls her eyes and speaks like Julie Andrews, 'At the Pub!'

She thinks she's rather tough…
'This case really p****s me off! I've f*****g had enough!'
'Don't speak to me like that, dar-lin'!'

She loves her dog to bits, but its bark gets on her…nerves.
It's not what she deserves.
She quite likes Paul (her hubby) too!

Her daddy's in the business, so she's got a head for figures
And can always spot a bargain, but she needs to know the facts

Billing Two

So to keep up with the gossip she is often asking questions
And she loves to have a bitch!
She's really into hygiene and she likes to keep things clean, but
She can be pretty mean...
When the car's wipers just won't go
And it's coming down with snow!

She has given up the smoking and you may think I am joking
When I say she's often choking from the clean air in her lungs.

She can be so polite...
It may give you such a fright.
'Well bugger me, with a pitchfork!'
'Cold potatoes, Harry Haddock, peas, brown sauce and mustard'

'L o v e l i e e e e e!'

Another lovely young lady was Leanne Wood who used to keep her Credit Control folder close to her chest. One day there was a 'snap' as the ring binder closed, and then tears as she almost gained an unwanted piercing! Ouch! Terry Browder had his own 'take' on office rules and liked to discard banana skins into the big blue paper recycling boxes.

There was always some gentle humour taking place during the office day. Paul, our CA, was well known for his silliness, for which he sometimes played to good advantage, in an otherwise busy and tense office. At one time when I sat at the desk opposite him, I used to throw a plastic dust cover over my PC screen before going home. As I raised the cover in the air, he always used to duck down and laugh, as he was expecting me to misjudge the distance and to land it on his head.

My GPO Family: Trilogy Edition

Debbie Chapman was a new manager who ran our team during this period. She had been with the company for a while, as she spoke of being a mini-skirted telephonist in her early career! Debbie was quite progressive and supported her people to do well by encouraging them to attend training courses (in Milton Keynes) and to take part in team-building events. Did we have fun? Oh yeah, yeah! On one occasion, we went to Priory Park for a sort of team picnic, to play softball. I recall we were using standard bats, but a tennis ball, in lieu of the usual hardball. In no way was I a sporting type, and on the second strike the team was worried that they were going to lose a player. At the third attempt, I positioned my arm back, lined up the ball and wacked it! Of course, the very soft ball simply flew right across to the other side of the park, and I easily got a home run!

PCBIS

As mentioned, the PCB computer system looked like an inferior version of CSS with its multiple databases. Every month we had to set the bill production runs ourselves and then manually envelope each bill by hand! Stats from the system were gained by counting the number of bills and adding up lists of revenue with a paper-roll type calculator. There was no way it was going to cope with the explosion of new services and the data-comms revolution!

The Private Circuit Billing Information System (PCBIS) was purchased off-the-shelf, but with a number of tailored features to make it fit for BT's purposes. PCBIS had a GUI (Graphical User Interface) based screen that (we were told) consisted of five separate sources which were displayed together to form a screen full of information. During our training course, Terry Tobin used to tell us not to 'wiggle the mouse' as this would cause the formatting to refresh, and it might slow the response time if everyone was

Billing Two

doing it! GUI systems seemed to take more learning as you had to remember under which menu the function you required was located. Another (serious) quip was that the new format bills for PCBIS now featured a SOFA (Statement of Account). One other feature was the ability to input ALAs, which were Account Level Adjustments, as opposed to the more usual circuit level charges. User input (financial) adjustments on the system went into a queue for a team leader/manager to authorise. PCBIS caused us many headaches, not least of which was the small sized font, though we finally got 19-inch VDUs as a consequence of this! [Thank you, Dave Bartle.]

Move to Exchange

By 1999 Telephone House was almost 40 years old and in need of major refurbishment. Southend Main was no longer full of switching equipment as the digital age had drastically reduced the need for large exchange buildings. A clearance programme to remove time expired equipment was ongoing across BT and thus a couple of floors of our local exchange were made available for office accommodation. The opportunity was taken to install new windows, lighting and air-con, as well as a new reception and staff restaurant. When we moved in, the new wavy profile, wire-managed desks with eye-level privacy boards were awaiting our occupation. On a personal note, I was now working in the exchange from which my father had retired in the 1980s.

Collaboration

Over the years, I'd built up contacts in other divisions whom I knew well, but had never met. Opportunities to take part in 'continuous improvement' projects had a habit of changing this premise, especially when I was 'volunteered' by my manager to take part! The well-established MCAT teams, now named CoGAT

My GPO Family: Trilogy Edition

(Corporate and Government Accounts Team) had a requirement to learn the new PCBIS billing system as it would impact on their Onebill work. Conversely, presentation and payment of Onebills often affected our PCB work. Claire Bullock (from Wolves) headed up the *Working Together* project and the scene was set for some long overdue collaborative work.

A meeting was scheduled at Midland ATE in Birmingham which meant a three-hour train journey each way. I can't recall who was there on the day, but, Nicola Ashley (from Wolves) had previously floor-walked for us when PCBIS was first introduced in Southend. And I'd spoken to Jackie Berry (from Croydon MCAT) many times. Both Jackie and Nicola were strong-minded individuals, but very personable. There was a short break in the afternoon before we were scheduled to catch our train home, so I had a wander outside and strolled around the building. I was pleasantly surprised to get sight of the Birmingham BT Tower, and I regretted not having my camera with me! Just a year or so later the tower was repainted and I wish I'd captured a photo of it as it was on that day at Midland ATE.

It was agreed that Southend PCBIS prepare a presentation to Croydon CoGAT. Croydon dealt with billing for larger and important customers, including those on Onebill. They had 'view only' or restricted access to PCBIS, so an overview of the new system was a worthy project in which to participate. I volunteered to compile some material which could be printed as slides and Cass Dolton agreed to present them. Cass wanted a partner to turn the slides over and support her, so as I had written the material it was decided that I attend too. I set off on the day, with the slides in my bag, but at the station Cass was nowhere to be seen! I boarded the train and began to wonder if I might have to do the whole presentation myself. At Blackfriars Tube, I turned around and Cass

Billing Two

was just behind me! Phew, it was going to be a good day after all. We completed the journey to Delta Point in Croydon and crossed the main road being very careful to 'beware the trams'! We knew a couple of people on the CoGAT team and chatted informally before lunch. We then set up the overhead projector and left them to begin their Team Talk. It was quite nerve racking waiting to be called into the meeting at the appointed slot, but we both knew the material and were prepared to answer questions as necessary. PCBIS was still quite new to us, but we made a good job of explaining some of its intricacies and enhancing our profiles. We were shortly on the train back to Southend, satisfied that our hard work was not in vain, though somewhat unaware that CoGAT's days were numbered.

Volume E & S 1999

Towards the end of the century I was dealing with Enquiry and Support work for PCB 'Volume' customers. These were SMEs (Small to Medium Enterprises) and sometimes larger companies who didn't have a dedicated SPOC (Single Point of Contact). They often made as much fuss as bigger organisations and took more convincing for a solution. I saw my colleague Jo Streetly working on the more complex SPOC cases and wanted to be involved. Angela was always good at listening to her team and helping them maximise their talents when the opportunity arose. Subsequently, when Nic went off on maternity leave it was arranged that I covered her SPOC role.

SPOC

At the time I took over Nic's SPOC role it was still a B2 grade, and the job entailed dealing personally with the PCB debt and queries for a small number of high-spend customers. The number of rented circuits ran into hundreds. I was supported by a team of Account

My GPO Family: Trilogy Edition

Managers who were BT's main advocate for the customer. There was a PRIME discount scheme for reduced connection charges for London-ended circuits. One day it was flagged from the Account Team that a Sales issuing error, over a long period of time, had failed to abate the connection charges and that the probable rebate due was in excess of one million pounds! The standard charge for one end of a circuit was about £4,500 and the reduced charge, (I recall) was £1,500, so the difference, multiplied by several hundred circuits soon added up. This was a sensitive issue as the customer was entitled to a refund, but our finance top-team weren't going to be happy at the loss of revenue! Adjustments to bills were strictly controlled and I had to seek sign-off concurrence at a very senior manager level. The majority of credits, I input at circuit level so that a full audit trail was visible. However, the older bills for certain circuits were no longer held on the system and I had to complete some 'account level adjustments' which weren't popular with finance or the system admin guys. Being a SPOC wasn't an easy job as potentially you had to upset people across many specialisms to get other people's errors corrected!

PCNBS (2002)

PCBIS evolved and was upgraded into what was named PCNBS (Private Circuit New Billing System). I attended one of the User meetings which was held in the developer's premises in London. It was a bit like going to a surprise party as we weren't entirely sure who had been invited. Steve Trennery and I travelled to the site independently and upon arrival we were greeted by Deb Webster who also worked in our office! System supremoes, Rockie Lee and Terry Tobin were part of the forum and I recall giving them a hard time by asking lots of questions, from a user's viewpoint. Rockie always gave a logical answer from a system perspective; it was a rare occurrence if you could ever catch him out. It was great

Billing Two

sparring with him, but it soon became apparent that if I didn't shut up, we wouldn't get home that day. It was certainly an eye-opener to learn how BT had asked for particular system changes for the developer to deliver within given timescales, and the compromises which had to be made to get as friendly a user interface as possible.

PCB Characters

The latter days of PCB saw the coming together of folks whose groups had closed down, so the teams were eventually of mix of either, very experienced, or mostly quirky people!! Regardless of this, everyone did their best to help one another, time permitting, and we had some real laughs along the way in our daily work. Linda and Giesla, *The Hub*: Sam and Marie, and too many others to mention. Lorraine Wood (aka Lol) was outspoken and rarely took any lip from customers. We used to cringe at her language, and fashion sense, but she was adorable!

SPOC Part 2

Over time, the SPOC roles became C2 grades, so I handed the duty to Rob Hickey and together we dealt with a select group of high-revenue customers, which tested our patience and resourcefulness! Karen, (another B2 SPOC) I had known from when she worked in the *Phoneshop* (a *94 High* girl), and the hand-over of her work to Rob and I was exemplary, as she had put a lot of effort into preparing her customers for the changeover. Patsy Shaxted, one of the Account Managers came down to Southend and we had a mini team lunch.

Of all the circuit variants, PPCs (Partial Private Circuits) were especially troublesome to administer. PPCs had been specifically devised to extend the reach of OLOs (Other Licensed Operators)

My GPO Family: Trilogy Edition

own networks. An agreed POH (Point of Handover) linked the OLO site to BT's SDH (Synchronous Digital Hierarchy) and thence on to remote (B end) sites. Charges varied depending upon copper or fibre nodes, the main link distances, and complex pricing rules as frequently amended and determined by the Regulator.

It was a battlefield as we tried to educate Sales to issue accurate orders, the customer to pay on time, and the Account Managers to update us on new contract deals which had been signed. In between this, we had to write robust Business Cases to justify huge credits to bills due to order deficiencies. Sales always promised to do better, but they had severe time pressures and glitches in the systems didn't help! The large customers were very astute; they had dedicated accountants to scrutinise our bills with a fine toothcomb! They often had the upper hand as they knew what they signed up for, as we sometimes struggled to obtain a copy of their original contracts. Threats of disconnections for delayed payments were meaningless as some companies operated essential public services. The 'GPO game' had many unwritten rules and it was always a challenge (and fun) to play.

BAS (Support) 2006 to 2008

In 2006 our PCB SPOCs took on the complete range of Billing for each of their assigned customers. This included Telephony, Onebill and other quite obscure data services. The SPOCs were now Billing Account Specialists (BAS) and I was a BAS Support. I'm pleased to say that Rob and I continued our 'partnership' and we were joined by Jess Nutting who took on the Credit Control role, while I concentrated on correcting bills which were clearly in error. Telephony was mostly billed on CSS in which I was well-versed, but Onebill was another complex GUI-based system, which took some mastering.

Billing Two

The *Onebill* concept had originated in Southend Telephone Area back in 1982 when it was simply a collection of bills loaded onto an early Personal Computer and processed for a few major customers. It had finally evolved into Onebill Plus or more correctly, CFB (Customer Focussed Billing) as it amalgamated bills from many different billing platforms, to produce a single invoice for the customer to pay. CFB fed receipts back to the source systems so that the debt was held solely on the Onebill. Certain amendments to the Onebill sent a debit back to the source account(s), so much care had to be taken when dealing with queries. New Onebill entities were created in COSMOSS and, with the right flags, downloaded to CFB as VP accounts ending in AC01. New PCB accounts also ended in AC01 so occasionally this caused some confusion in identifying which system to interrogate when a query was raised.

CSS accounts automatically downloaded into Onebill, but only when Sales had correctly populated the order field. Educating people in Sales was an ongoing task as perhaps they didn't fully appreciate the implications to Billing of getting these orders wrong. Of course, when I'd previously worked in Sales, we rarely had any feedback of orders which had caused problems? Did we?! Best not to mention those! I'd had some split bill problems where the dates of the incoming and outgoing tenants had changed. Luckily the DPCO had sorted them out. The overlap between Sales and Billing was always a dilemma, as Billing couldn't issue ANs, and Sales couldn't adjust bills. Teamwork was crucial, thus knowing friendly contacts in other divisions was most useful. The Organisation used to work together and the principle of ringing round other departments to get a solution or a progress update still held sound. There was certainly satisfaction in owning the billing of large firms. We knew the customers (almost personally), we knew the

My GPO Family: Trilogy Edition

Sales team issuing the orders, and we knew the Account teams running the show. We all talked to each other amicably (most of the time) and difficulties were usually overcome. Elsewhere in the BT, the *Front Office* concept was continuing to fragment meaningful contact between teams and creating automaton call centre staff!

Learning the tricks of Onebill could only be gained by experience, the hard way! Our overview training had only skimmed the surface and we had to pick the brains of ex-Onebill team members who were now dispersed over other groups. Automated tools, with fancy names, such as *Alchemist* were only as efficient as the software and support teams behind them. I had instances of accounts, which were correctly flagged, failing to load into the Onebill. It transpired that Noah had been offline for a while. Who on earth was Noah, and why wasn't he doing his job?! NOA (the correct name) was yet another robot which had to be run for the process to work. It was somewhat infuriating, to say the least, of having to dig around to discover the full extent of the processes involved. Once NOA was running again, the accounts were still failing, and a casual enquiry met with a response that my particular Onebill was on an exclusion list for NOA to ignore. Well, how was I supposed to know that! Instant erudition was never easy, though we were expected to acquire it.

Enquiries about process failures usually needed to be directed to senior systems managers who weren't very easy to track down. As system-experts they must have sometimes wondered why an earnest chap from the coal face was asking them stupid questions, especially when they'd already updated senior managers across the business as to the nature of the deficiency! It was a battle, but I usually found out the information which I needed, much to the aghast of Rob who had a far more laid-back attitude. These were serious problems as lines were getting automatically disconnected

Billing Two

by the payment robot and we were getting major earache from the customer, as well as being clobbered by our own managers as to why the debts weren't being collected! I did like chasing a problem and doing all I could to get a fix in place!!

Terry Smee wrote, *"John has very effective communication skills; he does not fear verbal or e-mail communication from seniors whether internal or external. I have yet to see an instance when John was unable to explain a complex case in Layman's terms."*

We all excelled in our own ways; Jess extracted payments from our debtors in a timely manner and Rob carried out the more delicate negotiations between management and the account teams. Rob did the awkward customer visits too! We did all we possibly could to ensure our patch had satisfied customers and paid bills. It was a real challenge, but the time soon passed. An added reward was incentive vouchers for meeting our targets, though this piled on the pressure as we chased other groups to ensure payments ledgered and fixes for order problems were in place. It was hard work, but the three of us did well together and we had some laughs.

After a couple of years the job didn't seem quite so daunting, but the pressure to work ever more efficiently continued, and everyone had to conform to a standard method of working. For many years we'd expected our billing site to close as there had been no new people join us, and with the trend of a reduction in the number of sites across the BT estate, it was only a matter of time? Experience had shown us that it didn't particularly matter whether a group was performing well, or not, it was usually about location, group size and ongoing costs. One quarter, although we had performed well, the expected reward vouchers were not forthcoming, and we were told that our site was closing, for good.

My GPO Family: Trilogy Edition

Our senior manager visited and offered redundancy packages for anyone who did not wish to remain with BT. Virtually everyone including our line-managers opted to sign up for release! This wasn't a sensible choice for our group as special authority had to be sought for so many leaver payments and there was speculation as to how many people would actually be allowed to go. It had been envisaged that only a quarter of the team might have wished to leave. Billing had signed its own death warrant; in hindsight if more people had chosen to stay, it would have been a viable proposition to move new work into the site for those who still wanted to work in Southend.

At the time I could not possibly contemplate leaving BT, and after all, how difficult could it be to find a new position in the Company? Thus, began a completely new chapter in my BT life...

Telephone House, Southend, (circa 1991)

Outlet 13: Scheduling

As a child, when we visited my dad's sister in Chadwell Heath, we always had to get the slower train which stopped at Romford, but I never recalled changing trains. So, I often wondered why so many people got on or off the train when it stopped at Shenfield. With five platforms, it appeared to be a key interchange on the route to or from London.

While waiting close to the platform edge looking to spot our train, one time my dad told me to quickly step back. A second later a long freight train seemingly appeared from nowhere and went thundering through the station. Although it wasn't going particularly fast, the sheer volume of high-sided goods containers produced a terrific back-draught which could have pulled me off the platform if I hadn't stood well back! Wow, that was dangerous, why weren't we given warning of the event?! Forty years later I was to discover the answers to these long-standing questions…

A New BT

By 2008, the once sleepy backwater of Southend Telephone Exchange had not changed very much. Modern 'wavy line' desks filled with flat-screen PCs and reliable Meridian Norstar phones suggested otherwise! Sensor controlled lighting and air-con was as close to a contemporary call centre that could be achieved in a 1930's building. The technology was greatly improved, though consistently we still cared about our customers and the quality of work which we produced.

Quietly, silently, almost unnoticed, the world had moved on. Computer skills (Word, Excel and PowerPoint), for which we had struggled to learn on the job, were routinely taught in schools, such

My GPO Family: Trilogy Edition

that any newcomers to BT already had these skills, or had been coached by their children! Younger, confident, socially adept people were now driving the company forward. The long-established clerical CA grade had virtually disappeared. COs were now predominantly call centre staff or the new field engineers. Higher grades were middle managers or well-educated number crunchers, manipulating complex staffing algorithms, or designing web pages!

Although 'customer-facing', and high-revenue earning, our Billing group had been remote from the mainstream call centre world of the well-evolved and new BT. Our skills were in manipulating the well-establish, sometimes legacy, billing platforms and influencing other teams to provide solutions. Our managers knew us well, they supported us, and we supported each other. As our group disbanded, the realisation of what we actually had, as individuals, to offer against younger, smarter candidates was beginning to dawn, and the prospects weren't looking good.

Finding a new job wasn't easy, as very few groups had budget to take on additional team members. I'd forgotten just how soul destroying this process could be. I was employed by a company who didn't want me on their salary bill and I was competing against hundreds of staff who were in a similar situation. In spite of this being the age of the PC, which made remote working from any worldwide location eminently feasible, potential new managers wouldn't trust team members to work responsibly on their own. Long service of ten, twenty, or more years counted for nothing. Positions as call centre staff working nearby, or from home, were readily available if one didn't mind the very strict time management and scrutiny of every single transaction, let alone the hassle from often upset and demanding customers! Field engineers were also in short supply, but the prospect of pole climbing on a winter's day at

Scheduling

age 50 plus didn't seem a very sane idea.

CSS Processing

Whilst trying to secure a new position, the daily supply of work to process was ever plentiful in the form of Short Term Assignments (STAs) from other divisions. One sunny morning, Lee (a fellow redeployee) and I headed off on a train bound for BT Centre to seek out a Billing Consultant who needed our CSS expertise to process multiple transactions in a short timescale. I knew all the mnemonic commands off by heart, so the fact that we were meeting a senior manager in the London HQ of BT wasn't particularly daunting. In fact, we felt rather important being invited to our own HQ as I'd only visited there once before, when the *Piper* logo was launched way back in 1991. Ironic too, as now we didn't have permanent jobs, we were finally getting to visit other parts of the BT world! Our chat with the consultant went well, up to the point when he asked us to demo our ideas on his laptop. I'd never used a laptop mouse before; my skill was seriously lacking. Lee wasn't much better, but thankfully our host toddled off and came back with a plug-in mouse to save our embarrassment! We assured him that we would be able to meet his deadline and thus we returned to Southend having secured a few week's work.

Our *Excel* spreadsheets contained 40 or more columns, that we had to populate with flags or values as a result of CSS interrogations. We managed something like 60 accounts per day, which was 2400 CSS transactions! This was an intensive task which required a lot of concentration as the transactions varied depending upon the products which each customer rented. We wrote a process paper and coached others on our virtual team, as this was quite a 'big data' gathering project. The consultant was more than pleased with our contribution, but didn't have any budget to reward us. By now

My GPO Family: Trilogy Edition

we were looking for another assignment, another manager to impress, and another hope of finding a job. It was dawning on us that for every new opportunity we would be judged on how we performed, and the fact that we were full-time employees of the company was purely incidental.

Another Sales Environment

Since my time in Sales (83-91) the technology of Call Centres had vastly changed such that the routing of incoming calls and scheduling of agents was handled by a single system with a local 'Command Centre' located in Brentwood. *Forecasting and Scheduling* (F & S) predicted and set out rules for the staffing and attendance patterns of Call Centres, whilst *Real Time* managed the routing of calls and the number of queue permutations to the agents. In the pay structure, Sales Commos had become the C2 grade which was the calibre of staff required for the scheduling operations.

Now, as a B2 redeployee, the prospect of learning C2 work was somewhat daunting although my manager had put me forward partly as a result of the accuracy and precision, which I had demonstrated, in the STA CSS role. My door to door journey to Brentwood was close to the limit of recommended daily travel time, but the incentive of securing a new position and once again belonging to a thriving office, spurred me on. Tony, a slightly eccentric, but eminently clever chap helped me to learn the scheduling rules by rote so that I was quickly able to build 'new entrant' class rotas.

Travel to Brentwood involved catching the early morning 'slow' train which conveniently stopped at every station on the line. For the return-trip I boarded the *Metro* to Shenfield and then waited for

Scheduling

a connecting fast train to Southend. If I timed the *Metro* link just right, I only had to change platforms and jump on the 'train now departing'! At least once a week, while I was standing waiting, I would hear the announcement, "The train approaching platform 3 does not stop here. Please stand well clear of platform 3." This was followed by a rumbling and whooshing noise as a 20-wagon goods train trundled through the station without stopping. Even as an adult, the through draught was still very noticeable, but significantly, now 40 years later, a timely warning was given!

Workstyle 2000

At floatation British Telecom had inherited a vast and rambling estate portfolio of telephone exchanges, engineering centres, offices, factories and radio towers, many of which were unsuitable to accommodate modern-day office equipment (PCs) and personnel. Additionally, office space in London was both outdated and expensive. As a solution, in the lead-up to the new Millennium, brand new *Workstyle 2000* buildings were constructed, close to the M25 (Motorway) to provide better working conditions and to allow the migration of staff out of London. With accommodation for up to 1500 staff, the *Workstyle 2000* buildings were both spacious and pleasant places in which to work.

Brentwood *Workstyle* had been constructed in the footprint of the former St. Faith's mental hospital by renowned architects Arup, and developer, Stanhope. One lunchtime I walked the grounds of the neighbouring church yard and it was very quiet away from the traffic of the London Road. Oh yes, like BT Southend, the Brentwood building was also located on a London Road! A shuttle bus used to run between the train station and the office, but this had long been disbanded by the date of my arrival. The office was a bit of a rabbit warren with numerous corridors, staircases and meeting

My GPO Family: Trilogy Edition

rooms off of the main corridors. It followed the contour of the land, hence the first floor was at ground level at one end! It was designed to be a very flexible building for a mix of teams and situations and to be adaptable as staffing needs changed. When I finally left, it was being sub-divided into accommodation for other tenants.

Like something futuristic, perhaps out of the TV series, *The Avengers*, it was a living building with venetian blinds which descended automatically when the sun came out! It was quite a sight to watch a section of 30 or more blinds slowly coming down in unison along the whole length of the building. There was a screen of glass around the outside of the building which directed airflow and maintained a steady temperature, even when the internal sash windows were opened. Circular air vents (Marilyn Monroe stylee) in the floor aided heating and cooling too. Of course, the system was abused by the users who placed magazines over the floor vents, disliked the darkness from the blinds, or complained about the windows being open! It was an impossible task to cater for everyone's personal comfort. The brightness of the fluorescent lights was controlled by dialling a number on selected phones, but when VOIP phones were installed there were only a few remaining Meridian telephones which still performed this function. The expansive canteen included a chef who regularly carved a joint of meat, so on those days I left my usual sandwiches at home!

Lee and I were tasked with helping the teams during the run-down of *Vantage* and the introduction of WFM (Work Force Manager). What started as a short-term project ran for about two years during which time we put in considerable effort to populating hundreds of agent's profiles and duties on WFM before it went live. We became experts at configuring new entrant builds and schedules. It was quite a learning curve, but the managers encouraged us while we continued our search for more permanent roles. The scheduling

Scheduling

teams were a mix of ex-Sales people, some of whom I knew from Southend, plus many who had joined the company in the late 1990s as the command centre was established. As C2s they were all bright intelligent people whose only excuse for not working would have been boredom, as opposed to any lack of ability. Some team members could instantly see the patterns in the rotas and it was almost second nature for them to spot any error, and to quickly figure a new pattern; they didn't have to concentrate very hard! I had to work at it the whole time, so as not to make a mistake. For many, it was a puzzle to solve and master, but I didn't regard it as so much fun!

My manager in 1981, Betty Keeps once wrote,

"John likes to be close to the heart of the business. A back-office role is not sufficient involvement for him."

Brentwood wasn't my ideal location at which to work, but it was still exciting swiping my security badge and entering the thriving hub of several hundreds of people, each performing their own functions to keep the BT machine operating smoothly. I enjoyed building the NEWTS (new entrant) profiles with training, grad bay, and eventually the standard schedules. It was a job I did well throughout the transition from *Vantage* to WFM. The train ride to work was fascinating on the occasions when I travelled up with another commuter who loved *Doctor Who*. There was always the uncertainty of getting a train home, which wasn't delayed by signalling problems, EMU breakdowns, or suicidal jumpers. It was a longer day than I would have liked and it often seemed ironic that I couldn't simply log-on in Southend to complete my daily tasks.

The Personalities

In Brentwood I caught up with a few names from the past which

My GPO Family: Trilogy Edition

included Jeff Wilkerson, Robin Peppiatt, Denise Norris, Lorraine Waymont, and Bobbi David. On my daily walk from the station I passed road names which I recognised from way back in the 1980s when I worked a split Sales duty of Brentwood Main with Lorraine. White Lyons Road and Romy House were memorable; I'm sure I never spelt them like that on my ANs! I also passed the lacklustre Amstrad building (now a Premier Inn) and often wondered if Alan Sugar was in residence!

Also joining us in Brentwood were Tracey, Darren and Brian, all of whom had the right temperaments to take redeployment in their stride. My new team headed up by Allan Sammy and Layla Bell was always welcoming of us and made us feel valued members. Jo Smith, Maude Matson (aka Catherine), Julie, Joe, Tony and many others made my days bearable. During training, I sat next to Tony as he had the expertise to teach me the NEWT building, but in later months I was placed next to Catherine, as she had a tendency to cause mayhem once bored! Catherine was an incessant talker, but eminently likeable, and most intelligent when she applied herself. Lunch in the canteen with Paul Williamson (another ex-Southend Billing colleague) all made for a more stimulating existence.

30 Years

Whilst working at Brentwood, I completed 30 years with BT and it was touch and go whether my official certificate would arrive in time for the onsite Level 2 manager to present to me on the day! I had to chase the paperwork which had been sent to one of my previous Transition Managers, to ensure it was forwarded on. That may sound a little trivial, but was I really proud to have completed so long a term with Post Office Telecommunications and BT. The guys in Brentwood had a special way of celebrating these events. When given the word, everyone got up from their seats and quietly

Scheduling

gathered round the desk of the 'victim'. When I looked up from my work, half of the office was standing to wish me well. It really was a nice gesture, as Karen Norton then presented me with my long-service letter.

End of Another Era

Eventually as WFM was up and running, we obtained permanent positions on a newly created admin team. The range of work was less stimulating and I wasn't particularly sorry when the senior managers took the decision to transfer all scheduling to another site, although once again it placed us in a very uncertain situation. Our HQ was now Brentwood, but Lee and I gained permission to return to Southend, if only while we hunted for yet another job!

BT Museum leaflet PHME 7665

My GPO Family: Trilogy Edition

Welcome to the telephone service (1970) CHQ/PRD for THQ

Outlet 14: End Game

The GPO game had frequently been one of bluff, counter bluff, standing one's ground, forging useful contacts, but above all, never going against the establishment. Two years of travelling to Brentwood for jobs which had disappeared at the drop of a hat had seriously worn down my resolve. The recession which began in 2008 was lingering on, and BT was continuing to rationalise and downsize. However, during 2010 it was with great hope that I allocated myself one of the spare desks in Southend ATE, still with the anticipation of securing a new position in the company. I'd always worked for BT, and I didn't for one moment expect that to change.

Lee had been a very supportive friend since we'd both been made redeployees in 2008 and once back in Southend we worked together at every opportunity. The assignments continued; we were expected to perform consistently well on every one, with minimal training, and little expectation of obtaining a job offer at the end of them.

Streetworks

As BT Retail employees, it was exceptional for us to be loaned to Openreach for a three-month secondment, and we looked forward to being part of the division. The processing of paperwork for the Streetworks Team required much attention to detail as it involved typing out 24-digit references. A special journey via Rayners Lane Tube to Pinner ATE, for an overview of the process, initially seemed to be unnecessary, but Jan gave us a warm welcome and it really helped to set us in good stead for the project. As usual, Lee and I worked to the required levels of quality and volume, but there was no budget for us to continue past the set date.

My GPO Family: Trilogy Edition

As BT's roll out of NGA (Next Generation Access) continued apace, we agreed that Openreach would give us the best opportunities of securing a job. We checked through some CBTs (Computer Based Training) of fibre deployment methods and were well-prepared and enthusiastic by the time we spotted the next job advert. Interviews with a prospective manager for *NGA (fibre) Admin* proved positive, until yet again the budget was pulled!

Call Listening

Upon ringing any large company an announcement usually warns, 'Calls may be recorded for training purposes'. I sometimes wondered at this statement as the sheer number of calls would surely require thousands of hours of tape? From my early days on '150' (Sales), this would not have been technically possible, or even practical, but I was forgetting that the digital world in the 21st century was now a reality!

Our next project was to evaluate an historic sample number of calls to determine how well the Call Centre agents had dealt with some specific customer queries and follow-up responses. This was surely to be a real giggle? No, it was one of our most challenging! Poor transmission, incomprehensible customers, offshore agents, all compounded even the most straightforward of orders. Some of the sample calls were more than 20-minutes duration, so we had to skip through the dreadful music-on-hold and attempt to find the most important sections of the conversations. We didn't know whether to laugh or cry when the agents clearly didn't have a clue, or when the customer(s) were shouting at them in sheer frustration! We had empathy for both parties.

Despatch of Broadband Hubs was a nightmare. Consequently, in later years, BT specified a slimline model which could be posted

End Game

through letterboxes, eliminating the need for the customer to be at home to accept a delivery.

It was a real 'ear-opener' listening to these calls and to discover the daily difficulties of a Telco operating in a highly competitive marketplace. Migration Authorisation Codes (MAC) were required for customers who were changing suppliers. Lines used for broadband were left with 'Tags on the Line' and it appeared that multiple telephone numbers at one property could exist in limbo without owners. Where once a line might simply have been 'stopped or started' the same day, contention over the lines and owners was clearly causing delays. And an extra five days to provide broadband on an existing line seemed ludicrous. I could imagine the poor exchange jumper runners working frantically to meet the daily churn of customers swapping Telcos. And with EOI (Equivalence of Input), BT Retail contact with Openreach, who held all of the records, was strictly limited. I despaired at the amount of time that must have been wasted by all Telcos and their customers in this unnecessary multi-layered and artificially created process. The days of the well-ordered and sensibly regulated GPO were long past! Public service had given way to a complicated profit-driven chaos, and I was glad to no longer be involved with provision of service orders.

Some agents handled the queries most professionally and clearly enjoyed their work, but we were mainly listening to batches of calls which had gone awry. Call listening was quite intensive as we too were targeted on our performance and were expected to complete a large enough batch sample to produce valid results.

As redeployees, we were doing some rather mundane jobs, but equally it was interesting to get an insight into the operational workings of other groups.

My GPO Family: Trilogy Edition

Other Divisions

Back in Retail there was no shortage of projects to be done and every group wanted work doing for free. We did many WFM projects to build profiles, check leave and run schedules. As Billing specialists, we applied for financial secondments, but these tended to be allocated to displaced teams, rather than singletons with experience. EOI stipulations discouraged Openreach managers from offering us short-term work. Monthly projects with deadlines meant that the days passed quickly and occupied much of our time, but the pressure of trying to find a proper paying job or exiting the company was ever present.

Searching through the lists of assignments, a familiar name, Howard Mapley rang a bell, and after a quick phone call, Lee and I were processing copy bills for the N3 NHS Billing Team. It was always good to work for people who we'd met in the past. On another assignment, I particularly enjoyed cataloguing of engineering drawings for BT Heritage, but that is another chapter…

Openings in Sales were always available, and for youngsters joining the business, these may have been ideal opportunities, but no longer for me. As Lee and I knew all too well from our scheduling work, nearly all desk-based customer facing roles were Call Centre orientated with all of the associated regimentation. OMD (Order Management Desk) looked promising, but after 30 years of working in Southend, daily travel again to Brentwood for another temporary role didn't enthral me.

End Game

Order Management Desk

OMD was for the progression of all types of Business Broadband orders in a Call Centre environment to stringent targets. Within the EOI (Equivalence of Input) rulings, a multitude of GUI-based systems had been developed to handle the management of these important broadband orders across an ever-developing product set. It was to have been a challenging, but interesting learning curve of a new specialism and well within my capabilities. However, by this stage in my career, the very prospect of becoming a call centre puppet, while still being tasked to search for another job was simply unacceptable to me.

BT wanted efficiency at all times; the days of winding down to retirement in any organisation was long past. Encouragement was given to early leavers in the form of retirement planning seminars, of which I had recently attended. The option of no longer 'playing the GPO game' allowed for a generous leaver package to exit. I'd had serious problems with my eyesight the previous year, and by now it had finally dawned on me that I wasn't immortal and that even I had to retire someday, so what better time than now?

With no one remaining to fight my corner, I lit the blue touch paper and waited for the notification of my last day of service…

"Let your fingers do the walking"
Yellow Pages slogan

My GPO Family: Trilogy Edition

BT Tower with its horn and dish aerials (2006)

Outlet 15: Post Office Tower

I'd always had a desire to visit the Post Office Tower; not because it was so high, or that the food in the restaurant was first class; simply because it was THE Post Office Tower and none other.

In the 1960s when the tower was open to the public, queues stretched around the block as it was such a popular tourist attraction. The famous *topofthetower* restaurant was leased and run by Billy Butlin of the holiday camp organisation. Lots of crowds, packed elevators and expensive food was not for me; and besides we didn't often travel to London, during my childhood years. The troubled 1970s and the bomb explosion on the 31st floor culminated in the whole tower being permanently closed to the public from June 1980. This did little to aid my ambition to one day visit the place! Or perhaps it did? For starters, the long queues of people waiting to gain entry, disappeared!

One of my favourite library books of my childhood was, *The Post Office* by Nancy Martin. One of the illustrations was a photo of the Post Office Tower, from which I took a tracing and then produced a rather cringeworthy drawing! Nonetheless, I treasured this drawing and kept it to remind me of my wish to one day visit the real tower.

By the 21st century, the world had changed, though the BT Tower was still a revered place to visit. Priority was given to entertaining potential corporate and business customers on the revolving suite of the ever popular 34th floor. Keen to maintain its social responsibility, BT partnered with ChildLine (now part of NSPCC) to offer exclusive lunchtime and evening visits for a one-off donation (set fee).

My GPO Family: Trilogy Edition

Having sent my cheque off, I eagerly awaited the due date for my very first visit to the tower! Here's my report of the day…

Top of the Tower (19 October 2002)

Today, you have to be very lucky to receive an invitation to the BT Tower, and more so, to get an absolutely clear blue sky to enjoy the fabulous views over London. Well, the opportunity arose and with a moderate donation to ChildLine, I was the proud holder of a lunchtime ticket to ride, in reportedly, one of the fastest lifts in the West End.

On the big day, my train was delayed and as I hurried out of Euston Underground (station), a new building on the skyline blocked my view of the tower, and the thought crossed my mind that *Doctor Who* didn't have this trouble back in the Sixties. For devotees, the modern 'war-machines' have brushes and a driver who aims to rid the streets of grime.

Close up, *The Stick* (as I've heard it called) showed as a mass of concrete firmly anchored to the ground and I was careful to mind yet another crane working in the narrow street. As I turned the corner, the fairly ordinary blue-painted building in a quiet road gave little clues of the major tourist attraction that was once open to all.

Camera in hand, I strode up the steps and through the automatic clear glass doors, which perhaps didn't really match the security within. The lowered ceilings and mood lighting cleverly hid the operational nature of the site. As the corridors narrowed considerably, I thought I was being led into the broom cupboard; then the lift door opened and I found myself on the flight deck of a 21st century elevator.

Post Office Tower

There was little sensation of speed as the car quickly climbed to the dizzy heights of the 34th floor. As the doors opened again, I was awe-struck at the truly spectacular views from a vantage-point, seemingly suspended in space. This was a dream and there was no correlation between the building and the ground, but I really, really was on 'Top of the Tower'.

I was greeted by the catering staff/waiters, who stood sentry like on either side of the glass doors, which opened out from the lift. The floor was surprisingly narrow and it didn't take (me) very long to do a few circuits, even though it wasn't revolving. As I sighted the tiny Millennium Wheel, far, far below, I was glad to hold the security bar across the otherwise full length, floor to ceiling, windows.

The singer of the trio kept a fairly upbeat tempo, which enhanced the overall relaxed atmosphere of the bar, buffet and comfy chairs in a space devoid of corporate identity of any kind. The tower, is BT. Branding is superfluous.

Back in the foyer, I collected my certificate, booklet and chocolate tower, and felt like simply another tourist, little the wiser about the significance of the building. Walking away, I turned and looked back up at the towering reality of the structure built with such insight into the communication needs of the modern world. On reflection, a fantastic day out: certainly, one not to be missed.

Surprisingly, my next visit was only a few months later, as a member of the Telecommunications Heritage Group...

THE (BT) Tower of London (2003)

For many years, members of the Telecommunications Heritage Group had wanted to visit the BT Tower which, for security, is

My GPO Family: Trilogy Edition

closed to the public. Through the kind offices of the Connected-Earth project team, this became a real possibility towards the end of 2002. As places for the event were strictly limited, a competition was held and the 70 or so, lucky winners who had showed 'their love for the tower', by answering the questions correctly, were invited to a *THG event at the Tower*, which happened to be on 14 February 2003.

As this was to be my second visit in a few short months, I wondered what surprises the occasion might produce...

Several days before the event, Ivor Flint rang to ask if I could scan a page of the 1961 *Post Office Telecommunications Journal*, which showed a model of the tower, for a *PowerPoint* presentation that he was preparing to screen in the auditorium. I took the opportunity to include my own drawing of the tower, which I had kept and treasured since I was just 10 years old.

On the day, everyone gathered in the Cyber Café area, meeting up with old acquaintances while Ivor and Simon made last-minute preparations. This was quite a momentous day for the THG; a large number of members had been invited and everything had to be just right, as there were representatives from both BT Group Archives and Connected-Earth in attendance. And of course, we were privileged, because the event was taking place at the very hub of the BT network.

In the Tower Auditorium, there was silence as all eyes focused on the podium, and Ivor began his carefully planned introduction. Appropriately, films of *The New Tower of London* and *The Post Office Tower - London* were screened. These gave a detailed account of the building's construction, its use and the early days as a major tourist attraction. As the films finished, I smiled quietly to

Post Office Tower

myself as my very own drawing of the tower was projected onto the 'big screen' and Ivor explained that there would be an opportunity later in the day for some of us to recount why the tower is so special to us. Richard Lloyd of BT's Connected-Earth remarked that to most people, the *Tower of London* is where the Crown Jewels are kept, but for him and others with telecom connections, the *Tower of London* means the BT Tower.

As I exited the south lift onto the 34th floor, my eyes were drawn to the spectacular views of London, far, far below. The sky was a little hazy, but it was great to be up in the clouds, once again. Lucy Jones from BT Group Archives greeted me.

On the table next to her was displayed the original brass GPO plaque and visitors book which had once been located in the foyer. The plaque read 'The Post Office Tower was opened by the Right Honourable Harold Wilson OBE MP on the 8th October 1965'. A carefully chosen selection of pamphlets and photos were also on display.

Of the event, Lucy tells us that she enjoyed the day, *"Not least because the THG is such an appreciative audience, but it was probably one of the only events to be hosted at the tower where the archive material attracted as much attention as the view!"*

Indeed, this was a leisurely event with plenty of time to sit down and chat, have a light buffet and a drink, and to enjoy the views, all courtesy of BT. I was doing just this and looking out of the window, when momentarily I felt a slight jolt, and sure enough, the mechanism for revolving the 34th floor had been switched on. This was noticeable as I could see the metal rims of the division in the floor slowly moving. It was fantastic to think that a complete section of the tower was turning and that I could literally sit and

My GPO Family: Trilogy Edition

watch the world go by and see the changing scenery below. The motion was very smooth and the speed just right so as not to be alarming.

Elsewhere on the floor, Simon was directing a professional video of the day's events and it was equally interesting to see the camera and spotlights being set up for colleagues to tell their very own tales of the tower. When it was my turn, I felt very important being 'miked up', but the lights were so warm and it wasn't so easy to remember my lines! Thankfully, I did a confident performance of own 'tower story'.

I left the tower, still curious as to what the other floors might reveal, but I was pleased to have taken part in such a special event, and only one other question remained; "When can I visit again?"

Stair Racing (2003)

The answer to my question came to me later that year with a *BT Today* news article inviting staff to 'Walk the BT Tower' for charity. The idea of climbing 34 floors, even at walking pace, seemed rather daunting and the added pressure of having sponsors to satisfy made it appear quite a challenge. However, an old newsreel clip from the 1960s of students racing up the tower excited me enough to want to be a part of the event.

I realised it would be prudent to do some training for this feat and luckily Southend ATE had six flights of steep stairs on which to practice, during my lunch breaks!

Here's a little bit of nostalgia for you about the Post Office Tower: *"In January 1969 the 2nd annual competition of 'stair racing' was hosted at the tower. Student union teams from eight universities*

Post Office Tower

took turns to be the fastest to run up the 798 steps. The winner, John Pearson from Manchester University, took just 5 minutes, 7 seconds to do the ascent and he was presented with a brass model of the tower.

In the previous year, Edinburgh University achieved a time of 4 minutes, 46 seconds!"

Of course, nothing like that would happen these days?

Well it did! And in 2003, I took part in a sponsored walk up the 34 floors of the tower to (what was once) the revolving restaurant. The event was to raise money for ChildLine, a charity that Esther Rantzen began in 1986. Here's my original report...

A sponsored walk up the BT Tower for ChildLine.

In September 2003, an article in *BT Today* (online) caught my eye. It said, "Sponsored walk up the BT Tower for ChildLine." I wondered, could I manage the 900* steps in one go and what if the stairs were crowded with would-be racers? Overwhelmingly though, the attraction of another visit to the BT Tower and the challenge of walking up to the 34th floor was simply too tempting.

*The steps are numbered with stickers, though when 'racing' one doesn't really have time to stop and check, especially when the finish is in sight! The climb to floor 34 has approximately 842 steps.

I e-mailed the organiser and she phoned back and stressed that for safety/insurance I would need a doctor's declaration stating that I was fit enough to compete. Initially it seemed a bit over zealous just for a stroll up a few stairs, but knowing BT's strong focus on health and safety, I concurred and duly sent off my entry fee.

My GPO Family: Trilogy Edition

Additional information stated that there would be no running and that a maximum of 8 people would be on the stairs in any period of 15 minutes. Also, that the event would be from 09:00 to 17:00 hours and entrants could choose their preferred time slot. Participants could walk up at their own pace or be timed as a personal challenge. I was satisfied that the conditions were favourable for both the casual walker and the serious competitor alike. Even so, the idea of trying to 'beat the clock' did appeal to me and spurred me on to put in some practice.

I found that I was able to walk up and down the six flights of our work's stairs to the equivalent of 36 flights without collapsing, albeit I was somewhat out of breath, so I knew the task was achievable. In the meantime, I canvassed sponsors in my office and then sweated that my doctor would pass me fit.

On 15 October, as I travelled up to town on the train, I knew that I must try my hardest to achieve a fast personal-time, but without compromising my ability to finish the task. Without seeing the course beforehand, there would be many unknown factors and I would simply have to play it by ear. As the potential runners (in shorts and trainers) gathered in BT Tower reception, I (in my long trousers and comfortable shoes) chatted to the others as we heard that Colin Jackson (the hurdler) had put in a time of about 8 minutes. It was suggested that a (non-BT) competitor had managed it in under 7 minutes!

Just before 11:30 I was given my number (26) and told to wait until I was called to the start, as entry to the stair well was being strictly controlled. As instructed I walked through the double doors and placed one foot on the first step of the stairs awaiting the OK to begin. This was exciting, and was going to be hard work too, but I was really hyped up and could hardly wait to start.

Post Office Tower

As only one person was allowed on a section of stairs at one time, I realised that I could dictate my own pace, fast or slow. The grey painted metalwork of the stairs looked really old and there were only about 8 steps before the section turned to the left (anti-clockwise), so the leg effort needed was minimal, but the number of twists and turns required seemed rather daunting. As I glanced down to find my footing I noticed sticky labels on the wall of the central core showing the step number (e.g. 132, 133 etc.). There still was a very long way to go and as the actual floor numbers weren't easy to spot, my only point of reference was the sticky labels, which weren't incrementing very quickly. I decided that I must keep going at all costs.

Much like a ghost train ride at a fun fair, on certain landings a head would suddenly come into view and an (almost) disembodied voice, from a seated person holding a clipboard, would call out "Hello and what number are you?" And then the static on the radio would crackle and the voice would report, "Number 26 leaving floor 7", but by then I was already out of earshot and wondering if any other surprises lay ahead. It was however, both exciting and reassuring that my progress (or lack of it) was being carefully tracked.

An added interest was the fire doors after every 7 or so flights, which needed a fair pull to open and pass through; this really was becoming a test of endurance.

As I was beginning to tire, another face politely asked if I would like a drink and I thankfully walked onto the landing through to a large room containing a table full of cups of water. Slightly disorientated, I asked what floor I was on and the voice replied "16". As I recovered my breath and took a few sips of water, I noticed entrant #25 was also in the room.

My GPO Family: Trilogy Edition

I quickly put down my drink and the realisation that I was about halfway up and doing rather well lead me to muster my efforts and go all out to get to the top. I did my best to increase the pace, but my breathing became rather laboured and as I panted for breath I had to slow down slightly once I was out of sight of the checkpoint. I looked at my watch, which showed 11:43 am, and I knew that a time of 15 minutes for the climb was within my reach. The radio crackled again and I noticed the legend 32 on the wall. It was great, and as I heard the voice check me through, I felt extra important. I was almost there!

Some seconds later, there was daylight as I entered the 34th floor another voice said, "Well done, come and have a drink and sit down", but all I could say was, "What time did I do?" As I was handed a drink the reply came back "9 minutes 36" and the official certificate was placed in my hand. "That's excellent", I managed to speak, as I recovered my breath.

Although I was due to begin my climb at 11:30, with the slight delay in waiting for the stairs to be clear, I was so intent of following the starting instructions and getting going safely, that I didn't stop to check my watch. It was truly amazing and I was really, really pleased to have done so well.

It was hard work, but I was so pleased that I had achieved a personal time of 9 minutes 36 seconds!
When I got my breath back some more, I used one of the Meridian phones (on the wall by the lift) to telephone my manager in Southend to let my work colleagues know that I had completed the walk.
I'd taken annual leave for the event, as the tower was a couple of hour's journey time each way. As I headed home, I wondered if I might one day do the climb again?

Post Office Tower

Postscript:

The fastest time was 6 minutes 16 seconds by Alex Tyrrell of BT Retail. Colin Jackson, (hurdler) the invited celebrity, completed in 9 minutes 5 seconds, though I think he did a faster climb, later in the day. The average time was 10 minutes 23 seconds.
It is said that Rachel Stevens (S-Club 7) did the walk in November 2001 and that BT sponsored her £1 per step!

I think I probably chatted to some minor celebs in reception whilst waiting my turn up the stairs, but without name badges, most sporty stars would have been unfamiliar to me! Most colleagues in my office were kind enough to sponsor me and I raised £216 for ChildLine.

My next visit was a 'Mother's Day Lunch' in 2004, again with a donation to ChildLine...

A Flying Visit to the Tower (20 March 2004)

It was a windy day, but not really cold and the expected rain was holding off as I waited patiently in Maple Street for my two guests, Malcolm and Carol to arrive. Every so often a black cab would pull up and two more visitors would get out and walk up the steps into the blue-panelled building.

At about 11:50 we entered into the reception where a queue had formed awaiting IDs and security checks. Long ago, the queues would have stretched the length of the pavement, but not today. My colleague Malcolm quipped that he didn't have this trouble in 1965 when he called in to check that the building could handle the expected numbers of visitors. And he later remarked how much the ground floor layout had changed since the almost 40 years that he

My GPO Family: Trilogy Edition

was there last.

We waited in the Cyber Lounge as parties were ushered in groups of 10 to ascend in the south lift. Upon seeing our host Karen, I commented that I wouldn't be using the stairs on this occasion as I remembered that she had started the stopwatch on my last visit.

In spite of the windy weather, the lift smoothly climbed the 34 floors, in well under a minute, aided by Dave Lemm (veteran lift operator). The glass outer doors leading onto the floor were held open for us as we were greeted by the waiters carrying trays filled with glasses of orange juice and champagne.

The cosy armchairs were not in evidence, but an array of tables and chairs, neatly arranged confirmed that this was a pre-Mothers' Day luncheon in support of ChildLine. To my delight, Karen told us that the revolving floor would be switched on later.

The sky was quite overcast and the two police helicopters that were hovering in the distance added to the dramatic overtones of the day as far below the 'stop the war' marches were taking place.

As the afternoon continued, the sky brightened up and the spectacular views of the London skyline were more discernible as the sun shone over Regent's Park. Having worked for many years in the capital city for BT, Malcolm and Carol were able to easily identify Mondial House, Faraday Buildings and Judd Street.

The only movement in the tower was generated from the revolving floor, but in the stairwell the strong breezes were borne out by the occasional slamming of the fire doors. A notice on the wall proclaimed that *Openzone* wireless (connectivity) for laptops or PDAs was in operation.

Post Office Tower

The atmosphere was very much a family one with a mix of ages in attendance from the very young to those of advancing years. A conjurer kept us entertained with his sleight of hand while David Graham of the *Tornados* led with guitar riffs and witty musical interludes. In discussion, Malcolm said that it was very apt for the *Tornados* to be invited to the tower as their 1962 hit record *Telstar* had obvious BT connections. David told us of his love for performing live music and of his recent concerts at Butlin's Skeggy. [Another connection here as Billy Butlin originally leased the tower restaurant.] He also spoke of how licensing issues are diminishing the opportunities for new musicians.

The buffet lunch was light and delicious and while there was plenty of space on our table for our drinks and cameras, there was little clearance between the central wall and the backs of the chairs. However, any disadvantage was far outweighed by the changing scenery as the floor slowly revolved every 22 minutes or so.
As we came down in the lift, there was general chatter about when the tower was built and how much had been modernised. Dave Lemm said that there used to be a mirror on the wall of the old lifts. Another visitor asked when the tower was built and Karen explained that everyone would be given a souvenir book. I added that the tower was opened on 8 October 1965 and Karen pointed out that I was an expert.

There is still so much interest in the tower and it was truly wonderful to be part of it again even if it was for just a few hours.

I did apply to 'walk the BT Tower' in February 2005, but with a nagging backache, I decided not to chance doing the strenuous climb, but another opportunity to visit soon presented itself!

My GPO Family: Trilogy Edition

Tower's 40th Anniversary

At the end of September 2005, *BT Today* (online staff news) announced…

"Twenty pairs of tickets can be won by employees to attend star-studded celebrations on Saturday 8th October marking the 40th anniversary of the opening of the BT Tower in London."

It further said…

"For the chance to win tickets, simply answer the question, 'Why should I be at the Tower's 40th birthday party?"

My colleague Claire Hogarth suggested that I enter and she entered herself too…!

"Why should I be at BT Tower's 40th birthday party… Well, I work with Mr John Chenery, a BT stalwart and ardent BT Tower enthusiast who has been kind enough to give me his empty Walkers crisp packets every day. Not because he's too lazy to put them in the bin, but because he wants me to win an iPod in recognition of the fact that I frequently get his overspill of phone calls and pass on his messages. It also happens to coincide with his birthday, so I kind of promised I'd do my best to enter and make his dreams come true.

I'd like to add that John is a great ambassador for BT and he even has his own telephone exchange in his back garden, as well as numerous BT paraphernalia. I know that although there will be celebrities there, for John, the real star will be the tower, for this I put him forward as a perfect guest for the Tower's 40th birthday party. If I win the tickets, they are his!

P.S. I notice there wasn't a word limit, hope this isn't too long."

Post Office Tower

This was my entry...

BT Tower's 40th: 8 October 2005

High up above London, the BT restaurant tower is turning
and the Children in Need are learning of 40 years ago
Tony Benn put on a show as the tower went operationally live.
He will survive (at 80 plus) so what is the fuss?

Well, the tower at night is a wonderful sight.
Twinkling lights abound, but there's hardly a sound.
The tower's come of age and digital's all the rage.
The Strowger floors are quiet, there's no need to shout!

The stairs are a creaking, although there's no one there speaking.
But in the aerial gallery above you can still send a message to your love...

As the tower is the hub for broadcasting pictures and sounds to the world all around.

After I sent off the poem, I speculated that the chances of being picked from hundreds of other BT-folks, who would want to go, would be slim. However, on 6 October at midday I received an e-mail...

"Congratulations! - I am delighted to let you know that you have won two places at the BT Tower celebrations on Saturday 8th October."

That was a real surprise as I thought that the twenty places had already been allocated. However, the e-mail went on to explain...

"The competition originally offered 20 pairs of tickets, but due to

My GPO Family: Trilogy Edition

an overwhelming response of more than 750 entries, the BT charity programme has doubled the number of prizes."

I arrange to meet my friend Simon outside BT Tower on the night. The red carpet was waiting, though it was cordoned off in readiness for the real celebrities' arrival! Inside, the four women who ran the BT Charity Programme got into the spirit of the 40th birthday history and were dressed in 'Sixties-style, Mary Quant', black and white mini-skirts and black caps. This nicely set the scene for remembering the tower as it once was.

With at least 80 competition winners expected, plus all of the celeb fund-raisers and guests, the place was going to be packed out. The celebs' party was on the 34th floor, but before then the BT staff and guests had a one-hour slot to visit the 33rd floor. With each group of about 12 (limited by lift capacity to go there and back), we had about 10 minutes at the top. And at only 17:45 hrs it was nowhere near dark enough to see all of the twinkling lights of neighbouring buildings.

At about 18:45 we all went into the auditorium and listened for five minutes to a dreadful 'warm up' act who made everyone get up and do a 'luvvies hello' to the people each side of them. *"Oh, hello darherling, wonderful to see you!"*

I wasn't impressed, though a screening of a short clip of the history of the tower was more of interest before Spangles (Natasha Kiplinsky) did her spiel about raising money for Children in Need.

Exiting the auditorium, we lined up beside the red carpet in the foyer to watch the arrival of the celebs. It was fun waiting to see who would turn up. Everyone was doing their best to lean over the handrail to get some decent shots of the stars who were eager to get

Post Office Tower

to their party on the 34th floor. The professional photographers had their own allocated space and proper SLR cameras, while nearly everyone else played with their digital 'toy' cameras and mobile phones! Camera angles were difficult, especially with so many spotlights which prevented my 'auto-flash' from operating, but the atmosphere was wonderful and it was exciting simply to be there and to try and put names to all of the famous faces! The full list of celebs was quite extensive, but those I spotted were; Vanessa (Radio 2 fame), Rick Astley, Pudsey Bear, Helen Lederer, Alan Davies, and Nina Wadia.

The parade of celebs seemed to go on for ages, the lights were very bright and *our* buffet was late! It was a jovial atmosphere, so it didn't matter too much. It was a good spread and the chocolate fountain looked very tempting too, but I was getting a little tired by now and the sleeve of my jacket got a dipping too, d'oh! For the number of guests, there weren't many chairs, so we ended up sitting on the floor. Jo O'Meara treated us to one of her songs and by then the crowds had thinned out a lot! She sang sweetly; it was pleasant. I must have left the tower just after 22:00, knowing that it would almost be midnight by the time I got home. It was fabulous to have taken part in the event, but I'd prefer a quieter scene next time...

I was to take part in two more stair climbs which were scheduled on consecutive Februaries; not a good time in the year as preceding months were rather cold in which to get additional outdoor exercise. Nonetheless, I was hopeful that I might better my original time, or at the least it was going to be fun taking part again!

By 2006 I had recovered from my first 'walk up the tower' and was ready to have another go...

My GPO Family: Trilogy Edition

This time was going to be fun as I'd bought a new shirt with the GPO logo on it and I decided to wear shorts and lightweight shoes. It was trying to sleet when I left home for the railway station, but was sunny from about 10:30. As my requested time slot wasn't until midday, I had time to take some exterior shots of what was once Bloomsbury Trunk Control. Even with my street map in hand, I thought I'd walked past it as it's tucked away behind the citadel/ventilation shaft. I was a little surprised to actually find it, before I had to hot-foot it to the tower.

I was hoping to improve my climb time, but didn't have the same energy and only managed 10 minutes 42 seconds. The view from the 34th floor was a little misty, but it was really great to have successfully done the stairs yet again! Upon leaving the tower, I walked to Upper Thames Street to capture some shots of Mondial House which was scheduled for demolition, but that too is another chapter.

Through sponsorship, I collected a handsome £281.50 for ChildLine. One of my SPOC customers (Sheila K) even sent in a donation and wrote, *"Dear John, Thank-you for doing the walk. The children will be glad."*

White Heat

In 2006 Dominic Sandbrook published a weighty tome entitled *White Heat* which was an in-depth history of Britain in the Swinging Sixties. 'The white heat of technological revolution' was a phrase coined by Harold Wilson (PM) at the Labour Party conference on 1 October 1963. It translated into the vision of a progressive Britain which would win through technological achievements, and the Post Office Tower was later seen to have been forged during this era.

Post Office Tower

I was thrilled to get a reference in Dominic's book where he cites: *'On the revolving restaurant, see*

http://www.lightstraw.co.uk/ate/main/postofficetower/t60.html a website devoted entirely to the history of the tower.'

My next stair climb was the following February, 2007…

The logistics of the event were carefully planned in advance with time slots of 15-minute intervals, allowing five or six participants to start during that period, provided that the earlier walkers had cleared the first few flights! A helpful e-mail informed, "If you would like to walk up before or after a friend, let us know." I opted simply for a slot close to midday to allow plenty of time to arrive at the tower, but with not too long a wait either.

Stair Climb (12 Feb 2007)

The weather was cloudy as I travelled up on the train to London and it was trying to drizzle by the time I reached the tower. I decided to stick to a casual shirt, long trousers and my favourite lightweight shoes, as this wasn't a spectator sport! Again, I managed to book my desired time-slot and following a quick drink and a bag of crisps, for energy, I was all ready for the start.

The lift doors were open and inside the compartment the walls were lined with a thick cloth and I remarked to the lift operator that he was in a padded cell today. Equally mad, I stood at the foot of the stairs awaiting the signal from the first aider/starter that the way was clear for my ascent.

After the first 100 steps, the counter clockwise spiral was taking its

My GPO Family: Trilogy Edition

toll and my head began to spin. I slowed my pace and by floor 17, I was looking out for the refreshment stop. Oh, that was supposed to be floor 16! As no one had dragged me away to have a rest, I continued on, keeping a more careful watch for the floor numbers. At about floor 28, I slowed to get my breath, knowing that just six more flights was achievable.

By 9 minutes 42 seconds it was all over as the rather cloudy view from the 34th floor confirmed that I had made it! I was well pleased with that time. It wasn't my fastest, but I'd beaten last year's effort. The windows were rain splattered, although I could see the Wembley 'halo' shining in the distance. I stopped to eat my sandwiches on the 34th, but before I could finish my Coke, we were asked to return to the foyer as the staff were going to lunch. As I left the tower it wasn't raining, so I jumped on the Tube to Monument, hoping to get some shots of Mondial House demolition, but by then it was absolutely tipping it down, so I turned back and headed for Liverpool Street and the train home.

I'd set up a *Just Giving* webpage and collected £45 via that, plus £248.50 in generous donations from friends and colleagues across BT. Denise Gates and Sharon Phillips very kindly circulated my sponsor form and collected £85 in the Bournemouth Onebill office, and the final tally was an impressive £293.50 for ChildLine.

By 2008, I was working in Brentwood *Workstyle* building and my colleague, Catherine Ralph had expressed an interest to visit the BT Tower. Coincidentally, I spotted a forthcoming event for the ITP (Institute of Telecom Professionals) Midland Region for a coach trip from Birmingham to London to visit the tower. A few polite words with the organiser and I arranged to meet them at the tower, with my guests Catherine and Paul. Brian Storer, a senior BT property manager lead the tour…

Post Office Tower

What a fantastic day out! (ITP 2008)

Although this wasn't my first time up *The Stick* it was still thoroughly enjoyable. The tower is a wonderful experience starting, as always, by trying to fit the whole building into the viewfinder of one's camera, while invariably standing rigid against a lamppost and trying not to move. Then in the lift, hearing the conversations of how many people's ears have popped as the car whizzes towards the 34th floor. And, of course, the breathtaking views of London as you look down on the Millennium Wheel, and other landmarks far, far below.
Brian's talk was most informative and really made a point of why we were there; not just to look out of the window, but to marvel at the pace of technological change that has taken place since the tower was first opened in 1965. And how the new developments have been integrated into the building, both socially and practically. Indeed, the tower is a strange mix of very old, e.g. the MDF blocks and very new, e.g. the orange fibre links. The original fabric of the building hides twisting passageways and staircases in a vast complex maze of lower floors, which lead off *The Stick*. The transition from old to new is striking as the corporate areas are so lavish by comparison, albeit crammed into the limited space of what still is, very much, a working building which in many aspects has been made obsolescent by the pace of change in the last 40 years!

Brian led us along many of the twisting staircases, and more than once!! It was slightly tiring, but really was a rare and privileged opportunity to see sections which aren't normally seen by corporate visitors. Watching the children run round and round the 34th floor, made me wonder if they understood just how lucky they were to be invited and if they would remember, 40 years on...

My GPO Family: Trilogy Edition

The TV Control was a showcase by itself, but the scale of the operation was perhaps diminished. The programmes displayed on the multiple screens were being fed from all over the world, but compared to the view over London, 30 floors above, I know which one I'd prefer. It's no wonder that a visit to the tower is simply out of this world. I would have loved to stay longer and seen more behind the scenes, but it was all credit to Brian that he was able to have taken so many people on such an extended tour. It really was exceptional.

An Aerial View

Fun as it is, the tower is a working building and an aging structure which has to be maintained. It may be for this reason that the aerials and associated equipment didn't form part of the 2003 Grade II listing status. The changing character of the building is true to the very nature of the tower in that it has evolved over the years, as communication technology has improved.

At the opening in 1965, the tower had four pairs of very large horn aerials which carried microwave traffic to four compass points:

"From London towards Birmingham, Coventry and the North; toward Southampton, Bristol and the West and also for the satellite communication ground station at Goonhilly Downs; toward Dover, Folkestone and the Continent; and toward Norwich and the North-East of England."

By the 21st century, the upper galleries were crammed full of aerials of every size and type; the external appearance of the tower looked very different to its 1960s profile. Silently, unnoticed, technology had moved on with underground fibre optic cables carrying far more calls and data than the microwave links ever

Post Office Tower

could.

The original horn aerials were thought to have been taken out of service between 1981 and 1986. Each of these pyramidal horns weighed 1 ton and were 27ft. high by 14ft. wide. The radiating aperture was enclosed by a Hypalon-coated *Terylene* sheet, which allowed the aerial and waveguide to be pressurised, by dry air, to keep the cover taut and to prevent the ingress of moisture. The air compressors were left operating to preserve the condition of the obsolete horn aerials, but a point was reached when it was no longer possible to maintain this equipment and thus the covers became loose and the weather began to erode the structures. Notably, DuPont ceased producing Hypalon® and closed the plant in April 2010.

Thus in early December 2011 the five remaining original horn aerials were removed for health and safety reasons. And 24 'modern' circular dish aerials, which were in service between 1986 and 2006, were also dismantled, leaving the galleries devoid of core aerials. It was expected that only a range of small aerials, for outside broadcast uses, would still be operational.

The tower continues to evolve and surprise as London too changes around it. Elaine Harwood of *English Heritage* once said,

"The slimness of it and the way that nothing was demolished to create it. It sneaked up right in the middle of Georgian London's townscape. It doesn't disturb historic London, it just adds to it."

50 Years of the Tower (2015)

As the '50th anniversary of the Tower' approached, I was wondering when my next visit might be feasible, as visits were still

My GPO Family: Trilogy Edition

like gold dust. I didn't have long to wait, as a renewed contact with the ITP (Institute of Telecom Professionals) via Facebook revealed that their schedule of *Insight* visits included a July trip to the tower. Places were strictly limited in number, so I had to write a 'tie-breaker' text to justify my place.

"A trip to the Post Office Tower is like none other. It encapsulates the essence of the 'white heat of technology' of the early 60s, but it still represents BT at the cutting edge of technology, with its LED display and continuing popularity as BT's public image. It's a unique blend of old and new and is a joy to behold. I've walked the stairs for charity, but I'd love to see some of the older parts which have been untouched by the decades of change! I'll give you a nice write up on my website too."

A few weeks later, it was very exciting to receive an e-mail from Adam Oliver (ITP CEO on secondment from BT), confirming my attendance!

I wrote a report of my special visit for the Telecommunications Heritage Group (THG) Journal…

50 Ingenious Years of BT Tower (2015)

This year is the 50th anniversary of the Post Office Tower which was operationally opened on 8 October 1965. It was built in the era of the 'White Heat of Technology' in the decade of Concorde, Apollo, the launch of BBC2 and the escalating Cold War. Constructed with 'Crown Immunity' the tower had to fit the constricted site which was available and was intended primarily as a working building rather than the massive tourist attraction which it quickly became. The tower was the hub of a communications network of microwave links, transmitting television and telephone

Post Office Tower

signals throughout the UK. Following the bomb explosion on the 31st floor in 1971, the public viewing galleries were closed, although the *topofthetower* restaurant, with spectacular view across London, operated by Butlins Ltd was allowed to continue until the lease expired in 1980. The Post Office chairman, Sir William Barlow affirmed...

"I would like everybody to realise the Post Office Tower is closed to the public for viewing and I'm afraid it's closed for good."

Today, more stringent fire, safety, and security regulations mean that it isn't viable to re-open either the restaurant or the building to the public, except for special events. Corporate visitors and guest numbers are strictly limited, though the tower has remained a national icon of BT and the UK. Some lucky THG members visited the tower in 2003, but requests for visits are numerous and opportunities to join a tour are rare. You can imagine my excitement when Adam Oliver, CEO of the ITP (on secondment from BT), wrote on Facebook, of a forthcoming 'behind the scenes tour' of the BT Tower, for ITP members. [The Institute of Telecommunications Professionals was previously the Institute of Post Office Electrical Engineers.]

I filled out the on-line *survey monkey* for the ITP tour, together with the tie-breaker answer of why I wanted to visit the tower, crossed my fingers and prayed for God's Poor Orphans (GPO). Then the waiting in anticipation began. First the e-mail to confirm my application, then the news that the event had been heavily over-subscribed. Would I be lucky? Yes!! I'd watched TV clips of Tony Benn and Charlie Luxton exploring the heights of the tower and hoped that I'd soon be following in their footsteps.

Our tour started in the foyer which links Museum exchange to *The Stick* (aka tower). As we climbed the stairs to the fourth-floor TV

My GPO Family: Trilogy Edition

Media Centre, Adam had already started snapping photos as a unique keepsake for the day. The team lead by James Mellor explained the standards and transmission rates of terrestrial HD TV and a typical end to end path from programme source to audience delivery, both for Freeview and BTTV. We discussed bandwidth against definition, network transport, resilience and cost. We had a brief overview of Agile Media, and RIDE (Recorded Information Distribution Equipment), which protects BT's switched voice network against overload when live TV phone-in votes are cast. There was a lot of information presented, but with opportunities for us to participate in exercises it was more akin to an informal seminar. The blinds of the adjacent room were then raised and we briefly looked in on the TV Media Centre which was filled with vast arrays of TV screen feeds, currently being monitored for quality, switching and scheduling. Feeds typically come into the tower from multiple studios and other programme sources for onward transmission throughout the UK via BT's core routers.

Back at ground level we donned helmets before descending into the semi-darkness via a vertical ladder which led into the catacombs, a maze of passageways between the solid foundations of the tower. Pipes and cables crossed above on gantries, while lightning conductors and earth bonding ran beneath our feet. Stooping low to pass through the cut-outs we emerged onto the pyramid (a vast sloping mass of concrete) and walked along a narrow wooden platform with a rickety handrail! It was a most unusual set-up, but the tower is no ordinary building and its foundations ensure stability and rigidity on the soft London clay base. For such an impressive structure, I may have expected the base to extend wider, but the site is very constricted and close-up it is difficult to comprehend the scale of the engineering. As I climbed the ladder back to the surface, I was reminded not to follow too closely to the person above, for want of getting kicked in the face. It was

Post Office Tower

important to pay attention throughout our tour as this was no office party! Thanks to our helmets our heads emerged unscathed as we then squeezed into the North Lift to ascend *The Stick*.

At level 14 we alighted to enter the disused TV control floor which was full of *Light Straw* painted racks of transmission kit. Of particular note were the units with metal telephone dials and *Trimphone*-type handsets. Time had almost stood still, though some much later blue/grey racks contained audio codecs. The curved wall of the core displayed a large chart, of plastic press-on letters, which detailed circuit routes and frequencies. Above the old control desk, a modern section of drop-ceiling acoustic tiles looked distinctly out of place. It was apparent that the available floor space was very limited and would not lend itself to other uses. It was just an amazing step back in time, as the technology of the tower spans 50 years of communications history.

Another short ride in the lift and we then stepped out onto one of the open aerial galleries, which are slowly being populated with new microwave dishes. For safety, we were warned not to stand too close to the live equipment. Our rigger expert pointed out the old metal supports which had held the original horn aerials, which were removed in 2011. Voids in the floor allowed cables to pass between galleries. The metal segments on the edge of the platform, although only just below my shoulder level, felt to be an inadequate barrier to falling hundreds of feet, in a gale-force wind! It was a calm, though slightly hazy day which gave a surreal feeling of standing in the open with such an otherwise unrestricted panorama of London. For our individual photo shots and record of the event, Adam instructed us to stand, back facing the edge of the platform. Back a bit further, don't trip on those pipes! It was a friendly, fun atmosphere and there was really no reason to feel ill at ease. Wow, I was standing on the aerial gallery of the tower! I thought better of

My GPO Family: Trilogy Edition

poking my head over the side to look down, as we had yet to conquer the roof and I didn't want to be phased part-way through the tour!! Adam held the camera high above his head while telling me to hold my tie in place for a good image. Click, flash, OK, onto the next one; we were on a tight schedule, as the afternoon tour had to follow us later!

On the 36th floor we exited the lift into the kitchen area where the staff were preparing lunch for my BT colleagues who were lucky enough to be dining on the 34th. The tower is always a hive of hidden activity and so much is crammed into a comparatively small working area. Another flight of spiral stairs led us to a vertical ladder with open treads. One of the team remarked that you could look down at the floor as you climbed, but the excitement of the moment spurred me on to complete the task and reach the landing. There was another ladder after this, but everyone was acting sensibly and there was no pressure to rush. It was a big step through the hatchway onto the roof, though the riggers were there to help if necessary and it was wonderful to finally be standing on the top of the tower. The sides of the tower were much deeper and wider here so there was no chance of looking directly below, but at this height the view of London was all around us.

A (1998) quote from Tony Benn (Postmaster-General who was responsible for the building when it was part of the GPO) sums it all up...

"Well this of course is the best view of all, from the very top of the tower, you don't have the windows. And you see the whole city (of London) and all the various monuments. There's St. Paul's Cathedral, where they worship God, and next to it is the Bank of England, where they worship money. And of course, all buildings symbolise for people, what it is they really worship, and I

Post Office Tower

suppose... Today, society worships communication, television, radio, mobile phones, Internet - It is communication that symbolises this period of civilisation, combined with the money-men."

While everyone was busy getting shots of London below, our rigger guide in full harness climbed the aerial mast to get a bird's eye photo of us all. Wow, the event had been very carefully planned to give us a most enjoyable trip whilst ensuring the safety of everyone in what continues to be a very operational building. We still had to descend those tricky ladders, but it really had been a 'once in a lifetime' chance to explore the places where few had trodden before. Thanks to BT and the ITP for making it possible.

I was thrilled to see an edited version of the above article appear in the ITP's *TELECOMS professional* July/September 2015 edition.

To me, the Post Office Tower will always hold a special wonderment of a Sixties' daydream come true.

GPO

The Post Office Tower was opened by

The Right Honourable Harold Wilson OBE MP
Prime Minister

on the 8th October 1965

Wording of the plaque which once hung in the foyer.

My GPO Family: Trilogy Edition

The author on one of the high-level aerial galleries of BT Tower (2015)

Outlet 16: Bleeping Computers

However non-sentient, machinery and computers always appear to have a built-in characteristic with which their human operators can identify. This may be a particular sound or a quirk of the operating system which makes them particularly memorable.

My first glimpse of a large programmable computer was on a day trip from secondary school to Essex University in 1975. A whole roomful of equipment was running to operate PAT (Parametric Artificial Talker) which spoke a very clipped style of English.

'One of the activities which you will see demonstrated is concerned with the generation of speech directly from English text. The system uses several computer programs running on two of the Department's computers (Digital Equipment's PDP9 and PDP11) and an analogue synthesizer which was designed and built within the Department.'

It was all rather James Bond (*Diamonds are Forever*), but at the time showed just how far away reality was from science fiction. The steady whirring of the disc drives and humming of the power supplies gave the impression of a powerful system, although the equivalent processor power and phonetics would soon be contained within a tiny silicon chipset and used for announcements on *System X* telephone exchanges.

On a visit to Westcliff library in 1977, I borrowed *Telephony* by Atkinson, volumes 1 and 2, to get an insight into the workings of the public telephone system or PSTN (Public Switched Telephone Network), as I later discovered it was named. Atkinson's seemed very dated and didn't appear to reflect the evolving electronics world, but the 'click-click-click, step by step' Strowger system had

My GPO Family: Trilogy Edition

hardly changed since the book's first impression in 1948. In comparison, the library had already dispensed with its long trays full of cardboard tickets. Stick-on barcodes now adorned the inside of the books, which were scanned with a light-pen, and a beep (confidence tone) was heard to signify that the computer had accepted the data. From afar, one could almost tell how many books were being checked-out by counting the number of beeps! The steady beeps, while useful confirmation of a working system, may have been somewhat irritating to the staff who had to listen to it all day, every day?

At college our 'mini' computer was a phone call away, at Chelmer Institute. The dial-up line was used by placing the telephone handset into an acoustic coupler, so that the tones (pulses of data) sent by the remote modem could be directed to our modem. Plug-in phone sockets and modems weren't commonplace back then, hence the use of the acoustic coupler box. In turn, the data operated a *Teletype* terminal which printed BASIC or FORTRAN programmes on a continuous roll of paper, or punched paper tape. The teletype made a clattering noise as it printed characters across the page and the stepping of the tape reader added to the impression that work really was in progress! There was always a humorous element to any session; simply that you had to type *BYE* to log-off.

"Dial-up users please BYE and wait for complete log-off message!"

Electronic and electro-mechanical machines had their own vocabulary and were becoming more-quirky!

Mainframe computers of the 1970s ran mostly payroll and accounting programmes. On a visit to the Computer Operations Division (COD) of my local Customs and Excise in Carby House, I

Bleeping Computers

first saw those (washing machine size) disc drives that were used to store large amounts of data. The thought of being in charge of all that equipment and computing power was exciting, though the level of maths needed to comprehend it was stretching both my ability and attention span!

In America on Ma Bell's telephone network, *Captain Crunch* was blowing his cereal packet whistle to imitate switching tones and place a free telephone call. *Touch-Tone* phones in the States sounded tones as you pressed each button and you could play a tune, given the right sequence of keys! Trunk calls in the UK used a different type of signalling and DTMF (Dual-Tone Multi-Frequency) phones weren't yet available.

In the UK, the keys of early press-button phones (circa 1980) had a 'fall-through' action, so that 'confidence tones' weren't essential to confirm that a button had been depressed. In any case, the UK signalling was decadic as many exchanges still used step-by-step switching. Intelligence was slowly being added to exchanges and one afternoon I was given an explanation of *Star Services*, which used the * and # buttons, on the 'new' *Statesman* telephones to signal to a programmable 'black box', which was an overlay on Southend Main's TXE4 exchange. *Star Services* allowed customers to programme their own reminder calls, three-way calling and other facilities in advance of the conversion to a System X or Y digital exchange. However, it was not until the mid-1990s that *Touch-Tone* signalling (and fast-call set-up) became commonplace on the BT Network.

Prestel

In 1979, *Prestel*, the Post Office Viewdata service, which used a modem to receive and send data over a phone line to a modified

My GPO Family: Trilogy Edition

TV, had just been launched. The idea of extra rental for the service, plus phone call access charges, plus page view charges made it appear less than ideal. *Ceefax* and *Oracle* teletext services provided by the BBC and ITV, didn't need a phone line and were free. The speed of page accesses was slow on all these systems, but they were the forerunners of the information revolution into the home.

I'd seen a demo of *Prestel* during my time in Traffic. It was available in Southend Area from October 1980. In Sales, I had details of how to use one of the *Prestel* sets and how to issue ANs to provide or cease the service. I seem to recall issuing a customer order for a Jack 96 to use with *Micronet* or one of the spin-off home banking services, a few years later.

One of my stalwart BT friends, Jason Ford, started his career in *Prestel* HQ, which was located in the former National Telephone Company (NTC) building in Temple Avenue, Embankment, EC4. The Grade II listed building dates back to 1900 and is resplendent with ornate figurines. Recalling his time in *Prestel* billing, Jason still wonders in disbelief at the reams of correspondence he had with customers disputing a 2p frame view charge!

One of his other responsibilities was operation of the massive bill enveloping machine which had a multitude of levers, flaps and buttons. Envelopes were stacked at one end, as the bills were fed through, folded, enveloped, moistened and sealed at the other. As a consequence, a trip to the pitch-black stationery store in the basement to collect another batch of envelopes was not without its trepidations. The ancient gates on the manually operated lift had to be pulled hard across before the whirring of the motor could be heard as the lift slowly descended through decades of grime which was visible through the criss-cross gates. Upon exiting, a few steps forward were needed to locate the light switch, always with the

Bleeping Computers

hope that no malevolent being was lurking in the darkness to grab hold of his arm. The thoughts of an 18-year old working alone tended to wander! Jason was diligent in his work and when tasked with re-indexing a bank of 12 horrendously untidy, four-drawer filing cabinets, he was later reluctant to allow his new system to be disrupted by others.

Computers in the Telephone Area

The 1980s heralded the widespread development of computer applications in British Telecom. Billing and Payroll programmes were already running on remote mainframes, and now everything else was under consideration! This was made possible by higher speed comm links to the remote centres and networked mini-computers in Area Offices. Small business computers enabled many more projects. This too spawned a multitude of new acronyms as each system was named. SPRET (Spare Plant RETurn), ACES (Accounting Control of Engineering Stores), ASM (Area Stores Module), NAS (New Accounting System). PRISM (Personnel Related Information Systems for Management). MICROTEX was the computerisation of Area Telex billing. These multitude of systems were eventually incorporated into sub-programs within CSS (Customer Service System), or were simply superseded by new working practices.

MOH

In our Sales Office (circa 1984), the MOH (Mechanisation of Order Handling) modems to the remote computer centre were BT type 30B operating at a giddy 9.6 kb/s via dedicated PWs (Private Wires)! This transmission speed was however adequate to send (in just a few seconds) an AN (Advice Note) to the Mainframe for storage and later retrieval. As back-up in case of PW failure, double

My GPO Family: Trilogy Edition

dial-up modem circuits were provided by two 'phones lines per PW. I seem to recall that when we needed the standby lines, a local cable fault prevented their use!

The MOH computers weren't noticeably noisy, as the air-con for the computer room made a steady rushing sound. The contract and advice note printers made a cacophony of zipping and trundling as three or four machines started up at almost the same time and sounded as though they were racing to finish their printing first! When a PT7 (MOH computer) was reset, it was more obvious that it had been making a whirring noise, albeit masked by other sounds in the room. Computers weren't the silent boxes that films portrayed! The lights on the modems winked and blinked and the power lights glowed steadily, confirming all was running as it should. And it was always the absence of lights which said something was amiss.

CARD

CRR (Customer Rental Record) cards had been introduced as early as 1973 with the details stored on a remote mainframe computer and the cards printed off for periodic despatch to Telephone Areas. Within Eastern Region the CR cards displayed 6375 as the Southend Area. MOH was just one of the early computer systems which paved the way for access to some of the biggest databases in Europe. The CARD (Customer Apparatus and Rental Display) service (mid-1980s) replaced thousands of individually filed cards which revealed exactly what each subscriber was renting. Access to CARD in Southend was by typing SD75 from the MOH menu. SD was an age-old abbreviation for Southend, and 75 co-incidentally was part of the database code? CARD log-on was usually restricted to the home telephone area, so that looking up of data for another area was effectively restricted. The 6375 database code was also that of Southend's Private Circuit Billing area; computer systems closely followed established Telephone Area hierarchy.

Light Straw

BT Internet was a brand name which offered UK technical support, user forums and hobbyist chat, and a free personal web space. Users were encouraged to create their own pages, and awards were given for 'site of the month'. I learnt how to design and upload a web page and my home site was to be found at www.btinternet.com/~fyneview/. The ~ symbol (known as tilde) was included in the URL of all *BT Internet* addresses. My 'techie' friends were all building their own telecom related sites so I wanted to choose a unique name for mine. I discovered that telephone equipment racks had (since 1959) been painted *Light Straw* colour. Thus, in August 1997 www.btinternet.com/~fyneview/light.straw/ was born! By 1999 the *Light Straw Domain* (hosted by Magic Moments) was available at

www.lightstraw.co.uk

The early days of *Light Straw* were a real blast as the site had an on-line guestbook, for which I had painstakingly customised a free script, to e-mail me every time an engineer (or visitor) wrote in the book. Any '404 errors' also generated an e-mail addressed to the Officer in Charge! Hobbyist sites were well catered for in terms of support by the emerging ISPs. BT engineers loved my site and I even got a mention on my firm's internal news web page *BT Today* under the heading *Take a step back in Telecom's Time*.

My GPO Family: Trilogy Edition

Light Straw kit… (see Outlet 15: Post Office Tower)

GEC control equipment, with Trimphone handsets in the disused TV control centre on the 14th floor of the BT Tower (2015)

Outlet 17: ERNIE

In chapter one, I marvelled at the thought of illuminated prize numbers from the Electronic Random Number Indicator Equipment (ERNIE), which was built by the GPO. Early bond numbers such as 2FL could be thought of as 'two flashing lights' of the machinery.

As we often played board games which required the roll of a dice, my father 'borrowed' the battery-powered motor from my *Junior Engineer* kit and, with some tin foil, made a single wiper which rotated over some screw heads and thus selected one of six lights. The whole contraption was fitted into a wooden box and was a far cry from ERNIE, but it did pick numbers in a random manner!

[In 2015 I met a school friend, Roger Philbrick, who I had not seen for more than 45 years, and he instantly recalled a memory of this home-built device!]

I believe the six lights on the front panel were arranged in a circle and were, of course, 6-volt lamps from the 'free line signals' used in the telephone exchange.

It was fun listening to the radio on a Saturday and waiting for the announcement, *"This week's £25,000 prize winner lives in...and the bond number is ..."* Radio documentaries told me that ERNIE liked to live by the seaside at Lytham St. Annes; he was an endearing chap, although rarely seen!

In those days I dreamt of a big win to help the (preserved) Bluebell Railway extend its line past Horsted Keynes. It was to be another 40 years before I saw the real ERNIE and 45 years until the railway reached East Grinstead!

My GPO Family: Trilogy Edition

As technology developed and more people bought Premium ERNIE was replaced to enable the draws to keep pace with the demand. By 2004, ERNIE 4 had been launched and an article on the Science Museum website held my attention. It told of an exhibition at which all four versions of ERNIE were on display. I wrote to the Curator of Computing, Dr Tilly Blyth to express my interest in seeing ERNIE Mk1 as, like many 1950s devices, it was built on GPO racking.

26/08/2004

Dear John

I'm afraid the ERNIEs were only on display for one day - 17th August - the day of the launch of ERNIE 4 by National Savings and Investment. The Science Museum has components of Ernie 1 and 2 in its collections, but they are not on permanent public display but kept in our store at Wroughton near Swindon.

I am sorry that you missed the ERNIEs while they were on display at the museum - it was quite a sight to see four generations of the same machine since 1956. The event was also attended by some of the original GPO engineers who worked on ERNIE 1.

It is possible to view these machines if you were able to visit Wroughton.

Kind regards

Dr Tilly Blyth

Tilly confirmed that she would arrange for me to see ERNIE if I visited their Wroughton storage facility, but I was busy at work and it would have been a long train journey simply to see some disassembled kit. However, in September I wrote to NS & I, asking

ERNIE

for publicity photos of ERNIE 4. Elen Thomas, Media Relations Officer, kindly sent me a selection which included all four machines when they were on display at the Science Museum. Elen also suggested changes to my website so that it gave a clear message about the historical nature of the content and to refer to NS & I for current details. With the new photos and updates in place I forgot about ERNIE, apart from waiting patiently for the monthly prizes!

Meanwhile I was in contact with Phil Hayes, an engineer who was part of the Colossus Rebuild which was nearing completion at Bletchley Park. Colossus, a wartime code-breaking machine was designed by Post Office engineer, Tom Flowers who later headed the research team to develop ERNIE. In 2007 Phil sent me some photographs of ERNIE 1 at Wroughton as he was investigating a proposal for Bletchley Park to seek permission to restore the machine to working order. Phil suggested that the ERNIE which had been dismantled and stored at Wroughton was the standby machine and not the working one with console desk and teleprinter network. In the era, the winning bond numbers were printed out on teleprinters in the filing rooms which held the drawers and drawers of record cards on which the registered holders were detailed. A later comparison of the photographs with drawing EX 29990 highlights discrepancies in the layouts, although the machine may have been modified over the years?

At this point I wrote to Tilly to express my support with such a project as I knew that the rebuilt Colossus was already a very popular attraction at Bletchley and to see another GPO machine come back to life would be really fantastic! Mark Brooks of NS & I gave me access to publicity photos of ERNIE which I added to my website. And David Hay of BT Heritage arranged for me to see some of the original Research Reports and diagrams for ERNIE, for

My GPO Family: Trilogy Edition

which I passed on the references to Phil. I received a very detailed reply from Tilly who explained that such a project was under consideration, but there were, resource, museological and practical issues to overcome. A loan of an exhibit to (at that time) a 'non-accredited' museum would have been complicated. There are strict ethics regarding the conservation or restoration of an original object as well as how the artefact is explained to, and interpreted by the visitors. With Bletchley Park still being developed as an attraction, the Science Museum was far ahead in visitor numbers and would elicit greater publicity and popularity for an ERNIE display.

Reading between the lines I felt a little humbled as it was more than obvious that much discussion had already taken place between all of the interested parties and that any project would require extensive funding and specialist support! Nonetheless, I was pleased to have engaged with some of the key players and to have shown my enthusiasm. It all helps to nudge people in the right direction and to get them thinking of what may be achievable. It was clear that a replica rebuild of ERNIE was more likely to be a practical solution, although due to its technical nature it would have to be built at a location where the expertise and resources were available. Bletchley's computer museum was still seeking funding and it was already an onerous task for them to continue developing the associated code-breaking machines, such as Tunny and Heath Robinson, to complement and complete the Colossus theme. However, the Colossus rebuild engineers would have been ideally suited to understand the follow-on work of the Post Office which had created ERNIE Mk 1.

ERNIE

In 2008, I received an unexpected e-mail

Dear John

You may remember that you contacted us in 2004 regarding ERNIE (see the email below). I thought you might be interested to know that the ERNIE 1 will be opened on the 26th June 2008 on the second floor of the Science Museum. The exhibition is part of the permanent display, so it will be part of our History of Computing gallery for the foreseeable future. I do hope you will be able to visit the exhibition and see ERNIE 1.

Dr Tilly Blyth
Curator of Computing and Information
Science Museum

Now this was exciting and I was so pleased that Tilly had kept my details on file to include me in the guest list! Did I want to go to the ERNIE preview, YES, and I was able to get Annual Leave, so all was well.

Visit to ERNIE in the Science Museum (2008)

I'd been to the Science Museum (London) on several occasions but this event was scheduled for 09:00 so it meant an early start and battling with the rush hour Tube. Arriving unscathed, I was pleasantly surprised to meet David Hay (Head of BT Heritage) outside the entrance and we waited for the doors to open. I'd previously seen photographs and schematics of ERNIE, but it was still a wonderful a sight to see the full-height of the five racks assembled in a shiny new display case. Much time had been spent conserving the equipment though in places numerous hanging

My GPO Family: Trilogy Edition

sockets were a reminder that this was only a part of the whole installation, which would once have included a console desk, teleprinters, and extensive cabling to an equipment room. Nonetheless it was fantastic that the separate racks had been re-assembled and formed into a permanent exhibition.

After the introduction by Chris Rapley (Director of the Science Museum), Tim Mack (Head of Communications NS & I) spoke with great enthusiasm of ERNIEs past and present and thanked all those who had worked on the project to bring ERNIE into the Science Museum. A special guest was Jack Armitage, an engineer who had worked with ERNIE 1 when it was fully operational, so I made a special point of finding him and having a chat. Naturally, I caught up with him already talking to Tilly. Perhaps for them it was another day's work, but for me was it so thrilling to be with the people who had looked after ERNIE. Tilly is very engaging in her passion for technology and Jack perhaps doesn't fully comprehend how awesome the whole concept of ERNIE makes it a life changer for so many. Over the years, Jack had featured in many publicity shots and had become the continuity between all ERNIEs. Jack is very 'down to earth' and doesn't expect to be thought of any differently because of his special association with Premium Bonds, but it's testament to his hard work that he is highly regarded as a key player in ERNIE's long history.

Thanks to NS & I, the Science Museum, BT Heritage and all the support teams for working to put ERNIE on display.

Update
After more than seven years (2008-2015) on public display, the ERNIE Gallery at the Science Museum closed on 1 September 2015.

ERNIE (2015)

I've got a friend named ERNIE, he's not from *Sesame Street*,
But when the postman brings his letter for me I have to have a seat!

ERNIE likes the seaside along the Fylde Coast,
And he produces numbers which everyone can toast.

The power is on and gently humming.
A celebrity so soon is coming.

The switch is thrown and the draw is underway.
Who will win the jackpot, no-one there can say?

The lights on the serial number generators flash.
Each one is signifying an awful lot of cash!

As the numbers step through hundreds more
There's going to be prizes galore!

The teleprinter starts its run.
Isn't this just so much fun?

A knock at the door, is *Agent Million* calling?
Another non-prize month's appalling!!

But then the post comes through the door
I've won a prize again, once more!

My GPO Family: Trilogy Edition

ERNIE Mk 1 display at the Science Museum, London (2010). The ERNIE gallery closed on 1 September 2015.

Location

Outlet 18: Location, Location, Location

In the constantly changing world of British Telecom, being in the right location, with the right managers was always essential to ensure job security. As senior managers re-located, work functions tended to move with them, whereas 'rank and file' staff remained in an Area and re-trained for whatever jobs were available. The onset of computer systems hastened this process as functions could be consolidated rather than retained at the numerous historically developed sites, which had once formed the GPO infrastructure.

Manchester

Manchester was a big Telephone Area, split (in 1967) into three areas, North, South and Central. It was also a fairly central location for British Telecom training with fast train connections to London, and good motorway links. By comparison, Southend Area was a backwater, though still an important player in the hierarchy of power! This was to become more apparent in later years of my work, but for Sales it was a key place to be trained.

Manchester 1983

Eve Allen and I were the only two candidates from Southend for the scheduled three-week Sales training course which was to take place in Manchester. This was to be somewhat of a proving exercise as we were given a list of bed and breakfast establishments and told to make our own arrangements. We were to be in different training groups, but at least we could travel together on day one. Costs would be reimbursed and we could apply for an imprest, but this was not going to be a luxury break!

I'd been away from home for a week when I was at college, but a

My GPO Family: Trilogy Edition

three-week stint on a training course was going to be a big adventure. Our train tickets were on a 'warrant' (a ticket much larger than today's travelcards). I'd not travelled on the Tube before and Eve didn't want to lug her heavy case about, so we opted for a taxi across London. Our mainline train was out of Euston and the two-hour journey to Manchester Piccadilly seemed to take an eternity!

British Telecom, London Road, Manchester was, and still is, a landmark building being a typical 1970s concrete-monstrosity at the junction of several main roads. *Victory House* was designed in 1969 to be a hotel, but tax relief legislation changed after completion in 1973. It was sold to the Post Office for £3.75M in 1976 and by 1979 all 600 staff had transferred from the old Whitworth Street location, which had been the north-west HQ since 1939. BT vacated during 2004 and the building was converted to a hotel in 2007! A unique feature was the 'ledges' formed around the outside of the building so that window cleaners could access, walk along (in harnesses), and clean any floor.

The route to my lodgings, the Kempton House Hotel, was a bus ride away in Chorlton-cum-Hardy. Way back then a weekly cardboard *Clipper* ticket could be used in lieu of cash on the bus, which was very convenient and useful to travel into town at lunchtimes too! Of a morning, the bus stopped opposite BBC New Broadcasting House (built 1976) in Oxford Road, and it was then a five-minute walk through the university sites and up through the subway of Mancunian Way to arrive at 'work'.

There was a bank of phones with acoustic hoods in the corridor of Telecom House and we queued to make calls to our homes. No mobile phones back then! In the guest houses we could ring the operator and ask for a *Service Call,* which was really a free call on

Location

official business – I think the TI (Telecom Instruction) allowed all officers a few of those!

Taxis were the most convenient way to travel around, especially with three or four people sharing, though we had a spot of bother with a minicab driver not knowing the way at one point; I think we were lucky he didn't crash the car, as his driving was erratic. A wiser colleague told us to always ask for a 'Bomber' taxi cab, i.e. a 'Black Cab', as then there would never be a problem. Our class had a meal out; I think my steak was underdone! On other days we saw an early evening flick at the pictures, *An Officer and a Gentleman*, but probably the best was the play, *Educating Rita* starring Annie Tyson and Alan Moore, which was running at the Library Theatre.

Telecom House was a longitudinal building and I seem to recall that you had to walk through other sections to get to the training rooms, though this was the case with the later *Workstyle* premises, as was Brentwood, but that again is another chapter!

Sales Office 87

British Telecom's in-house training was supplemented by external consultants' courses which were usually held off-site. One of these was *Sales Office 87*, in Felixstowe. Run by freelance trainers who had an appreciation of our company's inner workings, these forums encouraged lateral thinking which often led to proposed changes deliberately in conflict with traditional working practices. I imagine at a higher management level, these would have formed the beginnings of 'outward bound' events! Such early 'brainstorming' sessions would later beget Total Quality Management (TQM) and 'continuous improvement'!

Working in small groups we had to plan, and later present, a new or

My GPO Family: Trilogy Edition

better way of answering phones, gaining sales or increasing revenue. We were fully aware that revised processes would have to be agreed both by local management and the unions, but these exercises were just another part of 'playing the GPO game', so we had to indulge in them!

I was always a little wary of activities 'away from the desk', but this event was quite fun as there were sweets as rewards and the winning teams shared a bottle of champagne. The facilitator helped us build our confidence, while stretching the boundaries of our capabilities. Quirky rules meant that a few of us had to wear coloured silk bow ties for our presentation. Goodness, I could barely lace a tie, and stood no chance of being able to form a proper dicky bow! Luckily one of the pretty girls assisted me. These collaborative exercises weren't so bad after all.

Manchester PCB

By the turn of the century, Southend was one of three dedicated PCB (Private Circuit Billing) sites in the UK; the others were Wolverhampton and Manchester. Admin of the system was controlled from Manchester as were many residual functions which were key to our billing processes. Manchester was once again centre of our universe, managed by colourful characters such as Rockie Lee, Terry Tobin, Isobel Wilson, Darren Nixon, and headed by Chris Pearson!

On occasions, I went 'head to head' with several of these endearing people who didn't always quite appreciate that I was championing my customer to adjust a bill, whereas they were attempting to maintain the integrity of the billing system! Rockie and Terry were highly intelligent technical bods, several pay grades above me, and were sticklers for the correct processes to be followed. They

Location

innately understood the operation of every part of the software and were somewhat unforgiving of operator errors! I tried their patience many times, but they usually performed a system fix to allow my job to run.

Chris headed up the PQC (Process Quality Council) with the aim of better procedures, higher cust-sat and increasing revenues. As a senior-manager she ruled like the Iron Lady, but was sympathetic to team members who worked hard and participated in the improvement processes. Ultimately her job was no more secure than anyone else's and I think she left the firm before the accountant's axe fell. It was somewhat sad to learn of people with such drive and passion for their job becoming pawns in the Top Team's strategies, but the realities of big business are harsh.

PQC

The PQC group usually met in Manchester, but keen to be 'transparent', it alternated location every few months to Southend. Non-managers were invited to sit in and give feedback to the decision-making process, but these were long meetings and not many people were interested in taking part.

Angela G wrote... *"All, please see below some interesting feedback from John from his attendance at the PQC. Everyone that has attended so far has given positive feedback and John has captured his own impressions below. This might help to reassure those of you that think it is a scary event! I wish more people were prepared to come out of their comfort zones and give it a go."*

PQC Report (2004)
When I was asked to attend the PQC to be held in Southend on 9 June, I did wonder if this was going to be just another meeting?

My GPO Family: Trilogy Edition

As observers, on this occasion, we had to wait until a presentation had finished before we were invited into the meeting. This might have been a bit daunting, but as Chris Pearson welcomed us personally, it did feel that instead of being an interruption to something already in progress, we were more positively, valued guests whom they had been waiting to meet. Indeed, we were, and as introductions went round the table it was evident of a friendly, but business-like atmosphere where the managers were probably as curious about us, as we were to see how they spend their time!

Chris explained that some of the terms and abbreviations might be unknown to us and to speak up if things didn't make sense! Looking at the agenda it was obvious that the forum was well established. And as each manager reported back on his or her action points, it became clear that an awful lot of preparation goes on beforehand to give an accurate snapshot of work in progress for each function/responsibility.

This was an insight into 'the wider picture' whereby the 'top team' get valuable feedback, as to the debt and corres cases on hand. OK, 'stats, for stats sake' you might think, but you would be totally wrong! The PQC goes much further than that and encompasses a complete series of improvement plans, to address regulatory compliance, failures in processes, new product launches, system deficiencies and best working practices. In turn, this enables us to deliver the *My Customer* promises, customer satisfaction, debt collection and cashflow targets, as well as staff motivation and performance.

The objectives are clear; we are running a business to produce and collect billed revenue while delivering the services that our customers expect. If we are not performing, the fixes need to be in place to achieve this and very simply this is what the PQC is all

Location

about. It follows that the improvement plans are not restricted to Private Circuit Billing, as work impacts on COSMOSS, CAMSS, and SIEBEL to name just a few of the systems which extend both outside of billing and across of Lines of Business.

The meeting was an ideal opportunity to see the process making at work, with the chance to ask questions and suggest changes that really could make a difference to the way we do our jobs. You could be sceptical and think that budget restrictions might limit a valued suggestion. Of course, the only sure way to find out, is to be a privileged visitor at the next meeting and see for yourself.

After reading my submission, Terry Smee wrote…
"Chris, how about this for feedback! Fantastic stuff."
I certainly scored a few brownie points with that report!

And London (2005)

SPOC (Single Point of Contact) Billing work was high profile and because I spoke confidently during an information gathering interview, I was invited to join a 2-day seminar at BT's offices in the Angel Centre, London. Senior managers led the event with a serious objective to improve billing best practices, but it was also quite an informal meeting. It included several colleagues from our Manchester office. Over the years, I'd spoken to a majority of folks on the telephone and it was quite fun to meet them in person!

Those who know me will realise that I'm quite a reserved person, and not always comfortable at social events. The team had to meet up in the bar of our hotel before going onto dinner later. As I tend to be early, I was hanging about in the foyer waiting for the next person to arrive so that we could group up. Of course, the first person to get out of the lift was one of the real lookers, sexy as hell,

My GPO Family: Trilogy Edition

who I'd never dream of meeting in a bar! So, with some aplomb, I strolled up to her and said, *"Hello Sandra"*, and she did a double-take before casually replying *"Oh John, it's only you. For a moment, I thought someone was trying to pick me up!"* How do women do that, they just always know?!

The team dinner was nothing to write home about, as the service was late as I think it was nearly 21:00 before the main course was out. I remember sharing a taxi with Howard Mapley and although he wasn't the most popular Manchester manager, he did have the sense to get us safely back to the hotel.

I caught up with Howard again in 2012 when he was managing N3 NHS Global Billing, and he kindly provided assignment work for me. Manchester had begun my career in Sales, so it was fitting that one of my last assignments also hailed from that area.

Telephone House Manchester (1983)

Outlet 19: Retrospective

Retrospective

Throughout my Telecom career I had dealt with the situations, events, customers, managers, and colleagues in my own unique way. It was the only way I knew. With hindsight, I may have played the game differently, though probably not significantly. As an only child, my game scenarios were limited; so many situations had not been previously rehearsed, or the outcomes anticipated.

My world of Post Office Telecommunications in Traffic had been a 'non-customer facing' environment, so the transition to Sales had taken a steep learning curve. I had to play the 'GPO game' for real and learn the rules of 'how to play', and what to do, and how to react. Over the years my knowledge of the working environment was sufficient to overcome any difficulties, until the latter part of my career when the rules were changed and my managers themselves were vulnerable to the relentless financial cuts. A headcount of 250k was gradually reduced down to 91.3k by March 2008 and then 70.9k in March 2015. (BT Annual reports.)

Often at APR (Annual Performance Review) time, my managers would remind me that other solutions apart from the 'John Chenery way' were possible, but then I never saw them, or if I did, I choose to ignore them? Other times, some managers endorsed my 'take' on the world, knowing it would always be consistent.

Allan Sammy wrote... *"John builds open and honest relationships with his customers and this can be seen from the many thanks he receives from the virtual resource teams and managers."*

Creating a good image was always vital. Of course, it worked both

My GPO Family: Trilogy Edition

ways and watching and realising what was going on in the office was all part of the experience.

The Office (2016)

The office was a microcosm, a self-contained world,
Where thoughts and emotions of the workers constantly swirled.

Executives power-dressing and putting on a face.
A clear-desk policy with nothing out of place.

Gaggles of females going for a break,
Some of them anxious a fag for to take.

Slightly older women, strutting up and down.
Others with a heavy workload, showing a constant frown.

Younger office juniors, having a subtle bitch.
Watch them walking from behind, how their bottoms twitch!

Older colleagues struggling, slowly up the stairs.
People outside the room, for which nobody cares.

Chatting across the desktop, a billing problem to solve.
When the Day's Debtors are so very old!

Middle-aged colleagues, with glasses on their noses,
Looking professional with many change of poses!

Shouts and exclamations when 'dress-down' Friday's here,
Especially at home-time everyone can cheer.

Retrospective

A snapshot in time, of our office, revealed a wide age-range of people at varying stages in their GPO careers. It was a mix of agency people, who tended to be younger, as they were the new intake. Another age band of staff who had worked their way up from telephonists and were closest to retirement. And a larger group of middle-aged who were about half way, or greater, through their working lives. Recruitment had been halted during certain periods, so the profile of ages was not an even spread. New blood into BT was from university placements at the elite end, and agency fill-ins and the lowest level. As work moved to new locations, long established workplaces tended to stagnate and begin the almost inevitable run down to closure.

Dress Down and Duvet Days!

Over the years, changes in culture and accepted dress codes of the Civil Service era gave way to new corporate rules and ideas of behaviour. In my father's time, he always went to work in a suit and tie. When I started as a CA, I wore smart trousers and a 'hacking' jacket, though for much of the day, the jacket was hung on the back of my chair. During my years in Sales and Billing, we were classed as 'customer facing' so smart dress was expected, although it was rare for us to meet customers in our office. In 2000 a restructuring of BT produced the following divisions:

BT, BT Net, Yell, Ignite, Concert, BT Wireless and BT Openworld.

Together with the new business organisation, Sir Peter Bonfield (CEO) stated *"We now have the dress code that you can wear whatever you like. We're a pretty relaxed lot in this new wave."*

After this announcement, certain senior managers were frequently

My GPO Family: Trilogy Edition

seen without neck ties! In our Billing team, the concession was the introduction of 'Dress down Friday' when a more relaxed code was tolerated. A few team members took to wearing shorts and flip-flops and had to be politely reminded that although our town was by the seaside, such sights should not be seen in the office!

Another change was the formalisation of ad-hoc days off. Annual Leave usually had to be booked well in advance. A/L at short notice had to be for an exceptional reason. However, in a bid to improve the Sick Leave record, the 'Duvet Day' concept was introduced. Speculation was that younger Call Centre staff with hangovers were ringing in sick to avoid having to face work the next day. A 'Duvet Day' was simply Annual or Flexi Leave which was booked (and authorised) on the day it was required. In theory, anyone requesting immediate A/L could remain under the duvet for that day! In practice, DDs still had to be justified and if your manager refused, due to insufficient staffing on that day, then you were expected to attend work without fail, unless you reported sick!

Who's minding the Store? (2015 rewrite)

Telephone exchange (premises) were once a showcase for the Post Office. Thousands of operators and engineers worked in them to ensure that calls got connected and essential equipment was maintained. Strowger, electro-mechanical kit had to be kept clean to function, otherwise noisy lines and failed connections would result. Floors were polished and yearly *Telephone Fortnights* presented an opportunity for the public to visit them and be shown how their calls were handled. In 1968, key buildings in London which could be regularly visited included the Post Office Tower, Faraday, and Fleet Buildings. At the dawn of the digital age (circa 1990) exchanges gradually became unmanned, almost empty shells, where the MDF (Main Distribution Frame) almost occupied more

Retrospective

space than the modernised switching kit. Gone was the sense of pride, as no one engineer was responsible for their tidiness. Shared duties and the pressure to jumper a job and be on to the next allowed no time for housekeeping. Cleaning of near empty floors was low priority and maintenance of the buildings became an expensive liability.

In earlier times, the infrastructure was continually growing, with exchange extensions and new buildings being required to house the vast switching matrices. Now the situation is reversed as digital equipment requires a fraction of the space and no engineers on site for maintenance. In December 2001, the bulk of the BT Estate was transferred to *Telereal* and leased back as a mechanism to dispose of buildings that were no longer fit for purpose.

"In December 2001, as part of a wider property outsourcing arrangement, BT completed the sale and leaseback of the majority of its UK properties to Telereal, a joint venture partnership formed by Land Securities Trillium and The William Pears Group. Around 6,700 properties were transferred totalling some 5.5 million square metres." [Quote from BT's Report 2002]

Mothballing of empty floors in operational buildings presumably impacts on accounting costs, though also reduces the availability of office space for meetings and the opportunities for staff to work locally. LLU (Local Loop Unbundling) has resulted in 'cuckoo's nest' compounds in some exchanges as interconnections to competitors' broadband equipment dictates. Multiple cellphone aerials also require access by the named providers. Add to this the contractors 'working on behalf of Openreach' and it's probably only the BT engineers who no longer see the inside of an exchange. In short, no one is minding the store!

My GPO Family: Trilogy Edition

Is there a future in the Past?

Following on from *Who's minding the Store? (Looking after our Infrastructure?)* we see how the past and the present synergies can enhance the BT Brand, making valuable assets of our legacy network of buildings and culture.

So, is there a future in the past?

For devotees of BT's Heritage (myself included) the answer is an unequivocal yes. And for the BT Brand, there is a sound financial case for investing in BT's rich history, as long-established businesses, with a proven track record, are naturally perceived as being more trustworthy and perhaps have better associations of those that provide a quality service.

Supporting the past pays dividends (literally) as many shareholders would love the opportunity to visit the Post Office (BT) Tower, which although vastly expensive, and perhaps a liability to maintain (with its listed status), is nonetheless our company's most iconic symbol of communications technology. And yet the tower is decrepit and of great age (like some of BT's workforce) but still it manages to thrill and delight its public with its agility as it stages ever more spectacular lighting events and informational messaging across London.

The tower is a prime example of how investing money and resources on both preserving and enhancing an historical icon can strengthen the BT Brand, while satisfying architectural fans of Eric Bedford and those who might wish for its re-opening. Of course, getting the work/life balance just right is key, and although the tower's microwave carrying days are long gone, it still has the *BT Vision* (TV feeds) and location, location, location to make a

Retrospective

difference in our changing world.

Other buildings which have played key roles in BT's development, such as Mondial House, have fared less favourably. Mondial was the brilliantly white, stepped 'typewriter/PC building' which once stood next to Cannon Street Station. In its time, it was one of the largest telecommunications centres in the world, when international calling and switching hit an all-time high. Built of concrete, when telephone exchanges needed acres of space, its unique ziggurat design, clad with fibreglass, did not manage to save it from the wrecking ball as its prime waterfront location made it an ideal candidate for a re-development sell-off. And that was the right decision, as who would want to queue up and pay to visit another aging, under-utilised concrete monstrosity. As always, getting the balance between the historical value, the money spent, and a financial return is the tricky part.

Like draughty outdated railway stations, which were never designed for information technology, yesterday's telephone exchanges are no longer 'fit for purpose' and ideally might be replaced by prewired boxes, air cooled, open to the elements like the current day electricity sub-station transformers, albeit with remote links to every CP (Communication Provider) for instant on-line *slamming! Indeed, the new (NGA) green cabs complete with DSLAMs get a step nearer to this dream.

* Slamming was a term which meant transferring a customer to another CP without their prior permission.

People enjoy holding onto the past and they can become very nostalgic and wish for the olden days. It's great watching an old black and white film of a favourite actor/actress (of your choice) unless you have to pay for it. And nowadays you realise that it's

My GPO Family: Trilogy Edition

not in HD or surround-sound and perhaps it wasn't as good as you remembered it? Old buildings can be lovely to study, view and visit, but if you have to work in them every day, their innate charm can quickly disappear.

Many of my colleagues collect 'heritage phones' and while these can be great for demos of 'how it used to be', transmission sometimes leaves much to be desired and dialling with an old-fashioned dial soon becomes a chore!

However, people connect and can readily identify with the culture and ethos of bygone times and this is a great attraction if it can be properly channelled. BT's Corporate Memory does this with a mix of statutory duty to preserve the (written) past and as an incentive of leverage to enhance the BT Brand. Media in the form of films, slides, audio recordings, books and posters can bring alive past working practices and quickly paint a picture of 'how it used to be' for the both scholars and the general (buying) public alike. Fortunately, BT has a Heritage Policy so that the work of preservation can continue, albeit within financial constraints. It is mainly for this reason that all of BT's physical artefacts are devolved to its Connected-Earth Museum Partners who are spread across the UK.

The Partner Museums still get some funding and a lot of support from BT, but apart from UAX type buildings and the odd trailer, I can't recall any complete exchange buildings in preservation. Of course, BT is running a business and thus any value-add from the heritage side is a bonus rather than a necessity. Faraday Building, in London is a good example of a working building which has been extensively cleaned and refurbished and has people (BT Wholesale) 'living above the store'. And the 'store' is consolidated frames from nearby exchanges which have been offloaded. Two

Retrospective

complete blocks of Faraday were demolished, the North and North-East Blocks. The North Block was originally an extension of the Post Office Savings Bank, dating back as far as 1890, so a lot of history may have been lost?

It's almost impossible to preserve enough physical history of BT without turning every exchange into a static museum-piece! But the Corporate Memory (like the *Borg* from *Star Trek*) is built from the collective working reminiscences of GPO/BT staff who have been 'living the BT values' and doing all the jobs, from post boys, through Strowger installation, senior management and datacomms to mention but a few. Through its Connected-Earth website and from (recorded audio) of face to face interviews with staff, BT attempts to capture this 'work practice essence' and share it in the digital world. It's a work in progress, and really needs everyone's help, to make it come alive, but through the right partnerships, it's beginning to gain more recognition.

As one part of the industry does its best to preserve historical records and artefacts, the commercial side is more starkly focused on the bottom line.

Post Office Telecommunications van poster (c1970).

My GPO Family: Trilogy Edition

Heritage Trail

The Post Office Tower during the 50th anniversary year: Andrew Emmerson remarks, "Upper 6 GHz microwave gear for links to Birmingham and Bristol. Note the *Type 62* racks finished in *Light Straw* paint, also the proprietary *GEC* labels in the dials."

Microwave link equipment on the 14th floor of the disused TV control centre of the BT Tower.

Heritage

Outlet 20: Heritage Trail

The Post Office's long history created a unique heritage trail of papers, obsolete equipment, old furniture and mothballed buildings, all fascinating to a current-day urban explorer! The modernisation of the UK Telephone Network with System X and Y exchanges started the rationalisation and downsizing of the long-established Post Office infrastructure which had been steadily growing for many decades.

Until the 1980s, BT's telephone exchanges required ever more space as demand for national and international calls continued to grow. Impressive, bold, new designs of switching centres in the capital had been built to cater for this growth, but already miniaturisation of digital equipment was beginning to free up exchange premises on a scale not previously encountered. Staff accommodation had been growing too as more people were required to handle the mainly paper generated orders for new services. This also was to dramatically change as computerisation of office tasks steadily made inroads with savings of scale and efficiency.

Strowger exchanges had been supplemented, and in some cases already replaced with electronic switches, such as TXE2s and the larger TXE4s, as well as (hybrid) Crossbar TXKs, but the modernisation programme was to replace them all in an Integrated Digital Network (IDN). This was a 20-year project to take the Telephone Service into the 21st century. The implications of this impacted directly on my day job as Sales and Billing geared up for the associated changes in products which could be offered and the manner in which they were charged. As one who marvelled at the workings of the Telephone Service, where time allowed, I sought to

My GPO Family: Trilogy Edition

investigate these programmes and to seek out, and record, some of the passing history.

Baynard House

Was a typical 1970s-styled concrete telecommunications centre which was constructed to include a council car park, office space, and a resources annexe. The first System X digital exchange, a Junction Tandem was installed in Baynard House in July 1980 and the digital roll-out programme was underway! Nineteen eighty-two was Information Technology Year, so it was appropriate that the *Telecom Technology Showcase* (later known as the BT Museum) opened in the annexe. Curator Neil Johannessen brought together exhibits from all over the UK to form this new, interactive and exciting, National Telecommunications Museum.

Seven Ages of Man

In the public courtyard of Baynard House is a totem pole type sculpture which celebrates the many historic links of the site. A plaque reads:

"This Sculpture commissioned by Post Office Telecommunications and created by Richard Kindersley after inspiration from Shakespeare's seven ages of man was unveiled by Lord Miles of Blackfriars on 23rd April 1980."

Seven heads are stacked one above the other, each rotated from its neighbour such that you need to walk around the pole to view every face and fully appreciate the complete work. This is a most unusual piece and rather symbolic too, as people of all ages use the telephone. [See my poem *Seven Ages on the Phone* at the front of this book.]

Heritage

Inside *Showcase*, young and old visited to learn of telephones through the ages. I particularly liked the 60s and 70s display cases, which were full of examples of those decades. On THG swapmeet days, I mingled with a cross-section of enthusiasts who relived the telephones of their youth. The Strowger rack could be heard clicking away to test calls made within the museum, while Neil warned us not to dial 999 on phones that were connected to the outside world! Graham, of the Collections Team, staffed the resource centre, while ladies wearing the latest corporate image clothing kept the shop open. On one visit, I bought a number of phonecards depicting the latest 007 film (*Goldeneye*), a selection of books and postcards, as well as a few *BT Museum* branded pencils!

The Telecommunications Heritage Group

In late 1986, with support from *Telecom Technology Showcase*, Andrew Emmerson, a Technical Press Officer with British Telecom, conceived a small independent organisation, the Telecommunications Heritage Group (THG). The THG's aim was to promote the study, preservation and collection of the heritage of communications. Not that I needed much encouragement, but an article in *Telecom Today* staff newspaper prompted me to join, and so it was that I drove to London to attend their inaugural meeting and swapmeet in November 1987. In those days their newsletters and journals were really focussed on the collecting and hobby scene, and as British Telecom dismantled its old exchanges, those of THG members expanded! Swapmeets were a great way to buy 300-type Bakelite phones at a reasonable price and to chat to fellow telecom enthusiasts. Over the years, I have attended many THG AGMs and related visits where the enthusiasm for old telephones never diminishes. There is always a black 332 waiting to be polished in the minds of THG members, though for some it can be difficult to comprehend that the GPO stores depots no longer exist

My GPO Family: Trilogy Edition

and that one day the last Bakelite phone will break. British Telecom's exchange modernisation plan gave much impetus to would-be heritage enthusiasts as they realised that the Strowger era of switching was fast disappearing!

Rationalising British Telecom

The exchange modernisation programme slowly gathered pace during the 1980s as both the analogue networks and the switching equipments were replaced with digital kit. This was a time of unprecedented change in hundreds of telephone exchanges as whole floors of Strowger switches were turned off and abandoned to wait for the scrap man. The digital replacements required only a fraction of the space. Conversions of large exchanges yielded more space, although at smaller exchanges (UAXs) the turnaround to have the new equipment fitted first required a lot of careful planning.

Strowger tended to be housed in the older buildings and the larger exchanges often had different generations of equipment practice with a mix of *Battleship Grey* and *Light Straw* racking and covers. Type 51 and 62 equipments could be found in associated transmission bays. Pre-2000 type selectors with decades of dust on the wiring co-existed with the later 2000-type variants of selectors, linefinders and integrated panels of LR and K relays. Thousands of miles of intricately laced wiring and soldered contacts were to be savaged beyond recognition as the digital dream swept away a long-established regime. Constant in all this was the MDF (Main Distribution Frame) which usually had new blocks fitted to the E side, but otherwise was left intact. Bulky overhead cable runs concentrated and dropped down into shiny new blue and grey cabinets. The mismatch between the very old and the new was apparent. *Light Straw* ringing machines still whirred away on the

Heritage

MAR (Miscellaneous Apparatus Rack) and the pendulums in the exchange master clocks continued to swing and step the slaves, save for where they had been removed! In GSCs (Group Switching Centres) where the noise of RTs (Register Translators) stepping and releasing would once have been almost deafening, there was silence! Racks of meters no longer clicked up the bills. In the PCM (Pulse Code Modulation) section, the kit was still humming as selected inter-exchange circuits were still in use. With lights still on in working areas, it was a twilight world of change as the guts (and heart) of many exchange was ripped asunder for the passive digital pathways.

New equipment racks had strip lighting as part of the design, but none of the travelling ladders which, for so many years, were a unique feature of any Strowger exchange. Gone was the *Light Straw* paintwork and cream cabling, as brightly coloured yellow trunking and orange (optical) fibre cables took its place. The changed environment was clean, tidy and noise-free, except for the rushing of the air-con which (in some cases) was now required for additional cooling! Whereas the function of each kit was once quite obvious, the now (mostly) anonymous cabinets gave little clues as to what was housed inside.

In Sales, I had to issue ANs to de-share any remaining shared-service lines as well as persuading RCB (Renters Coin Box) customers to change to a modern payphone with SPM (Subs Private Meter) pulses. Unlike the 700-type RCBs which were very robust, the equivalent range of new payphones were plastic-cased, desktop or wall mounted versions not so well-suited to the conditions under which they needed to operate. Plug, Socket, Telephones (PST) had only been introduced in 1981, so the new equipment portfolio was rather lacking in offering amplifying handsets or inductive couplers which had been developed over

My GPO Family: Trilogy Edition

many years to easily fit the old-style products.

The cut-over of an exchange from the old to new equipment had not happened on any large scale since the gradual conversions from manual to automatic working which had finished in the mid-1970s. However, with the prospect of 6000 plus exchanges requiring replacement over a period of 10 to 15 years, the task was substantial. Early in the programme, tie cables between the old exchange and the MDF (Main Distribution Frame) were left in place for a while, but as confidence in the new exchanges increased, the switchover process was speeded up by cutting the tie cables as the transfer proceeded. The process is well-explained by Dick Landau in British Telecommunications Engineering (BTE) journal Vol 11, Oct 1992 *Exchange Transfer: Challenge and Innovation*. I did ask if I could watch the change-over ceremony at one of my territorial exchanges, but the events were often fully attended by local dignitaries, area managers and the press. The remaining space was occupied by the engineers performing the transfers!

Adaptations of telephone exchanges into office space for staff provided adequate, but not ideal working environments and by the mid-1990s a mix of new out-of-town offices around the M25 were created to provide a higher-quality *Workstyle 2000* standard of accommodation. Additionally, new office blocks were commissioned and rented as the roll-out of digital exchanges and office computerisation lagged behind the increasing demand for telephone service. The task of matching accommodation to the equipment and staffing needs was a continuing and expensive problem.

"In December 2001, as part of a wider property outsourcing arrangement, BT completed the sale and leaseback of the majority

Heritage

of its UK properties to Telereal, a joint venture partnership formed by Land Securities Trillium and The William Pears Group. Around 6,700 properties were transferred totalling some 5.5 million square metres." [Quote from BT's Report 2002]

A few key sites in London were not included in the sell-off as it was realised that these would yield large sums if sold directly to developers. The iconic Post Office Tower was retained, as a TV switching hub and a corporate attraction.

Connected Earth

Throughout its long history, GPO telephone engineers enjoyed building up squirrel-stocks of old equipment and telephones which tended to be tucked away in the deepest recesses of exchanges. Some of these collections became official museums and were appointed curators within the organisation; Oxford Telephone Museum was a fine example. Others were organised by members of the IPOEE (Institute of Post Office Electrical Engineers) and were tolerated and encouraged by local management. These were all great places for educational visits; the Post Office at that time had a culture of 'show and tell' and was proud to display its history. This was reaffirmed with the opening of *Telecom Technology Showcase*.

With the exchange modernisation programme completed and an aging property portfolio, BT could no longer subsidise its official collections and thus the *BT Museum* at Blackfriars closed in 1997. Following its wholesale property sell-off in 2001, BT moved quickly to set up a virtual museum on the internet and so *Connected-Earth* was launched in the following year. It was decided to transfer any historical artefacts of interest or value to its external partner museums. A cull of all collections on BT premises culminated in the 'Sale of the Century' in 2003, whereby thousands of remaining items were either sold or skipped. Ample notice of the sale was given and BT invested millions of pounds to assist the partner museums in presenting professional displays. Telecom enthusiasts might consider this as the moment that BT disassociated itself from the physical care of its own history, and this is perhaps a consequence of it becoming a commercial enterprise rather than a public service industry? BT Archives continues to care for the ephemeral and electronic records of the company and is instrumental in identifying any key artefact which should be preserved. I and other THG members often help, to catalogue databases of historic records, such as circuit diagrams, and to raise awareness and promote the heritage culture.

Enfield CB1 (July 2012)

The Enfield CB1 switchboard had been in long-term storage and was destined to become a major exhibit in the new *Information Age* gallery of the London Science Museum for 2014. For a few months during 2012 the switchboard was on display in the *Dugdale Centre* where it was the centrepiece of an exhibition and event to gather memories of the exchange and its people. I went down there to meet some of my friends from the Telecommunications Heritage Group and of course to check out the switchboard!

Enfield CB1 was the last manual exchange in Greater London (London Telephone Area) when it closed on 5 October 1960. The CB1 (Central Battery) Sections Switch was introduced into the UK as early as 1901. Each section of three positions had a total of 17 cord circuits. The 'A Position' sections were for subscribers' lines. The 'B Position' sections were for incoming junctions. Enfield CB1 had 65 positions of the 'A Board' and 11 positions for the 'B Board', although only a few positions were secured for conservation.

Heritage

The CB1 was a tall switchboard with a large number of jacks per position. The top section had the *outgoing multiple to local subscribers*. The middle section had the *outgoing junctions to other exchanges*. The lower section had the *calling subscribers* or *answering jacks*. A Manual Board was used in the far-off days before subscribers had dials on their telephones.

When a customer wished to make a telephone call…upon lifting the handset, a calling lamp would light up against a dedicated, numbered, *answering jack* on the lower switchboard section. The operator would plug into the jack, thus answering the call and enquire, "Number Please?" If the number required was for another customer on Enfield exchange, the operator could simply connect the cord into the appropriate numbered jack in the upper section of the switchboard, the *outgoing multiple to local subscribers*. If the caller wanted a number other than Enfield, then the operator would plug the cord into the *outgoing junction to other exchanges* and either dial the required number, if the exchange was automatic, or ask the distant operator to connect the call.

Actually seeing the switchboard helped to make sense of it, as the idea of every single subscriber having a dedicated calling lamp appearance was difficult to envisage! The CB1 had smaller sized jacks than the later auto-manual boards, as so many jacks had to be accommodated into a workable area. Along the front of the keyshelf, in the operator's jack, was plugged not a modern headset, but a breastplate transmitter, speaking horn arrangement, with a separate headband receiver. Conversely this used a larger plug than the later 420 series, which were used on Plan 4 customer installations.

To set the scene for the afternoon, a series of GPO films were screened, and these included: *The Coming of the Dial* (1933), *The*

My GPO Family: Trilogy Edition

Fairy of the Phone (1936), *The Retirement of Miss Brice* (1964), *Liz and Sally* (1966) and *End of an Era* (1970).

John Liffen and Hilary Geoghegan were our hosts for this gathering of many telephonists, who had operated boards at Wood Street, Faraday and Enfield. One of the original Enfield operators sat down at the switchboard and gave us a demo of how she used to connect the calls. For her it felt as though she'd never been away. Adjacent tables were filled with *My GPO Family* all reminiscing about their working days and the camaraderie which they had always shared. Cream teas were served and the place became alive with chatter about the switchboard. A photographer for the Science Museum captured the event for posterity as, for that one afternoon, everyone was transported back to the GPO of earlier times.

Studying the Culture

My heritage trail has been a long journey of visiting telephone exchanges, collecting Strowger mementos, taking photographs, attempting to absorb the culture and to keep alive the spirit of the GPO. It was often said that telephone exchanges had a unique *Essence of Oildag* atmosphere, which was a combination of switch-oil, parquet floors, arcing contacts and burnt-out coils!

Kelvedon Hatch (Secret) Bunker

During the Cold War a network of underground bunkers had been established where local government could shelter from the aftermath of a nuclear attack and (optimistically) continue to run the country. By the 1990s the bunkers and associated GPO communication links were in the process of being decommissioned. In 1996, I paid a visit to the Kelvedon Hatch bunker which had recently been purchased by the landowner and opened as a tourist attraction.

Heritage

Set back in a wooded area off the road was a 1950s-style bungalow, although the sturdy brick pillars of the veranda and the long run of steps leading up to it, cut into the sloping earthworks, suggested that this was no ordinary dwelling place! Once inside and down some steps, a long tunnel led onwards towards the blast door and bunker entrance. It was a little daunting walking into the bowels of the earth while imagining what it may have been like in a wartime situation. In fact, it was rather grim and with one of the many rooms laid out as a fake (medical) operating theatre the reality was too harsh to contemplate. With the heavy blast doors closed and sealed, the staff might have been entombed for many months; their only contacts with the remains of the outside world being the numerous comm links that the GPO had provided. Conditions inside would have been very basic and I soon formed the opinion that a quick demise within the blast zone (outside) may have been preferable.

Cold War planning was extensive and many resources were committed to ensuring that law and order continued in what would have been desperate times. It has only been in more recent years that the full extent of these preparations has become apparent, as more sites have been declassified and decommissioned. As to whether their utilisation would have been successful is for speculation, but this dark past was certainly an integral part of the GPO for many decades.

Cold War Bunkers (Feb 2016)

Cold War bunkers were deep underground.
Not the place you'd want to be found.

Dark and damp and cold inside.
Stark accommodation in which to hide.

My GPO Family: Trilogy Edition

Telephone exchanges hidden away.
How long for, none could say?

All part of the defence of the realm,
With the GPO at the helm.

Vast complexes stretching for miles.
Government offices ordered trials.

Declassified and cleared now the world's in a different state.
Hopefully another war, a long time will wait.

Telephone exchanges were always built to be functional, industrial buildings and were fabricated using the materials available during the era of their construction. Thus, those built before the 1970s were often of brick, while those which followed were made of reinforced concrete and tended to be of unique designs. Historically, exchanges had to be close to the national and international cable networks (particularly in London) and this frequently dictated that they be built on constricted sites of irregular shape. The standby power requirements of electro-mechanical switching together with the perceived threat of the Cold War led to fortress-like brutalist designs on a grand scale. Prime examples of these were Mondial House (1978) and Keybridge House (1978).

The Digital Programme had a long development period, but once it had gained momentum, it quickly overtook the comparatively new analogue equipment which had been provided in the big international centres. Several were re-equipped, but the days of these massive purpose-built buildings were somewhat numbered!

Heritage

Mondial House

Mondial was once the largest telecommunication centre in Europe, switching terminating and through-traffic for thousands of international calls. [It's described in detail on my *Light Straw* website.] The building was a ziggurat (stepped) design of concrete which was clad in glass fibre to give it a gleaming white appearance that stood the test of time throughout its short-lived life. It was a massive bulky structure which was outdated almost by the time that the last mould of concrete had set. It was loved and hated, in equal measures, by many, and was a unique example of 1970s style architecture. Long before my visit, the digital switching, which had displaced some of the earlier electro-mechanical Crossbar, had already been removed and two floors had been adapted to provide accommodation for BT Internet, which was a high-profile division.

In his 1989 book, *A Vision of Britain*, Prince Charles wrote:

"As you continue down the river (Thames), it is poignant that you can only just glimpse Wren's Monument to the Great Fire as you pass the dreadful Mondial House. To me this building is redolent of a word processor. I don't see that people particularly want a perpetual view of a word processor when they find themselves living with them all the time in the office or at home."

Visit to Mondial House in 2001

As I hurried along Upper Thames Street the noise and vibration of the four lanes of vehicle traffic was quite overpowering in the dim confines of the Cannon Street railway bridge that was above me. I stopped for a moment to get my bearings and to take a few shots of the exterior of Mondial. Almost immediately, a security guard

My GPO Family: Trilogy Edition

asked if I was taking photos of the security cameras and I replied that I worked for BT and was going to meet a colleague in Mondial. This was the aftermath of 9/11, though at the time it surprised me that events in America could have such impact upon our own lives. Ironically, the area once switched calls for the rest of the world, and now the ripples across the oceans were felt in another way.

Inside I met up with Mark Rippingale and he showed me the *BT Openworld* spaces which had been designed to accentuate the industrial nature of the building, while providing for a modern office space where people and ideas could gel. The open plan incorporated internet pods, which had been sourced from the decommissioned Millennium Dome, a very colourful café setting and discrete lighting. I started to take some more photos, but my analogue camera gave up! Mark kindly found some new batteries for me and I was able to take a few internal shots, though my initial enthusiasm for that day's photography had already waned. The fourth-floor decking led outside to a rest area and from there the Post Office Tower could be seem in the distance! On the balcony below, the huge cooling pods for the power generators showed that this was a real 'working building' and not simply an internet play area.

Other parts of the building were virtually abandoned with test desks gutted of their wiring, and floor tiles, which had been lifted to access underfloor cabling channels, had become a dumping area for litter. TXK5 (Crossbar) racks were devoid of their electro-mechanical switches and other floors were completely empty with only the tell-tale marks on the floor that they had ever been in use. The sheer scale of floors the size of football pitches with lofty ceilings made me wonder what equipment they had once contained, and I was also somewhat saddened that a magnificent building was

Heritage

quickly becoming surplus to requirements. Locked rooms still emitted the hum from their transformers and there was hope of future use, but the era of large scale switching with many engineers on site had ended.

The staff canteen was still open and I had a pleasant meal there on the seventh floor with views across the Thames. That was my one and only visit inside Mondial, though my website subsequently inspired others to create their own tributes to the iconic building, as I was later to discover.

Mondial 2006

In 2005 Mondial House was sold to UBS for £51M pounds. Originally, the designs for a replacement building were to have incorporated elements of the integral Dowgate Fire Station, but in the event only the lower floors were retained. In 2006 after I had completed my charity walk up the stairs of the BT Tower, I schlepped over to Mondial to take the first in a series of photos to capture the exterior before it was razed to the ground. Fellow photographer Leon Baird got in touch with me and kindly allowed me to use much of his work on my website.

Leon wrote…

"I am just writing quickly to inform you that sadly, when I was walking over London Bridge the other day, I noticed they have started to demolish Mondial House, and half of it has gone already. Was looking for some good pictures of the building in its former beauty and was very pleased to find them on your website. It was such an amazing building and I am very sad to see it go. You may want to see if you can get some pictures of its demolition while it is still happening, as a sad concluding chapter to your informative website."

My GPO Family: Trilogy Edition

Kim Laughton and Rob Telford also displayed excellent images on their own sites, so that as much detail as possible, on limited budgets and time, was recorded. Ian Coxall sent me a wonderful account of his work on the exchange recovery team, so Mondial became quite a collaborative little project. Guildhall Library allowed use of archive material and Jason Hawkes, aerial photographer supplied a stunning shot of Mondial from the air. Tali Febland, a BA student of Fine Art, wrote that she was so captivated by the design of Mondial House that she made a short animation of the building as part of her second-year coursework. The clip included an original theme (*wish upon wish*) composed, written and sung by her.

In 2015, I received an e-mail from Frances Smith, whose father Peter Hodge had designed the glass fibre cladding for Mondial. Frances was pleased to read reports that the GRP cladding had outlasted the life of the building.

Mondial Steps (Feb 2016)

Mondial was a ziggurat clad in white
Shining out an international light.

Calls worldwide were routed through
Another vast building on the Thames to view.

Crossbar switches and digital too
Filled with operators to connect you.

A web presence global wasn't to last
Yahoo took over the e-mail task.

Heritage

A Cold War fortress of concrete so strong
When bulldozers moved in it took so long...

Reinforced levels on a scale so vast.
This building wasn't going anywhere fast!

Power generators the size of a ship
Just in case the breakers did trip.

The fire station now is clad in glass
It's so much more upper class!

Fleet Building

Designed in the 1950s, Fleet Building was one of the early projects to create a giant telecommunication building in London, as the demand for automatic telegram and telex services, and International Subscriber Dialling (ISD) required both staff and equipment accommodation on a grand scale. Although sprawling and capacious within, the external appearance of Fleet was of a large office complex, whereas the later Mondial and Keybridge exchanges were of brutalist 70s concrete with industrial functionality! As the GPO was a public utility service in the 1960s, it exuded civic pride and so Fleet Building included public artwork to showcase the advancing technology of the era.

On my travels (in 2006) to study disused telephone exchanges, Fleet Building at 70 Farringdon Street was on my list to visit. I recalled that the other entrance at 40 Shoe Lane may have been a *Onebill* address, but by this time the premises appeared empty and I didn't know of any contacts to arrange access, so I had to be content with a walk around the outside. A series of nine distinctive (but weather-faded) tiled artwork panels were displayed at street

My GPO Family: Trilogy Edition

level and I took my time to capture a photograph of each one, with my Sony P200, being aware that a repeat visit was unlikely.

Upon reviewing the photos I pondered over the signature on one of the panels which appeared to read Damman? After much Googling, I determined that the artist was Dorothy Annan, but by 2007 I had still not realised that each panel had a specific title. One of my yearly visits to BT Archives may have provided the information, although I feel it may have been tucked away in a Post Office journal, of which I have hundreds. I added the titles of the murals to my website to annotate the earlier photographs and thought no more of it.

To my surprise, in January 2011 I received an e-mail from Lara Schroder (caseworker) of the 20th Century Society. She wrote, "Through general research I've come across your brilliant photographs which are up on your website. I wonder if I might be granted permission to use a few of your images in the listing application to English Heritage." She continued, "...perhaps you might feel some pride in knowing you are helping to save this excellent mural!" I duly e-mailed her higher quality photos together with my agreement for their specific use. Lara wrote back, "Currently English Heritage are not receiving submissions for listings until April, so unfortunately it will be quite some time before we know either way, probably the autumn!"

The murals depict aspects of telecommunication practice of the time:

1 - Radio communications and television.
2 - Cables and communications in buildings.
3 - Test frame for linking circuits.
4 - Cable chamber with cables entering from the street.
5 - Cross connection frame.

Heritage

6 - Power and generators.
7 - Impressions derived from the patterns produced in cathode ray oscilligraphs used in testing.
8 - Lines over the countryside.
9 - Overseas communication showing cable buoys.

I don't know for certain that my photos were actually used in the application to English Heritage, but I certainly inspired Lara in her efforts to gather relevant information. Much later in the year I read on-line that the 20th Century Society and the Tiles & Architectural Ceramic Society had together secured an English Heritage Grade II status for the murals on 21 November 2011. The listing was supported by Frank Auerbach, artist and Penelope Curtis, Director of Tate Britain. It was satisfying to know that, in a small way, I had helped with the process!

Although the murals had been successfully listed, they were still under threat as the new owners (Goldman Sachs) of Fleet Building wanted to completely redevelop the site. It was another couple of years before I read that the Annan murals had been relocated (in 2014) to the Barbican Centre and thus in July 2015 I made a special journey to London to seek them out in their new home.

The Barbican is a bit of a rabbit warren with high-level walkways which appear to double back on themselves, but after studying a strategic 'you are here' wall map, it didn't take me too long to locate Speed House and the wall upon which the murals were now displayed. Unexpectedly, the murals looked brand new and it was obvious from seeing the vibrant colours and textures that they had been extensively cleaned and restored. Wow, they really were a fantastic legacy from a bygone age which had almost been allowed to slip into oblivion! An information panel adjacent to the display explained how Miss Annan had been commissioned by the GPO to

My GPO Family: Trilogy Edition

produce the special telecommunication themed murals and how she had carried out extensive research to enable her artwork to accurately reflect the subject. The panel even included a photograph of her at work in her London studio as she created the patterns. It was like time had been turned back as the murals once again emanated the optimism and forward thinking of an era long past. My new Sony HX90 camera in 16:9 mode was ideal for snapping a complete mural in a single-framed shot.

Upon reflection, I wondered why Goldman Sachs had obviously taken so much care in the relocation of the murals. City of London documents confirmed that it was a condition of the Grade II listing that the artwork was to be professionally handled and furthermore that a sum of £100,000 was to be set aside for its cleaning and ongoing maintenance, for the foreseeable future. Preserving the past can be expensive! Upon completion of the restoration, ownership of the murals passed to the City of London Corporation, where it is hoped they will be in safe hands.

Keybridge House

In 2007 another brutalist building, Keybridge House received the un-coveted title of BT's ugliest, worst maintained property in London. In its heyday, Keybridge was both a telex centre and an international call gateway. In later years, it switched *Cellnet* mobile traffic and data throughout the capital. In November 2014, Keybridge was sold to Mount Anvil and A2Dominion for the sum of £92.5M. The Vauxhall Society stated:

"It is not possible to refurbish Keybridge House – although the architects spent three months trying to find a way to do it. The construction methods used and the fact that it was purpose built for very specific equipment of gigantic size, mean that it is not possible to adapt it internally. Nor would it be possible to gut it and rebuild

Heritage

within the shell, due to the type of construction. There is therefore no alternative to demolition."

Keybridge Words (Feb 2016)
Keybridge was a monument of the telex age,
When buildings were spacious, and concrete was all the rage.

Polished metal on an industrial scale.
It was all part of the Brutalist tale.

A towering block of cellular design
Exhaust ports outside, looking fine.

Another bastion of the Cold War race
Technology was changing too fast apace.

Its cavernous floors no longer filled
Where office workers once over-spilled.

Frontier switching and servers remote
Property prices rising to gloat.

A new vision, housing a different space
More people's homes to call their place.

In search of Light Straw at Keybridge House (2013)

The vastness and complexity of the 1970s exchange buildings have always fascinated me, but in my 32 years with BT, I seldom had the time or opportunity to visit many. As the digital world expands apace, the building closure programme seeks out those long-forgotten bastions of the analogue era, as sadly most are no longer fit for purpose.

My GPO Family: Trilogy Edition

Brutalist London: Keybridge House (2013)

Heritage

Their unique designs, often on constrained sites, whilst being an innovative solution to the technological demands of their time, simply don't lend themselves to what is fast becoming a multi-nodal, intelligent communications network.

When Jeremy Flashman, a former engineer at Keybridge House, told me that BT had agreed to a nostalgic final tour of the building I was somewhat intrigued to be included in the invitation. Surprisingly, Jeremy could not make it, but my hosts Brian Storer and Amanda Sherry accompanied me on a whistle-stop tour of the cavernous floors from whence telex, voice, and data traffic was once routed throughout the world.

Seemingly endless corridors lead off to lofty equipment floors, the size of football pitches, which were once crammed floor to ceiling with kit. Remnants of *Light Straw* racking in the form of older PCM 30 equipment looked rather anachronistic next to the blue and grey cabinets of later practice, and more so when compared with the fibre optics and LAN (Local Area Network) cables of the server areas. With HV power risers and AHUs (Air Handling Units) at every turn, together with oversized goods lifts, the feeling was very much of an industrial working building, which sadly has been left behind in our rapidly changing modern world.

Brian enthralled us by giving a potted history of the development of networks and switching, from copper to fibre, and analogue to digital, which has ultimately lead to the demise of these monstrous, but once magnificent buildings.

For a moment, we stopped to reflect upon the daily routines of the many technical and support people who would have worked in the building throughout its heyday. Then, with hardly a second thought, we checked our smartphones and headed outside…

My GPO Family: Trilogy Edition

Outside, a new sign (The Central Hotel) was being placed over *Keybridge House* as BT had hired out sections of the building to filmmakers. In one of the lifts, a call sheet listed some of the productions that were in progress.

ITV's *Breathless* (2013), BBC's spy thriller *Legacy* (2013) and *The Interceptor* (2015) were just some of the series which made good use of the empty floors.

Places like Keybridge and Mondial were hard, industrial buildings, built to maximise the much-needed equipment space, often on a comparatively tiny site. Constructed to satisfy planning constraints of the time, but with a 1970s grandeur of concrete and steel. Fabulous during their era, but utterly useless in the 21st century! I loved 'em.

Keybridge House (2016)

A return visit to Keybridge on a bright sunny day in January yielded some good contrast shots of scaffolding creeping up the tower section as preparations for the demolition were well underway. The main building was shrouded in plastic sheeting as is the usual practice nowadays. *Keybridge* will live on as the new development retains the name, and another tower block will rise to capture the stunning views across the City. London keeps reinventing itself and this site is typical of that process. It was sad to see another unique design being laid to waste, but it had served its purpose. Buildings which are adapted for another use are often a compromise and reinforced concrete has a finite life. So Keybridge takes its place in a time of when telecom's architecture was magnificently bold!

Heritage

Industrial Waste? (2016)

Keybridge and Mondial exchanges now past
Seventies architecture built to last.

Magnificent buildings of the concrete age
Designed while the Cold War still did rage

Industrial bastions ever so vast
Modern technology dated so fast.

Both were landmarks in the City
Though many thought they weren't so pretty!

Crafted before the digital revolution
Achieved complex planning solutions.

Now IP protocols can route anywhere
Central London is looking bare!

Burne House

Keybridge and Mondial were feted by their sheer size and inability to be converted into use as anything other than for what they had originally been designed. In the 1960s when these buildings were on the drawing board it would have been difficult to envisage the later scale and speed of miniaturisation in the emerging electronics industry. Provision had to be made for the rapid growth in telephone switching, with proven equipment, and thus the 1970s saw the most extensive building programme as these now legendary schemes were realised.

Michael Pearson's commission to design an extension to NPTE

My GPO Family: Trilogy Edition

(North Paddington Telephone Exchange) included the specification of a standard floor-to-ceiling height of 13 feet. With space allowed for three AMCs (Auto-Manual Centres) and a DQ Suite, as well as switching kit and power plant, this was to be another massive telecommunications centre! Burne House used modular interchangeable cladding to give it the flexibility for future change. The sub-contractor for these specialised panels was Crittall who had supplied the curtain walling for the Post Office Tower.

When Burne House opened in 1977 its façade was coloured *08 B 15 Magnolia*. The concept that glazed panels could be easily interchanged for louvred ones, to transform office space into equipment rooms, as automation displaced staff, would perhaps secure its future?

Michael Pearson: *"Burne House was planned like a warehouse... It can be used for anything."*

References:
The Power of Process: The Architecture of Michael Pearson by Chris Rogers.
IPOEE Red Paper No. 228 (1967) *The Utilization of Large Telecommunications Buildings* by TJ Morgan.

Strowger Exchanges

Strowger exchanges always seemed to have an urgency and importance about them, as each call could be heard to progress through the system. The electro-mechanical switches uttered a unique language, revealing to the practised ear exactly what they were doing! A typical call set up and clear down was very animated.

Heritage

Strowger Calling (2016)

The line relay energises as the handset lifts
A uniselector round the bank does shift.

A free group is found and dial tone is heard
All before the sub speaks a word.

The dial is rotated and the A relay flicks
As stepping up the selector clicks.

Then hunting to another group
While an engineer adjusting contacts stoops.

At last a final for the two digits remaining
At this speed no one should be complaining.

The testing relay says it's fine
And ringing current hits the line.

After a pause the meter clicks
Revenue earning very quick!

The conversation says it all
I've been waiting for your call.

Handsets slip back into place
And all the selectors now do race.

Home to where they started from
Another call won't be long!

All STD (Subscriber Trunk Dialling) calls had to seize an RT

My GPO Family: Trilogy Edition

(Register Translator) in a GSC (Group Switching Centre), which was usually co-located in the Main exchange for an area. In Strowger ND (Non-Director) areas RTs used a 'bunch' of electro-mechanical uniselectors, initially of the Type 2 design, but later the miniature Type 4s. RTs were a form of Director, such that the equipment translated the subscribers' dialled number into routing digits to send it across the trunk network. On every call, the equipment was pulsing out a whole string of digits, which was a much more intense sound than that of decadic group selectors stepping.

A few recordings exist of busy Strowger exchanges, but as with the Industrial Revolution, many of the routine and once distinctive sounds of the daily workplace have simply faded into the past, as time and new technology has displaced them.

Southend ATE (Old Building) 2016

Outlet 21: Faraday Building

"Faraday Building, named after the great scientist Michael Faraday, whose discoveries have done much to make modern telephony."

While on my 'heritage trail', Faraday Building was one of the most deserving of being associated with *My GPO Family* and is steeped both in the history of London and trunk switching. The site was known as *GPO South* and was the Savings Bank HQ. The original building was finally demolished in 1929 and the newly named Faraday South Block was completed in 1933 to house the City and Central automatic exchanges. The South Block is a vast expanse of stone with ornate telephone carvings above the windows. Even more impressive was the elevation of the North Block (circa 1890) to Addle Hill and Carter Lane. The North Block was built as an extension to the Savings Bank, but it soon became the home of the Post Office's first (manual) telephone exchange in London, named *Central*, which opened on the 4th floor on 1 March 1902.

I first became aware of Faraday Building(s) during my visits to the BT Museum in Baynard House (annexe), which was just across the road in Queen Victoria Street. Further investigation was required!

The International Exchange, for which Faraday Building is renowned, opened in 1933 as a sleeve-control board of 121 positions, on the 1st floor of the North Block. With portico entrances, on Carter Lane and Knightrider Street, inscribed VR (Victoria's Reign), this was a rather grand building. A tablet on the side of the portico, above the entrance to Bell Yard, a few paces east, recalled the Bell Tavern...

My GPO Family: Trilogy Edition

> UPON THIS SITE FORMERLY STOOD
> "THE BELL" CARTER LANE
> FROM WHENCE RICHARD QUINEY WROTE THE
> LETTER TO WILLIAM SHAKESPEARE DATED THE
> 25TH OCTOBER 1598. THIS IS THE ONLY LETTER
> EXTANT ADDRESSED TO SHAKESPEARE AND THE
> ORIGINAL IS PRESERVED IN THE MUSEUM AT
> HIS BIRTHPLACE, STRATFORD UPON AVON.
>
> THIS TABLET WAS PLACED UPON THE
> PRESENT BUILDING BY LEAVE OF
> THE POSTMASTER GENERAL 1899.

A hundred years later, in 1999, I took a photo of the above plaque, although it wasn't until 2001 that I got a look inside the building. Two noticeable blue plaques on the South Block were:

Doctors' Commons

Site of Doctors' Commons demolished 1867.

The Doctors' Commons was a familiar name given to the College of Advocates and Doctors of Law which was founded in 1511. They had shared facilities, such as a common dining/meeting hall, a group of clerks and scribes, and probably a common waiting room.

Thomas Linacre

In a house on this site lived Thomas Linacre, Physician 1460-1524.

Thomas Linacre established the Royal College of Physicians and became its first president.

Faraday Building

Trunks and Tolls

Historically, telephone traffic evolved from centres of population and radiated out from capital cities. In the 1920s, it was envisaged to interconnect the UK with just 12 Zone Centres for all of the trunk traffic. In those early days of the telephone service, calls over 15 miles were handled as trunks and had to be connected via an operator. Subscriber Trunk Dialling (STD) of long-distant calls was not possible before 1958. Consequently, the London Zone, controlled by Faraday operators, covered a 70-mile radius around the capital! By 1934 the North Block boasted 435 positions, the switchrooms being named, Inland, Trunk, Trunk Provincial, Trunk Country, Toll Manual, as well as International. *Toll A* handled outgoing calls from London, whilst *Toll B* handled incoming calls to London. The Trunk Exchange(s) dealt with longer distance calls.

Over the years, thousands of operators and engineers worked in Faraday, and the building evokes treasured memories for many. Although there isn't room to include their stories in this particular book, colleagues who have shared memories of Faraday and have encouraged me to write, include: John Burt, Malcolm Knight, Barbara Ball, Helena Wojtczak, Richard Truscott, and Robin Edmonds (aka The Loon).

The Citadel

This was the wartime bomb-proof extension of Faraday (North East Block) on the corner of Carter Lane and Godliman Street. The scheme for the Citadel was planned to meet the following two principal conditions:

1. To provide a limited trunk service if both the Faraday North and South Buildings, which accommodated the existing trunk

equipment, were destroyed.

2. To operate in conjunction with the trunk switchroom in Faraday South Building if the switchrooms in Faraday North Building were lost.

Citadel manual trunk exchange was fitted with 204 standard sleeve-control switchboard positions. Barbara Ball (nee Parkinson), telephonist, writes "I remember that in the winter, we did not see daylight. There were no windows and it was dark when we arrived and dark again when we went home."

Calling Trunks (2016)

In Faraday the lights are twinkling
Dancing along the board and blinking.

Trunks, number please or do you want Toll?
This is an important operator role.

Provincial, Country or further abroad?
I'll plug it up on my switchboard.

The lights are flashing another call.
On demand I'll connect them all.

Lines in delay, I'll find a way,
And call you later in the day.

International

By the 1970s the switchrooms were predominately for international calls.

Faraday Building

Continental:

Faraday Linguist 3M (3rd floor Main)
Faraday Linguist 4M (4th floor Main)
Faraday 4A (4th floor Annex)
Faraday 5M (5th floor Main)

Intercontinental:

Faraday 2A (2nd floor Annex)

Closure

By the mid-eighties, operator assistance had moved to other sites and the Strowger switchgear in Faraday was obsolete. Mondial House was the dominant international exchange, although direct dialling and digital switching was soon to lead to the demise of many once great buildings.

Visit to Faraday (2001)

Faraday was laid waste, the builders were in and the whole of the south elevation was covered in plastic sheeting. Conversion to office space with a new look entrance onto Knightrider Street was the longer-term plan. The building looked abandoned and devoid of staff. Racking uprights, once full of equipment were empty. Strowger kit was bound up with hazard tape, awaiting removal. Audio patching suites (VF CO TJF) plug-up and test jacks were no longer in use. A carousel of circuit set-up cards suggested that perhaps everyone was simply on a long tea break? A stack of empty waste paper bins, a 1990 calendar and a Buzby sticker which harkened back to another time, proved otherwise.

My GPO Family: Trilogy Edition

Faraday North and South blocks were, unusually, connected by bridges; these were metal walkways suspended on girders attached to the outside of the building! There were at least four and although they looked hideous they were nonetheless very practical for quickly getting to the opposite side of the building, without changing floors. The interiors had polished floors to match the decor such that, excepting the external windows, it wasn't apparent that these corridors were actually suspended in the air! It really was like stepping into a 1930s-styled workplace, where time had stood still.

At the entrance to the repeater station, a six-inch thick metal blast door secured the area and remnants of a dated fire alarm system was hanging off the wall. Long black cable-runs snaked off in all directions. One of the large MDFs had a narrow mezzanine platform and I climbed up for an inspection. It was rather cramped and I imagine it would have been hot and uncomfortable working there for any length of time. The older equipment had *Battleship Grey* can covers. A pair of slip-on shoes left on top of a stool added to the impression of this corner being more than just a normal place of work! Elsewhere in the complex, neatly laced and tied wiring ran on. Parquet floors with shorn-through cables emerging were the only sign of recent activity. A few metal-framed chairs still with the orange and yellow seat covers didn't seem out of place in this setting. It had been a whistle-stop tour of a once glorious building, but I was fascinated to have had a glimpse of areas where the bulldozers would soon be decimating.

Postscript

The Grange (St. Pauls) Hotel has stood on the site since 2009. A blue plaque now declares:

Faraday Building

Former site of Faraday Building North, City, Central, Long Distance and International Telephone Exchanges 1902 - 1982.

Additionally, the two original VR porticos have been restored and incorporated into the design of the hotel.

Faraday's End (2016)

Faraday has taken its last Toll
It's almost lost its very soul.

Trunk operators no longer call.
STD has removed it all.

Continentals are now far away
Assistance traffic's had its day.

Switchrooms are empty and shadows are tall
No footsteps walk its hallowed halls.

No supervisors at their desks
Or loo lines plugged to take a rest.

No tangled cords or speaking keys
Or ticket marking if you please.

No swivel chairs or working time
Its *Hello Girls* were so sublime.

My GPO Family: Trilogy Edition

References:

POEEJ Vol 24 *Demand Trunk Service* by IH Jenkins
POEEJ Vol 35 *Replacement of London Toll Exchanges* by RC Devereux and CN Smith.

Faraday (North Block) plaque (2016)

Outlet 22: BT Archives

Amid the changing world of telecommunications, it was recognised that there was a duty to preserve the written history of BT. Referred to now as Corporate Memory it also acts as a publicity tool for the company to promote its fascinating past.

BT Archives website: *"Records produced before the date of privatisation are public records under the Public Records Acts, 1958 and 1967. We undertake the company's statutory responsibilities under these acts to preserve and make available BT's archives to members of the public after 20 years. BT Archives has been appointed an 'official place of deposit for public records' for this purpose by the Lord Chancellor."*

I first visited BT Archives as part of a THG (Telecommunications Heritage Group) Study Day, way back in 1999 and every couple of years thereafter. The archives are located in a stylish, but unobtrusive telephone exchange in High Holborn. On a few occasions, I was adventurous enough to energetically climb the three flights of stairs up to the Search Room, as the tiny lift can be a little claustrophobic when filled to capacity! The shelves of the public room are crammed full of journals, books and publications which date back to the turn of the 20th century. The vast size of the room distracts from the sheer volume of information which is contained within. Long corridors lead off into the depths of the building to where the temperature and humidity-controlled storage room is located. A noticeable chill is felt upon entering, although the rest of the building is perhaps too warm? As far as the eye can see is rack upon rack, each completely filled with box upon box of carefully catalogued archive materials. In the adjacent sorting room, more piles of boxes await allocation of a shelf space.
In the Search Room, strict archive rules are observed such that

writing is by pencil only, although the use of laptops and tablets now make the older process rather superfluous. The world moves on as the cataloguing can be accessed by a few strategically placed PCs and a large selection of photographs can be viewed via the web. Talking isn't encouraged and the atmosphere is one of a library setting; one of study, concentration and whispered utterances! The step back in time is all encompassing as a few display cabinets show off once 'state of the art' telephones. A floor-standing wooden switchboard, and *silence cabinet* completes the scene.

THG Study Days at the archives were always poignant as during lunchtime we met up at a local coffee shop to reminisce about the GPO. Some of us had been engineers, others clerical, and a few simply enjoyed collecting, studying or building their own kit, as a hobby. Whatever the background, we could all talk authoritatively about our passion, and intuitively understand the conversations. Favourite topics were number routings, exchange names, stories of 'misdialling' and other irregular practices! These tales of the workplace soon evoked the nostalgia of long ago. Reality returned as we forged a path through the crowded 21st century streets, back to the sanctuary of the archives.

Every visit to the archives is a fresh experience as little gems of history are unearthed. On a singleton visit in 2016, my document requests ranged from, reports in a *General Post Office* folder, memos headed *G P O*, and leaflets printed for *Post Office Telecommunications*. The styles and layout transport one back to the era, as the everyday processes of long ago, are recalled. Vivid colour brochures headed with 'tramline' typeface trigger memories of the Post Office organisation as it once was.

BT Archives

BT Archive Projects

After leaving BT in 2012, I decided to continue some voluntary work with the Archives, and Dave Shawyer asked me to concentrate on the *Relay Sheets* section of the THGR (Telecommunications Heritage Group Resource) database. *Relay Sheets* were originally cards which gave the build and adjustment data for the Post Office 3000-type relays, which were used in every telephone exchange. There were thousands of permutations of relay coil and contact spring assemblies, and a separate card was produced for each one! Cataloguing each card (from a PDF) only took a few minutes, but required attention to detail to ensure the correct figures were typed into the database. After many months of work, I was quite excited to find RS 11749 XA, which was the F-relay in a Strowger Final Selector!

There was quite a story behind the origins of the cataloguing project, which was recounted at several of the THG AGMs...

BT Archives at the AGM – An overview by John Chenery (2012)

The Aperture Card project in partnership with UTEL, aims to capture and catalogue just some of the 650,000 microfiche records which were previously held by BT's central SDD (Specifications, Drawings & Diagrams) Unit in Harrogate Spa exchange.

The microfiche cards are converted to PDF format by means of a dedicated scanner and are then loaded onto a database which can be viewed at www.thgr.org.uk. Special thanks go to Paul Grafton for designing and hosting the system, and Dave Shawyer at BT Archives for managing the project. The website holds a library of drawings, diagrams, and specifications of all kinds of

My GPO Family: Trilogy Edition

predominantly GPO documentation. Of particular interest to THG members are the AT/ATW circuit diagrams of telephone exchange apparatus, which are a great aid for anyone who is restoring relay sets and associated equipment.

To date, 276,000 cards have been scanned and digitally preserved. Each diagram has to be manually read, its title and condition typed into the database, and takes thousands of hours of labour, which normally would be prohibitively expensive. Fortunately, BT was able to enlist the services of a virtual team of (up to 200) redeployee employees and volunteers who all worked remotely to catalogue 104,500 diagrams! The project has been running for several years and is currently tackling diagram notes and specifications.

Notes from THG AGM (Oct 2015)

Paul Grafton gave an update on THGR, (www.thgr.org.uk) the extensive database of PO/BT diagrams and technical instructions. The project began many years-ago when Kevin Dodman asked Paul to catalogue a collection of TP drawings which were held on aperture cards. Paul bought a special scanner and used his own company resources to design, host and maintain the THGR website. BT Archives requested that another 144,000 cards be added and Dave Shawyer led a virtual team of available BT staff who painstakingly catalogued the on-line database. To date only 4000 diagrams remain uncatalogued. In Paul's team, Alan May did the scanning while Richard Larkin handled the database and website software. Kevin Dodman scanned EIs and TIs (Telecom/Engineering Instructions) while John Chenery catalogued an amazing 10,000 *Relay Sheets* (and diagrams)!

BT Archives

I'd always found that BT Archives people presented a professional image to staff and public alike. Special thanks go to David Hay, Lucy, Siân, Ray, Dave, Keith, Liz and many others who have assisted my research enquiries over the years.

References:
BT Archives at the AGM (2012) John Chenery TH Journal No.81
Study Day at BT Archives (2013) John Chenery TH Journal No.87
THG Conference Report 17 October (2015) TH Journal No.92

BT Archives leaflets-The corporate memory and heritage policy of BT

My GPO Family: Trilogy Edition

BT Archives (2016)

Outlet 23: Bletchley Park

During my early timeline, Bletchley Park was a government training centre, and as part of the Civil Service, the GPO (General Post Office) sent thousands of staff to its RTC (Regional Training Centre) on courses between 1948 and 1992. The park was one of the few places which encapsulated the spirit and empathy of working together as one 'GPO family' in a well-ordered, government run establishment.

Bletchley Park is famous for its role in the wartime code-breaking of Enigma and the use of the GPO-devised Colossus which cracked Lorenz messages. The Government and GPO associations are strong and make for an intriguing history, and although the war is not of particular interest to me personally, its influence on my parents has shaped my own development and ideas.

My GPO family connection with Bletchley Park dates back to World War II, when (in 1943) my mother was lodging in Cromwell Road, Letchworth, working at BTM (British Tabulating Machines) machining parts for the CANTAB project. CANTAB was the code name for the Turing Bombe which was a vital part of the Enigma code-breaking operation at Bletchley. And the Bombe used some standard GPO components in its construction. Banks of GPO (Creed) teleprinters transmitted important messages, so from the very beginning, GPO involvement was paramount. Of course, the full extent of the wartime activities at Bletchley were unknown to many, none more than my mother who used to (somewhat jokingly) tell us that she made mechanical parts for bombs; she supposed it was the release catch on aeroplane bomb doors? She simply didn't know. Such was the secrecy of the time, and more so for piece parts, the machinists were not aware how the parts they were making would be utilised! The Bombe was actually a combination

My GPO Family: Trilogy Edition

of many mechanical rotary drum switches, with brushes and commutators, which could search for and indicate a particular sequence of numbers/letters and thus greatly assist in determining code-breaking patterns.

My father received Telephonist training at Bletchley Park in 1965 and he brought home a little booklet detailing the history of the park. There was no mention of anything to do with the war, or of any possible connection with what my mother had manufactured on her Capstan lathe, and CANTAB wasn't ever a word to be spoken. Over many decades, Bletchley hosted training courses for teachers, civil aviators, Ministry of Labour, Post Office counter staff, engineers, and management grades. The GPO dominated the site with the numbers of staff it trained and it would ultimately shape how the park developed in future years.

I am told that shared rooms, without en suite, was the standard of accommodation at the park. Wartime buildings which once housed electromechanical GPO kit were converted to house GPO engineers! The wartime *F Block* had become *Gifford House* where the majority of GPO apprentices stayed during their courses at the park. These building standards were still acceptable in the 1960s, but from 1971 some of the wartime areas were cleared to make way for Clare House and Villiers House. In 1980, Leon House was the newest addition. Decades of stability at the park were about to change as the recently commercialised BT required modern, up to date training facilities if it was to become a world-class telecoms player!

From about 1986, Milton Keynes Council and the Development Corporation were considering business and housing plans once the park was officially decommissioned. In 1987 the Central Training School of GCHQ moved out of the park, and perhaps it was no

Bletchley Park

coincidence that British Telecom then demolished *Gifford House* which, during the war, had housed seven Colossus code-breaking machines. The Colossus machines had been dismantled at the end of the war, so there appeared little reason to only now clear the site, when the majority of other wartime buildings were still standing? BT finally vacated Bletchley Park in 1993 as its outdated buildings and site obligations (a Grade II listed mansion in 58 acres) were a burden. Land ownership deals are often complex, particularly with government holdings, but BT usually manages to negotiate the very best deals with developers, to increase its cash flow and thus support core activities and shareholder value. However, behind the scenes, those who knew the true nature of the wartime work at the park had a story to tell.

Tony Sale's interest for computers began in about 1965 when he joined the British Computer Society (BCS). From the mid-1970s, information about the wartime work at Bletchley Park had started to be declassified. If the UK had developed the world's first programmable, digital, electronic computer it was going to be of interest to Tony! In 1989, in partnership with the Science Museum, he started a specialist group of BCS which was the Computer Conservation Society (CCS). One of the aims of the society was 'to develop awareness of the importance of historic computers'. At the launch meeting of CCS in November 1990, Dr. Tom Flowers, designer of Colossus, was present.

Tony writes, *"When I and some colleagues started, in 1991, the campaign to save Bletchley Park from demolition by property developers, I was working at the Science Museum in London restoring some early British computers. I believed it would be possible to rebuild Colossus. In 1993 I gathered together all the information available. This amounted to the eight 1945 wartime photographs taken of Colossus plus some fragments of circuit*

My GPO Family: Trilogy Edition

diagrams which some engineers had kept quite illegally, as engineers always do!"

Bletchley Park was owned by the Government, although British Telecom had claim to certain areas. Circa 1993 CCS leased *H Block* and Faulkner House from BT with the intention of setting up a computer museum, which would also house a rebuilt Colossus.

By 1994 public support to save Bletchley Park was growing. The Bletchley Park Trust, which had been formed in 1992, had ideas for a range of high-tech museums on the site to include computing, telecoms and aviation (air-traffic control). This diverse mix would, together with recreational areas, attract a high number of visitors and be self-funding. On television, BBC2's *The Net*, programme 5 (topical computer news) showed Susan Rae visiting Bletchley Park and talking to ex-Wrens who had worked on Colossus, a GPO-made code-breaking machine. It looked a very intriguing place to visit, as many of the huts and outbuildings had been boarded up, giving the impression of a place untouched for decades, with mysteries to be solved! It said the site was open to visitors; now that was a place I wanted to see. I didn't have long to wait for an opportunity to go there as the THG (Telecommunications Heritage Group) was holding a swapmeet on 1 October.

Bletchley Park (1994)

I was keen in those days and my notes tell us that I caught the 07:02 from my local railway station. The total train fare to London, across on the Tube and thence to Bletchley was £20.50 cheap day return. Exiting the Underground, I had to walk round to Euston Square for the mainline train and I paused to capture a rather murky shot of the BT Tower. Nowadays that's more difficult as an NHS building blocks the line-of-sight view. Nonetheless, it's always

Bletchley Park

exciting to catch a glimpse of the tower!

By 10:30 I was walking the long path (enclosed by high wire netting either side) to the entrance gates in Wilton Avenue, upon which a sign declared, *Government Property Unauthorized Entry Prohibited*. I could see my colleagues in the grounds and the gates were open; the security wasn't very good! In retrospect, we were some of the very first visitors in those early years of the Bletchley Park Trust and what was the beginnings of the National Museum of Computing. Wow, the awe of walking the grounds and stepping towards the mansion from where the code-breaking activities were coordinated. The boarded-up huts untouched since the ministries moved out...

I'd bought with me a '126 sized' disposable camera for the day, which with 26 shots, I considered adequate! It even had a built-in flash and was lightweight to carry, and cheap to have developed. The quality of photographs produced was almost as good as my Canon *Sureshot*, such was the technology of the era, with my first digital camera ten years away! The grounds were much like a time capsule with huts and buildings of a style from an era long past. Parts of the site looked derelict and abandoned, but the grass had been cut back and the mansion house looked, well, just like it had on TV! The park is a very large area and I did well to attend the (private) THG swapmeet, purchase a few old phones; complete the guided tour of the mansion and huts, as well as tracking down the Enigma Trail.

The Enigma Trail lead to the *Colossus Rebuild Project* which was underway in *H Block*. In years to come the room was to be filled with racking housing 2000 or more electronic valves, uniselectors, relays, and lamp strips, but way back in 1994 the only evidence of 'work in progress' was some grey metal angle iron, stood up to form the Bedstead (to house the tape drive) and two other empty racks! I glanced Tony Sale, deep in conversation, at the far end of the closed room, so I took a few shots through the glass viewing window and hoped they wouldn't be too dark. In the scheme of things, this was an historic photo, although much research work had already taken place to enable the build team to get to this simple stage. Further along the corridor, other viewing panes showed rooms with cord switchboards, wartime radio sets, and an office layout (tables and chairs), very much Civil Service style. And on the wall a Churchill poster declared, '*Let us go forward together*'. A period dressed mannequin (Wren) stood next to a bicycle, as this was the main form of transport for staff who had lodgings close to the park. It was all very atmospheric, although I would have liked to have seen the racks of equipment close-up, rather than through glass.

Elsewhere in the extensive grounds the spurs of *D Block* with its many boarded-up windows stretched into the distance and merged with buildings on other levels. In its heyday, it would have been a labyrinth of interconnecting passages spanning across the whole site. It was all rather derelict, though as neat and tidy as it could be, and I felt privileged to be allowed a glimpse at what was once a very secret establishment. A stand-alone outbuilding with RSJs supporting its leaking roof was the heavily reinforced Bombe Unit which was soon to be another rebuild project for the CCS.

A visit to the shop had me purchasing the obligatory tea towel and postcards plus *Britain's Best Kept Secret – Ultra's Base at Bletchley Park* by Ted Enever. This became a useful reference book as it told the story of the site and the work of the Trust to date. I was already thinking about my next visit.

Bletchley Park

Kents Hill Park (1996)

BT's Kents Hill Park, a brand-new build, had opened for training on 13 October 1993. Unlike Bletchley, the facilities at Kents Hill were more akin to a modern hotel complex, having a gym and a pool. Covered walkways between the accommodation and training blocks ensured that the worst of the weather was kept at bay. The en suite bedrooms, had TVs, and the meals in the restaurant were very good. I particularly liked the self-service early morning breakfast of scrambled eggs, bacon and toast. The training? It was self-evaluation with more role-play exercises, time management and confidence building. I remember educating the facilitator that daleks had been able to climb stairs since *Remembrance of the Daleks*!

Bletchley Park (Oct 1999)

By the time of my second visit, the Bletchley Park Trust (BPT) had been granted, on 10 June, a 250-year lease on the historic core area (28 acres) of the park. This appeared to be fantastic news, but a careful study of the site map revealed that most of the areas previously occupied by BT were outside of the core zone! As a wartime building, *G Block* was within the overall conservation area, but would not form part of the Trust's responsibility. It would have been a wonderful opportunity to have created a national telecom museum in *G Block* and thus continued BT's historic links with the park. Instead it appeared that the remaining 30 acres were to be sold off to developers. It has to be noted that the negotiations between BPT and the landowners (Government and BT) had been complex, difficult and very protracted, and the result of saving only half of the site for posterity was a very hard-earned compromise, but was still a great victory in the circumstances.

My GPO Family: Trilogy Edition

The THG swapmeet was held in the building that was later badged the *Enigma Cinema*. In the car-park adjacent, Ken Bennett drove his resplendently restored Post Office Telephones Ford Anglia in *mid-bronze green* livery. It absolutely gleamed in the hazy autumn sunshine! It didn't rain on this visit, so I was able to spend more time exploring the other areas of the park. There were several tours taking place and one could almost imagine the hive of activity of when the site had been fully utilised. I walked through the arch of the clock tower by the stable block and remembered to glance at the 'time-warp' clock which Ted Enever had described in his book. A time-warped park; it was surprising that apparently so little had changed, especially as the site had been used extensively for civilian training after the war.

In *H Block*, the Wren mannequins still adorned several of the displays, but the Colossus Rebuild now filled a whole room and was clicking away as though it had always been there. It was a fantastic achievement for Tony Sale and the team to have reconstructed this from just a few faded photographs. A tongue-in-cheek notice read, '*Colossus is year 2000 compliant*'! Outside in Hut 11A, the Turing Bombe Rebuild had started and a test 'wardrobe frame' and a wooden mock-up were on display. Since my last visit, I'd had access to the internet for several years and John Harper's website had kept me up to date with progress.

Ongoing fund raising for the repair of other buildings in the park meant that *C* and *D Blocks* still had boarded up windows and the whole site was still easily accessible, apart from where vegetation had taken a hold. Comparatively low visitor numbers meant there was little need for strict segregation of derelict and unused areas. The walls of *G Block* still displayed signs with the blue *British Telecom* logo. Another notice warned that '*ALL persons entering must wear an industrial safety helmet to B.S. 5240 (1975)*'. I

Bletchley Park

decided not to wander far from the footpath in that area! The grassed area known as *The Mound* was an earthed bank behind *D* and *G Blocks* and it proved a good vantage point to capture some shots of that corner of the park. I think this was close to where the 'field of telegraph poles' used to be sited, but on checking, it was the former aerial mast site as some of the anchors still remained in the ground. I walked up to Faulkner House and with its red paint peeling it reminded me of the 'lino' finish of my 5 + 20 PMBX switchboard. On each visit, a little more of the puzzle of 'which building was what', was revealed. I wish I'd had the time to explore further as by my next visit the developers had moved in.

Bletchley Park (July 2007)

After a week of very wet weather, I had hoped to dodge the showers for *The Post Office goes to War* special event at the park, which was to include preserved vehicles from members of the Post Office Vehicle Club (POVC). Access to the park was now via a newly built entrance and road off a realigned Sherwood Way. This made the park much less of a secret, but served a dual purpose of making it easier to locate, as well as providing the road infrastructure to allow housing developments to occur outside of the non-core museum area. It was strange for the gates to be located so far inside the established tree line, but this was the reality of how the park was about to be 'carved-up' by development.

B Block was now the ticket reception and, in the basement, was the completed Bombe Rebuild, which had been working since 17 July, although it was not being demoed during my visit. Wow, one of the equipment panels had been hinged open to reveal precision-made mechanics together with an extensive, multi-cable wiring loom of a single colour (red). Although bulky, this was a very compact unit of phenomenal complexity. The mechanical engineering was more

My GPO Family: Trilogy Edition

impressive than Colossus, which had used predominantly ready-made components, whereas the Bombe had been custom designed for its function. Adjacent display cabinets highlighted an extensive range of tools and sub-assemblies which were used in the fabrication and I stared intently, wondering which part my mother used to machine, during the war?

Site maintenance was much improved; *A* and *B Blocks* had been repainted and new curb stones and paving highlighted the repaired roads and walkways. I paused by the serene setting of the lake to open my sandwich box, while the resident duck population waddled quickly across the grass thinking it was their feeding-time too! Would-be code-breakers and GPO apprentices may well have enjoyed the same experience. As I walked in the direction of *H Block*, a row of townhouses stood boldly on the site of Faulkner House, with their front doors just a few feet away from the grassed area of the long-demolished *F Block*. A contractor's wire fence and plastic sheeting divided off the remainder of the *F Block* site and a concrete mixing tower confirmed its use as a 'temporary' building compound. The park had been totally spoilt! Although Faulkner House had been of no historical value, to replace it with housing facing towards the park, with no screening of trees, was just sheer greed on the part of the developers. It was now patently clear as to the limited extent of the BPT boundary, with half of the *F Block* site and all of *G Block* totally excluded. Tony Sales and his BPT colleagues had worked hard to get Grade II listing for as many buildings on the site as was possible and this was the final compromise. The whole story of the post-war period of the park is perhaps more troublesome than at any time during the war!

Bletchley Park

Grade II listed building status was granted as follows:

- The Mansion in 1990
- The Bungalow, stable(s), cottages 1, 2, 3, and the Gatehouse in 2001
- Blocks B and H in 2004
- Blocks A and D in 2005
- Huts 1, 3, 4, 6, 8, 11 and 11A in 2005
- Block C finally in 2012

In the mansion, the Milton Keynes Telephone Museum displayed an interesting collection of telephones, switchboards, and GPO hand tools. At 2 pm in the ballroom, Tony Sale gave a special talk about how a German Enigma operator's mistake led to the eventual breaking of the codes, the development of Colossus and the later Rebuild Project. I had seen the rebuild start in 1994 and learnt that by 2004 his Mark 2 Colossus was able to set 'all five K wheels on the BREAM cipher text,' just as the original would have done!

Tony had achieved what others had believed was impossible. I had followed his work via the web for so many years, so I was pleased to have attended one of his lectures, and heard him in person, before his death in 2011 at the age of 80.

Bletchley Park (June 2012)

In May 2011 I'd received an invitation to attend the official switch-on of the newly completed Tunny machine rebuild, but as usual, places were strictly limited and I'd wanted to go with my friend David. A year later we made the trip and I wondered how much the

My GPO Family: Trilogy Edition

park might have changed since my last visit?

As we entered through the gates, a bright red banner on *C Block* proclaimed, '*Sorry my décor is lacking, but post-refurb I'll be just cracking*'; Google funding and lottery grants had been secured to transform the block into a new visitor centre. Increased visitor numbers meant that the reception had changed to the rear of *B Block*, presumably to allow better segregation of those waiting to purchase tickets and less crowding of the exit from the building. The once ramshackle hut (of no significance) adjacent to *B Block* had been replaced by a brand new 'cabin' and was now the home of the NRC (National Radio Centre). BPT was making steady progress in creating a viable and professional museum site.

The now open Tunny gallery looked authentic with its overhead *Battleship Grey* ironwork linking the racking and power units. Next to it was a recreated scene of a radio intercept station together with rows of teleprinters and paper tape perforators. And the Heath Robinson rebuild (a predecessor of Colossus) was underway. It was all a wonderful recreation of the era. In the Colossus room, the modern-day ceiling tiles had been removed both to allow better ventilation for the heat generated by the thousands of valves and to enhance the display, which was now in a 'walk-round' enclosure. Fantastic! Phil Hayes (senior rebuild engineer) showed me the MUGs (Motor Uniselector Groups) being stepped one pulse at a time, whereas in GPO exchanges they would normally drive to an outlet. Such is the originality of Colossus to use standard kit in a different circuit configuration.

Next door in the National Museum of Computing, main block, I popped in to grab some shots of the recently restored WITCH. The *Wolverhampton Instrument for Teaching Computing from Harwell* used Dekatron tubes for program and storage data. It was partly

Bletchley Park

constructed with standard 3000-type Post Office relays, so it was of particular interest to me. The designations on the relay armatures were, SAX, SBX, SCX, SDX, and finally SEX! The WITCH was officially rebooted on 20 November 2012 to become the world's oldest original working digital computer.

Another room was full disc drives and operating units for an ICL 2966, a mainframe computer of the type on which BT's VME applications would once have run. In the corridor, a GPO Master Clock (36), and a slave was steadily ticking away. This would also drive the slave clocks in the Tunny Gallery.

Bletchley Park (October 2012)

For my second visit in 2012, I took time to walk round to the (closed) Wilton Avenue gate and take some up to date photos before the old hall and canteen were demolished. The sign read, *'For Sale 0.8 acres of land approx., with derelict former canteen building'*. Of course, I then had to walk all the back to gain entry to the park, but I do enjoy tracking the ever-unfolding story of the area! The problem with taking shots of individual *Blocks* is identifying them later on, as one span of brickwork looks much the same as any other building on the site. However, the process of simply soaking-up the atmosphere of the place and trying to turn back time in my mind is one of the reasons that my visits are never boring! Tunny and Colossus were operating in *H Block*; they are fascinating to watch.

Bletchley Park (May 2013)

I had arranged to meet the new Archivist, Richard Lewis, to discuss some of the GPO history of the park. He dug out some photographs which clearly showed the steel-framed Faulkner House during its

My GPO Family: Trilogy Edition

construction circa 1968. I had also wanted to see the video footage of the demolition of Gifford House (*F Block*) which took place around 1986. He managed to find hand-held video camera footage of *F Block*, depicting a contractor's wrecking ball doing little damage to the single storey block. A copy of the film had been transferred to DVD, and so I eagerly sat for 20 minutes viewing the crane and jib attempting to raze the building to the ground. *F Block* originally housed an impressive seven Colossus code-breaking machines, which were dismantled after the war, though it is strange that the building itself stood for another 40 years before being demolished for no particular reason. The later name of Gifford House was designated after the family who owned the land in Norman times. Papers with the site photos listed the 'spurs' off the main corridor and confirmed that spur 'x' was a cinema. There was a first-floor tank room where *F Block* spanned the road and joined to the annexe. Other GPO areas mentioned were the 'wet weather sheds' and a 'propane store' to supply the workshop in *G Block*.

Elsewhere on site, a framework of scaffolding had been constructed around *C Block* in preparation for its restoration and redesign as the main visitor centre. Work had already started on removing asbestos from some of the codebreakers' huts as Lottery money was becoming available. In TNMoC (The National Museum of Computing) a Commodore *PET* with a built-in cassette (data) tape player looked very primitive and I remembered that this was once the top of the range BASIC machine before the Apple II, BBC Micro and later Commodore products became popular, in home, and small-business use computers.

Bletchley Park (June 2013)

David Shaffer joined me at Euston Station and we chatted about his early employment as a computer programmer, so he was

Bletchley Park

particularly interested to visit TNMoC, which was building up an extensive collection of 1980s kit. We tried writing a few lines of BASIC on the demo BBC Micros; quite a laborious process, though it took us back a few decades! I left David busy landing planes in the 'air traffic control room' and I walked out of the park and round to the new housing estate at the back of *G Block*, to take a few photos. The access roads had been named after the codebreakers; Turing Gate, Colossus Way, Faulkner Drive, Enigma Place and Ultra Avenue. *G Block* is in the conservation area, though the building remains derelict for now. Back at TNMoC, Robert Dowell kindly gave us an ad-hoc tour of the development of the Micro, from QDoS to the iPad. In the mainframe area, a Ferranti *Argus* took my attention and it appeared massive compared with a *Raspberry Pi*! It was an interesting and enjoyable trip. TNMoC has such a variety of working exhibits.

Bletchley Park (August 2015)

As I approached the park from the railway station, I glanced a new housing estate on the periphery and the very latest was Tiltman Lane, where once Clare and Villiers Houses may have stood. The park's new wide entrance at the rear of *C Block* was impressive, although it was obviously intended for easy access by car and not very secret! However, with the green-painted windows and remnants of the original granolithic floor inside, it felt like I was stepping into a far earlier time-zone and it was apparent that a lot of time and money had been spent on its redesign and renovation.

From *C Block*, the exit into the park led towards the lake and across the lawn to the mansion house. A newly created expanse of lawn in place of a peacetime car park together with a *keep off the grass* sign gave a feeling of tranquillity in an otherwise bustling visitor area. The once dilapidated Codebreakers' Huts had been skilfully repaired and with the 'crossed-tape' on the windows, they looked

My GPO Family: Trilogy Edition

ready to engage in another war! The lack of motor vehicles crossing the area was good, but the reason was a large metal gate which effectively cut-off access, for both cars and pedestrians, to the rest of the park. Thus, to visit TNMoC and see Colossus it was not possible to walk past hut 10. The route is to double-back and exit *C Block* as if leaving the park, and then walk all the way up the hill adjacent *to D Block*. The gates are officially part of the pedestrianisation scheme, but press report suggest it's really to segregate visitors to the BPT (Bletchley Park Trust) and TNMoC due to the ongoing dispute over separate ticketing and funding of the two charities. This rather spoils the overall visitor experience, although each trust is worthy of support. Funding of the museums has always been a controversial topic and it is hoped that a consolidated solution can be found.

I chatted with Phil Hayes, engineer for the Colossus Rebuild, and he was excited that so many older computers are being restored and their true histories in the timeline of computing are finally being revealed. We had a discussion about MOSAIC (Ministry of Supply Automatic Integrator and Computer) which was designed at the Post Office Research Station. MOSAIC storage used 'delay lines' and there was speculation at how early these had been developed in order for the computer to have used them. Known dates varied between 1947 and 1955; it's difficult to be certain about the past, unless one was actually there!

A few days later, my neighbour Richard told me of his crown bowling friend, ex-Wren, Beth Bedford. He had seen a photograph which depicted her having tea with Lady Churchill at Bletchley Park. Co-incidentally, I had worked with Beth during my early years at BT!

Bletchley Park (October 2015)

On a somewhat overcast autumn day, I once again headed for the railway station to catch a train to Bletchley. I made it to the park entrance without getting wet, but had to dodge between the trees and the huts to remain dry. The trees gave adequate shelter and from my vantage point I could look across the lawns to either the lake or the mansion. I snapped some shots of the area before my camera got too wet and then headed for the mansion hoping that the lens would soon dry!

On display in the ballroom was *The Imitation Game* exhibition which had a wide selection of props from the (2014) film. These included Benedict Cumberbatch's costume, the bar, *Christopher* (Bombe machine), an Enigma machine, and lots of paperwork, spread over several period desk settings. With their Bakelite phones and official-looking papers the desks could equally have been set in a GPO manager's office. And there the co-incidence happened. When my 'GPO friend' Dawn later viewed one of my photographs, she exclaimed, *"That's the ink stand that they bought from me on eBay! I was so chuffed to see it in your photo."* Other rooms in the mansion had been populated with office furniture of the period; it was a typical Civil Service environment!

With the rain persisting, I dashed off towards the Codebreakers' Huts for a first look inside since they had been refurbished and retro-fitted. The green and cream colour scheme of Hut 3 was welcoming, although the low light from the ceiling pendants shone down onto bare floorboards; the corridor was narrow and spartan. I could see doorways leading off into the distance; it was a large hut! Some rooms had connecting doors; it was quite a warren. With the blackouts drawn I wondered how anyone had enough light to work efficiently, but then I suppose, there was a war on! Desks, tables,

My GPO Family: Trilogy Edition

wooden chairs, typewriters and filing cabinets, all the basic-essentials for work and not much else. Strategically placed S.O. books completed the scene. S.O. books were standard issue when I started working for the Post Office, as the *Stationery Office* supplied all government departments. Earlier in the month, when I had visited a colleague in the Science Museum, he too had an old S.O. book on his desk!

As the weather was brightening up, I had a leisurely walk back to the main gate and then doubled back up the side path to TNMoC, as the security gates still blocked the shortcut past Hut 10. In the Tunny Gallery, a guide was explaining the Enigma code-breaking process in detail; a lot of effort goes into telling the stories of wartime work at the park.

I found Phil Hayes, the Colossus Rebuild engineer, in his office. He gratefully held up a photo of the *Band Response Tester* which I'd located on the BT Archives' site for him. The tester generated tones derived from the patterns on a glass disc, and was once used to check the frequency response of telephone transmitters and receivers. Phil had used such equipment many years ago, and was rather pleased to have confirmed its existence. We chatted about the expected refurbishment of *G Block* and I looked forward to a time when it would be completed.

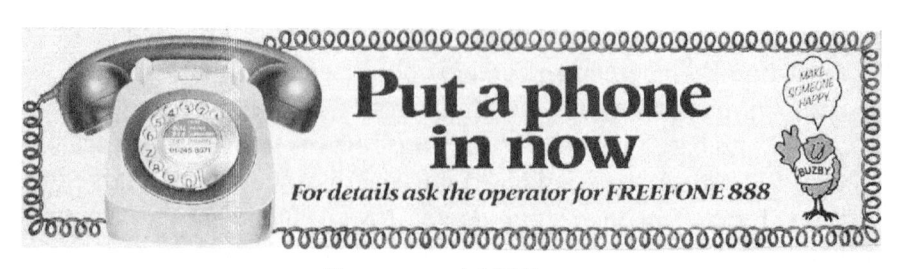

Van poster (c1977)

Bletchley Park

An Enigma? (2016)

In a place where time stood still
GPO machines once again do thrill.

Bletchley Park entrance forbidden
Secret codes within were hidden.

The ticking of the Turing Bombe
Cylinders turning right or wrong?

Code letters broken at a stop
Enigma revealed the overall plot!

Lorenz on Colossus wheel settings to find
Trying to break the enemy's mind.

Checking on Tunny the messages true
All the Wrens knew what to do.

On my infrequent visits to Bletchley Park, my good friend David Shaffer has observed my enthusiasm and content demeanour and has remarked *"You'd be happy to die there, John!"* (Followed by one of his characteristic guffaws.) David is sincere and he recognises when I am 'in my element'.

My GPO Family: Trilogy Edition

Engineers at Bletchley Park Regional Training Centre (1966)

Final Tally

Outlet 24: Traffic Record Final Tally

The *Peg Count* was a traffic record taken to tally the number of calls in a given period passing through an exchange. As a CA, I worked on A 5590 forms (Half Hourly Distribution Record) which were used to calculate the operator staffing requirements of an AMC. Typically, call types were: controlled untimed, controlled timed, alarm call (bookings), alarm calls (connected), 999 calls, incoming, enquiries, and directory enquiries. These allowed calculations of staff justified against staff authorised. It was a very manual process of estimating how many operators should be on duty.

My GPO Family would not be complete without a special mention of just some of those colleagues and friends who sadly did not make it to retirement, or have passed on since.

Harold Chenery (2000)
My father was a TPST (N) at Southend Exchange from 1961 up to his retirement in 1981. Aside from new operating procedures, I think the only change to the switchboard, during this whole period, was the replacement of dials with keysenders! His weekly starting pay was nine pounds and 18 shillings. In 1971, he received an award of three pounds for his suggestion of an amendment to the LPA DQ (London Postal Area, Directory Enquiry) records.

Harry Scrafield
Harry worked in the Switchroom with my father. I used to say good morning to him as I passed by his lock-up garage, when I used to walk to secondary school. In a cartoon drawing he was once known

My GPO Family: Trilogy Edition

as 'the females' friend', because he used to shut the switchroom windows when the ladies said it was draughty! [The temperature of BT offices was always a discussion point.] I think he was a considerate man. He often gave my father a lift home from work.

George Miller
I did CA work for George in *Traffic*. I remember one morning I was standing at the bus stop (almost late for work) and he came along in his car and gave me a lift. Magyar (as his boss called him) at times spoke with a Hungarian slur. And he was often asked, *"Vot is loss, George?"* as office humour made fun of him!

Terry Hopper
Early on, as a CPSA Rep. I spent some time on the Area Safety Committee, of which Terry was the secretary. Later, she transferred from Personnel to Sales and was my manager for some of the time that I was MOH Site Officer. I recall that Peter Pratt took us both to a meeting in Colchester and we had tea and cakes in town afterwards.

Monty J Hall Ellis
Was a TTS whom I met at several of the THG swapmeets at the BT Museum in Blackfriars. He wrote three excellent telephone histories: *The Early Years of the Telephone Service in Bristol*, *Weston 100*, and *The Early History of the Telephone in Bath*.

Ken Tate
Ken worked exclusively on the machinery which folded and enveloped the CSS Sales contracts. I would often take my tea break (a coffee from the nearby vending machine) in his 'office' and we'd chat about the state of the world! Ken's 'office' was the small room which housed the contract printers, and a second one in which the enveloping machine was located. The mechanical

Final Tally

tolerances (of the machines) were very fine, and whenever Ken had a day off, the relief operators tended to end the day with a serious paper jam that warranted an engineering call out! I think for the comparatively small volume of contracts produced, and the number of times the machine jammed, it was only just within budget. Being invited into Ken's domain was a privilege and I was always pleased to stop and chat when the opportunity arose.

Doreen Tate
Ken's wife, Doreen worked in the Sales Bureau (a desk in reception) and later on she was on 'stats duty' issuing *Office Records Only* ANs for *prime instrument* returns. Stats was one of the duties I covered during my tenure in Sales. Doreen was 'old school' and she used to recount the time when she worked in Kynaston's, during the days before she joined BT. I kept in touch with Doreen and Ken for many years after they had retired and they always sent me a birthday card.

Denise Cleveland
Denise had worked in Southend AMC, transferred to Billing, and later joined our group. She was known as Dopey Denise as she wasn't terribly efficient at her job. She was always kind and polite to me.

Barbara Buckingham
I worked alongside Barbara in the office and sometimes met her in the canteen at lunchtimes. Her catchphrases were, *"Is it?"* and *"Laters Johnchenery."* Sadly, she left this world well-before her time.

Paul Tyler (2009)
Paul our CA was a unique character who had Cerebral Palsy, though this was not revealed to us until after his death. I think if

My GPO Family: Trilogy Edition

others had known they would have made more allowances for some of his seemingly quirky habits.

Maureen Billington (2013)
I met Terry Billington and his wife, in the 1990s, at a THG swapmeet in Milton Keynes. We kept in touch by phone and it was sad to learn of her passing.

Ron Sewell (2014)
I'd never met Ron, but he was a high-profile THG member. It still felt strange when a colleague on my *Linked-In* network asked me to pass on news of his demise to the Group.

Sandra Ryan (2014)
Sandra worked in Business Sales and was often spotted wearing her crash helmet as she dismounted from her moped, and walked through the office doors. I probably changed her VDU a few times when I was MOH Support.

Iris Vicary (2014)
My father was, on occasion, Iris's supervisor and I knew her children at the time she worked in Southend AMC. Many, many years later I met her socially just a few days before she was called to the great switchboard in the sky, where my father doubtless still watches over her.

Mark Rosney (2015)
In 2014 Mark e-mailed me, and we compared notes about the Post Office *Dial-A-Disc* service, so that he could update his blog at

https://retroscoop.wordpress.com/2014/02/05/dial-a-disc/

Although I'd only known Mark for a short while, it was still

Final Tally

shocking when I opened his Facebook page one morning to read that he had died in his early 50s. Mark had worked for the Civil Service, so the culture we shared was much the same as the GPO.

Rob Stapleton (2015)
Rob worked as a Commo on Bus Sales (Special Services) and although I wasn't on his team, I reconnected with him years later, on Facebook, during his chats (and snorts!) with Yve Collins. Another GPO family member taken before his time.

Dawn Dick (2016)
Dawn was a good-natured lady on our Billing team and she'd had long service in the Exchange during my father's era. She once told me that my father had 'worked-time' for her on occasions.

At Dawn's service, I sat there with *My GPO Family,* and although it was a sad time, we were all together once again...

Janet Butler (2016)
Janet was the BT CFB guru who knew all about Onebill systems, and utilities such as NOA and Alchemist.

Tony Nesnas (2016)
Tony could often be seen riding his pushbike as he travelled between telephone exchanges to expedite some priority jobs. Given the correct bar-pairs he would set to work and jumper-up my urgent provides, or renumbers.

Vernon Fitzpatrick (2016)
As a Night Staff operator, at Southend Exchange, Vernon worked with my dad on the switchboard.

Brian Storer (2017)
As a senior property manager, Brian knew the BT Estate in detail.

My GPO Family: Trilogy Edition

He was an excellent tour guide of operational buildings and a great ambassador for BT.

Other Friends
Good friends tell me of their own GPO families and are proud to share a few memories. Here are some more names to be remembered...

Brian Hembling (2015)
Mark Hembling writes...

My father joined the Post Office in the 1960s from the local bus company in Basildon, Essex due to the higher wages on offer, as he had a wife and three young children to support. To develop his career, he attended regular courses at Edinburgh and Bletchley Park training centres.

As a cable jointer at Basildon TEC (Archer's Field) for a number of years, Brian worked on coaxial (copper) and then optic fibre cable. He subsequently gained promotion to Senior Technician (Foreman), serving at various times at Basildon and Widford TECs, with the challenging role of managing the workflow of dozens of men.

Brian took redundancy on 31 July 1992 along with 37,000 other colleagues who left BT on the same day. He enjoyed a long and happy retirement with his wife Patricia, giving history lessons to children at his local school, tending his garden and relaxing with his family, until he sadly passed away on 31 October 2015.

[A photo of Brian and his colleagues at Bletchley Park RTC is included on page 336.]

Final Tally

Ken Pike (2014)

Yve Collins writes...My father was an AEE (Assistant Executive Engineer) responsible for Mechanical Aids, Gas and Equipment testing for the whole Telephone Area. His office, with secretary, was based at the TEC in Stock Road, though he also had an office in Telephone House. He travelled all over Essex, making sure both the field equipment and the engineers were working safely. Sometimes the engineers weren't where they were supposed to be, or doing what they should. He used to catch them out, having tea in local cafes! He retired at MPSC salary band in 1986, after 31 years-service.

Make your career in the Post Office PA 25 (7) (2/69)

My GPO Family: Trilogy Edition

THE OLDHAM
G.P.O. LAMP
Nº 13
MARK II

- SWING
- ROTATE TO SWITCH
- CARRYING HANDLE (IN PROJECTOR RELEASE POSITION)
- POCKET CLIP BEHIND PROJECTOR
- REFLECTOR HOUSING RELEASE
- SWIVEL
- BATTERY POCKET CLIP

Part of Ken Pike's field equipment

Final Tally

Donald Prince (2016)

Maureen Mckenzie recalls...My dad joined the Post Office as a counter clerk and took the exams to progress to a management role in the telephone business. He became a Chief Telecommunications Superintendent (CTS) in Traffic, working in Lutyens House, Finsbury Circus, London. Responsible for the forecasting and procurement of telephone kit, he sometimes travelled to Edinburgh by plane, which was exceptional in those early days. Maureen adds that her father used to participate in conference calls between offices while she was at home playing on her roller skates!

At sixteen, Maureen was encouraged by her father to join Post Office Telecommunications as a Tracer, in a London Drawing Office, copying and redrawing engineering circuits and diagrams. She later went on to art school as her talent for drawing developed beyond stencil work.

Conferencing Muses

I wondered when the technology had made conference calls commonplace? Conferencing today is a valuable business tool, and current Meet Me systems use a special 'bridge' to ensure that the transmission quality is maintained, even with a large-number of participants, who dial-in from their Meridian extensions, ordinary telephones, or possibly mobile devices too, from potentially any worldwide location! Upon dialling into a BT Meet Me call, one is greeted by the upbeat and optimistic voice of the exchange sub-system module who in other guises might say "Sorry, the number you have called is not available."!
In medium-sized meeting rooms, my manager had used a 'spider' containing multiple microphones, placed in the centre of the table, to pick up the conversations, but the quality varied depending upon

My GPO Family: Trilogy Edition

the acoustics of the room. In the past, I'd spoken to Heads of Division on their LST4e loud-speaking phones and the conversations had been very clipped and echoey.

In 1997 Kerry Wood, as PA to Steve Dibley, demoed an ISDN2 (Integrated Services Digital Network) video-link to our Brighton office, but the bandwidth, screen-size and quality was somewhat inferior to today's instant Skype calls!

I took part in many audio conference calls from my desk, in a sometimes busy/noisy office. With multiple participants, one always had to listen carefully to figure out who was speaking, and depending on their status in the (external) company, determine if it was acceptable to interrupt them, or to simply carry on listening! These calls frequently required delicate handling, especially when bills which amounted to thousands of pounds were being discussed.

(Good old) Yellow Pages

In July 1965, the right to sell advertising space in telephone directories, was awarded to Thomson Directories Ltd. Thus, in June 1966 the Brighton Area directory was produced as a combined Alpha/Classified book. The classified listing of business customers was printed on bright yellow coloured pages. Growth in classified entries spawned a separate *Yellow Pages* directory. The final printed volumes were produced during 2018, as on-line listings then dominated the market.

'Wise buys begin with Yellow Pages!'

Outlet 25: Supplied for the Public Service

Supplied for the Public Service
Items from HMSO Stationery Office (S.O.) were marked *Supplied for the Public Service*. Notebooks, in particular, were noticeably endorsed in this manner. The GPO, as a *Public Service* was thus supplied!

"During the 1950s, the Stationery Office operated eight production factories, and subcontracted work to an additional 1,700 private firms."

The S.O. branding and the crown was predominant, although in later years, many items were marked *Government Property*.

```
         ♛
─────────────────────
Supplied for the Public Service
HMSO Code 28-616




     S.O. Book 616
─────────────────────
  Indexed at front 256 pages
```

Stores
Stationery, pens, pencils, rubbers, scissors, letter-openers and more, were supplied by Her Majesty's Stationery Office. HMSO was responsible for the printing and distribution of many publications as well as sundries for use within the government.

My GPO Family: Trilogy Edition

Engineering stores were requisitioned from approved suppliers and issue of items was strictly controlled. *Tally Cards* aided the storekeeper to accurately account for items.

Tally Cards (A 521s)
A system of cards used to keep track of stores stock levels.

						A 521	
						(STORES, Stkprs., A 0501)	
Tally Card No.	Item Description	PAINT LIGHT STRAW UNDERCOAT	1 PINT	Item Code No.	15 0364		
Section Stock/Pole Stack	SOUTHEND		E or RD control or special circulation	Unit of issue	Valuation Group		
Forecast Monthly Demand	1	Price £	0·160			00	
Order Level	3	Maximum Issue	2	Minimum Stock	1	Order Quantity	12

	Monthly Issues (excluding stock transfers) during 19											Lead-Time (Weeks)
MAR.	APR.	MAY	JUNE	JULY	AUG.	SEPT.	OCT.	NOV.	DEC.	JAN.	FEB.	MAR.	
	NIL	NIL	1	2	3	9	5	4	1	4	1	1	2

Date	Document Reference	Receipts	Issues	Stock Balance	Date	Document Reference	Receipts	Issues	Stock Balance	Date	ON ORDER		Date Rec'd
											Requisition Reference	Quantity	
	JAN 1971			9	7/8	8/527/8		B/F 2	12 10	20/5 19/6	141/014 00/1059	12 12	11/6/7 3/6

Of the many stores items, hand tools used by the engineers were the most often discussed…

Pliers Wiring No.2
Although I never worked as an engineer, the question of "What were 81s?", often arises. In historical 'lists of stores' e.g. the *Rate Book*, items of tools were allocated numbers and descriptions. The standard nomenclature was, the type of tool, followed by the activity for which it was intended.

Thus in the original list, number 81 was *tool, instrument*.

Supplied for the Public Service

An E.I. (Engineering Instruction) for Tools and Transport, Hand Tools, A 0090 dated 20.4.1948 explains in more detail...
In 1936 the items in the *Rate Book* under the heading *Tools, Instrument*, were grouped together into a separate sub section, which included tools for adjusting apparatus and instruments. The method of describing *Tools, Instrument* by numbers was discontinued and new titles were adopted.

The new title for number *tool, instrument* no.81, was *Pliers, Wiring*, No.2.

In summary, 81s are pliers, which engineers use(d) for twisting and bending, wiring. They have a tapered nose with serrated jaws. They most likely had a multitude of other non-approved uses too!

Batch Sampling
Was carried out by TOs from the London and Birmingham Test Sections, who would take samples from a manufacturer's production line, to inspect and test, those items.

The sampling plan allowed for the batch under test to have a set number of defects, both major and minor. If the number and type of defects found were within the set limits, after any defects found were corrected, the batch would be accepted.

If the batch was rejected, the whole batch would have to be reworked to find and remedy the defects found. The batch would then be re-submitted and another sample taken.

Those items that the TOs had passed, were marked with their personal numbered stamp. All items in the accepted batch were stamped *Batch Sampled*.

My GPO Family: Trilogy Edition

My GPO Family of Books by the Author

My GPO Family: Supplied for the Public Service (2017)
1. *My GPO Family: Trilogy Edition* (2018)
2. *My GPO in London* (2019); *London's Trunks, Toll, and Telex* (2020)
3. *My GPO Legacy* (2021)

My GPO in London explores the growth of the Post Office (and its estate) as the postal, telegraph, telephone and telex services gradually developed to serve the whole of the UK.

My GPO Legacy - further recollections and reminiscences of the Public Service.

⎡ GPO ⎤

For details of other publications about the Post Office for use in schools, please enquire in writing from your Head Postmaster or Telephone Manager.

This notice appeared in many educational books which were written for schools. (1960s)

Visit: www.lightstraw.co.uk/mygpofamily

Glossary

Continuous Improvement
Was a phrase from the *problem-solving wheel*, which was introduced during the early TQM (Total Quality Management) period of British Telecom.

Crown Immunity
A set of special powers granted to Her Majesty's Government that, among other things, reduced its responsibilities to its employees in matters such as personal safety. This effectively allowed defence and other installations to be quickly constructed without potentially onerous planning obligations.

Flexitime
Clerical grades worked Flexitime with start and finish times that could be varied to suit the individual. An agreement between the Union and Management allowed for this, subject, of course, to *the operational needs of the Department*. Going home earlier than others was to *flex-off*.

MBORC
Matters Beyond Our Reasonable Control. This term was usually applied to compensation schemes to avoid paying out under *Act of God* situations, such as storms or lightning strikes.

Oildag
Oildag was the name of a mineral-based oil containing fine graphite particles, which was used to lubricate Strowger switch mechanisms.

Outlets
Outlets was the name given to the connections on the two-motion switches, which had ten routes in or out. Subscribers' uniselectors had 25 outlets.

Right First Time
The phrase *Do It Right First Time* was introduced into Aberdeen Telephone Area as early as 1968 and was part of an ECR (Error, Cause, Removal) management scheme, originally from America.

To Work Time
This was simply to cover another operator's duty, usually for a cash payment.

And Finally...
In taking pre-orders for this book, some respondents included a brief summary of their career, as beyond doubt they are proud of their GPO service.

PO *Batch Sampled* Marking
Was a quality control stamp, indicating that stock from the contractor(s) had been checked and was approved for use. This progressed to *Authorised Release* and later developed to a full QA (Quality Assurance) process.

```
P.O. BATCH SAMPLED
```

Printed in Great Britain
by Amazon